On the Law
of Nations

Also by Daniel Patrick Moynihan

On the Law
of Nations

· · · · · · · · · · · ·

Daniel Patrick
MOYNIHAN

· · · · · · · · · · · ·

Harvard University Press
Cambridge, Massachusetts
London, England

This book is printed on acid-free paper, and its binding materials
have been chosen for strength and durability.

Library of Congress Cataloging-in-Publication Data

Moynihan, Daniel P. (Daniel Patrick), 1927–
On the law of nations / Daniel Patrick Moynihan.
p. cm.
Includes bibliographical references.
ISBN 0-674-63575-2 (alk. paper)
1. United States—Foreign relations—20th century.
2. International law—United States   I. Title.
E744.M79 1990   90-33227
327.73—dc20   CIP

For Timothy, Maura, and John

Acknowledgments

A survey of American attitudes toward international law from the eighteenth century to the verge of the twenty-first leaves an author with many debts, but most especially to persons more learned and more diligent who have been willing to read the manuscript. I would especially thank Alfred P. Rubin, the most recent of those members of the faculty of the Fletcher School of Law and Diplomacy who have attempted over the past forty years to educate me in these matters. The others know who they are, and they know my gratitude. However, I dare not implicate them in the result!

Frank Fenton has been indefatigable in devising English equivalents for the Latin phrases that festoon the literature of international law like swags in the interiors of Victorian households, diminishing what little light seeps through. There are but three remaining; only one more, as I count, than will be found on the Great Seal.

Eleanor Suntum, Curtis Kelley, Seth Rosenthal, and Stephen Rickard toiled over the text with patience and forbearance beyond all expectation.

The Congress shall have power . . . To define and punish . . . Offenses against the Law of Nations . . .

Article I, Section 8

. . . Treaties . . . shall be the supreme Law of the Land.

Article VI

The Constitution of the United States

Introduction

This volume was a while in the making. The story begins in February 1979, with a talk to the Council on Foreign Relations in New York City. I took as my theme the proposition that a certain disorientation in American foreign policy derived from our having abandoned, for practical purposes, the concept that international relations can and should be governed by a regime of public international law. Further, this idea had not been succeeded by some other reasonably comprehensive and coherent notion as to the kind of world order we do seek, or which at all events we do accept and try to cope with.

I referred to the vision associated primarily in the American mind with Woodrow Wilson. No man in the history of the world—and certainly none other in our century—so engaged the passions and the hopes of mankind as Wilson did in those months of 1918 and 1919. The idea of a world ruled by law is as old, almost, as the idea of law itself. But it was only with the latter part of the nineteenth century that it came to be seen as a practical vision and as a reasonable choice that governments might make in determining their own behavior. It is probably fair to say that at the turn of the twentieth century most statesmen in the West expected such a future for the world. It was part of the prevailing optimism of that time, and closely associated with the confident expectation that liberal democracy—with its great emphasis on law as the arbiter of relations among citizens with equal rights—would become a near universal form of government.

Now, toward the end of the century, something had changed. My talk was not well received; nothing notable in itself, save that this was the Council on Foreign Relations, where what I had said was once doctrine. The origins of the council can be traced to discussions between members of the British and the American delegations to the Paris Peace Conference of 1919. It was founded in 1921 to continue the quest for American involvement with the League of Nations and the then Permanent Court of International Justice. To say again, a half-century earlier a subject such as mine would have been the standard fare of Wednesday afternoon teas at the council. A friend suggested that the audience thought I had been defending the war in Vietnam.

Thus the catalytic quality of the subject. Introducing international law into a discussion almost invariably sets off a reaction. This reaction will vary according to the environment. If on that same Wednesday afternoon I had given the same talk to a gathering of the Center for Security Policy, in Washington, I would almost surely have been judged to be *opposing* the war in Vietnam. (The war was over, of course, but it was still being debated.)

I left the council gathering puzzled and thereafter, from time to time, wondered what had prompted me to bring up the subject in the first place. There was, to say again, no crisis at the time which turned on issues of international law. Nine months later there would be, when the United States embassy in Teheran was seized and American policy seemed incapable of grasping that there was an issue of law involved. But that was yet to come. I have to suppose that I chose to talk about international law because there was, at that time, so *little* talk of it. As in the celebrated exchange in Conan Doyle's "Silver Blaze":

> "Is there any other point to which you would wish to draw my attention?"
> "To the curious incident of the dog in the night-time."
> "The dog did nothing in the night-time."
> "That was the curious incident," remarked Sherlock Holmes.[1]

Now I think I have it. I was by 1979 a member of Congress. Congress makes the *laws*. Our time is passed in considering what is law, what ought to be law, how faithfully laws are executed. This was for me a new perspective. I was elected to the Senate in 1976. As the only former ambassador at hand, I was immediately assigned to the newly formed Select Committee on Intelligence. Legal issues were constantly before us; at length the absence of any consideration of international law began to seem curious.

Little things began to take on a larger aspect. As ambassador to India I had developed a considerable interest in visiting the old Portuguese possession of Goa on the Malabar Coast for the sufficient reason that I was forbidden to do so. India had invaded and occupied Goa in 1961. At the United Nations Adlai Stevenson was adamant. India was in violation of law. We would never recognize its conquest. "What is at stake today is not colonialism; it is a bold violation of one of the most basic principles in the United Nations Charter . . . But if our Charter means anything, it means that states are obligated to renounce the use of force, are obligated to seek a solution of their differences by peaceful means."[2] It was my turn to be at the UN when Western Sahara was invaded and partitioned by Morocco and Mauritania, and when Portuguese Timor was invaded and conquered by Indonesia. But I found myself, if not exactly defending, then certainly not opposing, these equally clear and concise violations of the very same United Nations Charter. (It was left to the representatives of the Soviet Union and the People's Republic of China to do that.) As time passed my thoughts returned to the partition of Western Sahara. It happened that the General Assembly had asked the International Court of Justice to deliver an advisory opinion as to whether the Spanish colony had a sufficiently credible prior existence as an independent entity to be entitled once again to freedom and independence. Most assuredly, advised the Court, not five weeks before that right under the Charter was, for the moment, extinguished by two of its neighbors. The American judge on the Court had called on me in the anteroom of the Security Council, bringing an advance copy of the advisory opinion, to be certain I got one. I had thanked him, and had even read the opinion. But my instructions were to ignore it.

In 1978 I described these episodes in *A Dangerous Place*. American policy had proceeded from a simple formula. The Communist powers had clients, we had clients; what our clients wanted we wanted, the more so if "their" clients, Algeria, for example, wanted otherwise. That this was a formula for ethical ruin was obvious enough. I believe I saw this at the time; in any event I later wrote it. Only slowly, however, did the thought come that larger American interests were involved and that these interests were not well served either.

In 1984 I published *Loyalties*. The concluding essay, "The Idea of Law in the Conduct of Nations," went over this subject with particular reference to the 1983 invasion of Grenada by the United States. The official version of what happened there did not quite extend to the claim that we acted in self-defense, but it was not far from that. It was the clearest possible violation of Article 18 of the Charter of the Organization of American States, a document as much of our drafting as was the Charter of the United Nations. It was a violation of the latter also. I noted that the director of the International Law Institute at Georgetown University Law School, while supporting the invasion, acknowledged that the legal defenses offered by our government "embarrass people who believe in law."[3] But the discomfort was minimal; few seemed to mind. A *Wall Street Journal* editorial began by recounting a dinner-table conversation in which a guest declared, "We are only going to be able to talk sensibly about Grenada if anyone here who is an international lawyer agrees to keep his mouth shut."[4] To anticipate and, in a sense, to repeat, this editorial seemed to me to reflect a new attitude. It was defensible.

> The good old rule
> ... the simple plan,
> That they should take, who have the power,
> And they should keep who can.[5]

But *different*. Would the *Journal* editor's dinner guest have felt that the Iranian mob was quite within its rights in seizing the American embassy in Teheran, given that it clearly had been able to do so? What about executing the diplomats there? Dependents?

One *supposes* that the *Journal*'s dinner guests would have argued that Iranians had no right to be shooting Americans. One assumes, however, that any number would have just previously been defending the right of Americans to be shooting Grenadians. In point of fact, these are not incompatible views. But do not expect to sort them out without reference to international law. It cannot be done save by embracing the most extreme form of nihilism, such as would place in jeopardy the very rights of property, which is hardly a proposition likely to be advanced at a dinner table expecting favorable references from the *Wall Street Journal.*

I asked, in this final essay, whether American opinion is moving "away from an era in which we set great store by customary international law and expected fruitful development of treaty law, which would result in a comprehensive body of rules that would govern the conduct of nations." I suggested, with reference to Grenada, that we might have benefited from "a weekend's pause in which we could have considered our interests rather than merely giving in to our impulses. That, largely, is what law is about."[6] (The invasion followed by two days the destruction of the marine barracks in Beirut. It was carried out, in part, by marines on their way to the eastern Mediterranean.)

Loyalties was in press when the decision was made to mine Nicaraguan harbors in an effort to overthrow the government of that country. But when Barry Goldwater and I protested that this was a violation of international law, we were easily discredited by officials of the Reagan administration. It was put about that we were merely trying to cover up our own failure, as chairman and vice-chairman respectively of the Senate Intelligence Committee, to pay attention to what we had been told. This was a lie, as Robert C. McFarlane, the national security adviser at that time, later conceded under oath before the congressional committees investigating the Iran-Contra events. But without notable exception, the lie was believed. (Why would anyone raise the subject of international law save as a lame excuse for poor performance?) Whereupon a practice of deception mutated into a policy of deceit. As I write, criminal trials are still going on in Washington involving men who once held positions of honor and trust in the United States government, men who would have done well to consult their own as well as their nation's interests before giving way to *their* impulses. They did not then, nor do any, McFarlane possibly excepted, seem to have subsequently acquired any notion of what was wrong about what they did. Rear Admiral John M. Poindexter, who succeeded McFarlane as national security adviser to the president, evidently feels that liberals are responsible for his troubles.

Seeking funds for the Poindexter Defense Fund, he has written to a potential contributor in Delmar, New York:

> ... because I care more about the long term security of America than I do about myself, I must now face the liberals' accusations surrounding the "Iran-Contra affair."
> And as I stand, one man, alone against the massive onslaught of liberal special interests who want to imprison me for serving my country, I must turn to you for help.[7]

This is painful not least because it is not true. Even as Admiral Poindexter's fundraising letters were flooding the mails (the gentleman in Delmar received three), the admiral was demanding in court that he be allowed to consult former president Reagan's personal diaries, presumably to demonstrate that he was only following orders. Which in the event would hardly have originated in liberal precincts.

On the other hand, liberals did have a say in the matter. The Select Committees which investigated the secret military assistance to Iran and the Nicaraguan opposition included persons of strong conservative views, but clearly Daniel K. Inouye, chairman of the Senate committee, and Lee H. Hamilton, chairman of the House committee, are to be seen as political liberals, and each chose political liberals for committee counsel. Still, there is no more discussion of international law to be found in the massive *Report of the Congressional Committees Investigating the Iran-Contra Affair* than was evidently considered in the dinner-table conversation reported by the *Wall Street Journal*. In 690 pages of text, the term *international law* does not once appear. Chapter 27, "Rule of Law," begins with a felicitous citation from Robert Bolt's *A Man for All Seasons.*

SIR THOMAS MORE: The law, Roper, the law. I know what's legal not what's right. And I'll stick to what's legal ...

WILLIAM ROPER: So now you'd give the Devil benefit of law!

MORE: Yes. What would you do? Cut a great road through the law to get after the Devil?

ROPER: I'd cut down every law in England to do that!

MORE: Oh? And when the last law was down, and the Devil turned round on you—where would you hide, Roper, the laws all being flat? This country's planted thick with laws from coast to coast— Man's law, not God's—and if you cut them down—and you're just the man to do it—d'you really think you could stand upright in the winds that would blow then?[8]

In real life Thomas More would have been decidedly of the view that there was something called the law of nations which was prior to and above the laws of England. But no such awareness seeps through the thickets of statutory law which the Iran-Contra report discusses. Chapter 24, "Covert Action in a Democratic Society," treats in great detail the requirements of domestic law but does not even touch upon the subject of treaty law, albeit the mining of Nicaraguan harbors was in elementary contradiction to at least one treaty in force, one that under Article VI of the Constitution "shall be the supreme Law of the Land." Two developments were at work. The idea of international law *had* faded. But just as important, in the 1980s it had come to be associated with weakness in foreign policy. Real men did not cite Grotius.

The Iran-Contra events would have provided grounds for returning to the subject of international law, although they would hardly have been compelling. But then came the extraordinary events of 1987–1989 in the Soviet Union, Eastern Europe, and among the nations describing themselves as Non-Aligned, but which objectively have been instruments of Soviet policy for much of the postwar period. George Will described the spring of 1989 as "the most momentous months in mankind's history", Leon Wieseltier called it "a political and philosophical epiphany."[9] Nothing like it had happened in our lives. Finally, in our time, something on earth truly to be thankful for.

During these months I visited Southeast Asia and later Eastern Europe. The world was reshaping itself with momentum and logic. The cold war was ending. The Soviet Union, and Marxists pretty much the world over, were giving up their claim to be the next stage in history. Normalcy was returning to the relations of states, which is not to say peaceableness, or even harmony, but even so the end of protracted ideological conflict. We were at the end of the Twentieth Century War, which began, in my reckoning, with the Paris Peace Conference of 1919. This was a systematic effort to establish a regime of law in the world based on the sovereign equality of states, which effort the Soviet Union just as systematically rejected. Curiously, during the tumultuous months of the spring and summer of 1989 the Soviet Union began to assert a great interest in international law, which it had once dismissed as an epiphenomenon of the late stages of capitalism, a delusion at best and in any event unavailing in the face of historically determined conflict. There was nothing casual in the Soviet shift; a decision was made to press this new position, and it was soon to be encountered in forums everywhere. In what may prove their final act of obeisance to Moscow, the Non-Aligned nations convened a conference at The Hague in June 1989 and called for the United Nations to declare a Decade of International Law.

From the outset it has frequently seemed that international law is an idea espoused in about equal proportion by people who would believe anything and those who believe nothing. Frequently the mark of simple honesty has been to deny that there is any such thing, save as a set of beliefs belonging to the realm of ethics more than to the world of affairs. On the other hand, there is a school of legal reasoning which seems to hold that law exists when and as it is *necessary* for it to exist. This view is typically to be found in the texts of seventeenth- and eighteenth-century jurists. In his *Course of Lectures on the English Law,* delivered at Oxford in 1767–1773 and composed "in association" with Samuel Johnson, Sir Robert Chambers opens with "this necessary law of nations," a term long in use. (We will see that Chancellor James Kent's lectures on American law, given at Columbia University a generation later, begin in this same manner.) Chambers speaks of "politic law,"[10] something Roman lawyers understood: *Quod ad statum republicae spectat*, "as regards the condition of the state." So it was with the law of nations.

> This practice is therefore not voluntary but necessary, so necessary that its neglect would make the world a desert, and the nation, that should violate it first, would probably be extirpated by a general confederacy of mankind against it.[11]

Previously he has told us, on the authority of Strabo, that "the Eretrians and Chalcidians . . . agreed to use no arrows or other missive weapons in their wars with each other"; further that in the great war carried on by Queen Anne against the French in Flanders it seems to have been agreed, though perhaps only by a tacit compact, that the French should consider as lawful enemies the refugees whom they should take prisoners fighting for us, and that the English should treat in like manner Irish papists taken in the French army.[12]

Here we come upon a matter of considerable interest but no very great consequence. As regards, that is, the law of nations.

How does it originate?

For the longest while it was held that nations, like individuals, were subject to preexisting laws. Divine, if you please. Natural, if you like. In the view of many, both. "The Laws of Nature, and of Nature's God," to cite the first sentence of the Declaration of Independence. Commentators of Chambers' period (important to us, as it was the period of our beginnings) were, in Alfred P. Rubin's nice phrase, "desperate to find an 'objective' underpinning for morality." Hence the attraction of natural law, something that might be learned from observation, much as natural science was to be learned by patient inquiry and fidelity to facts. Alas, Rubin continues, "[This] was doubted by Aristotle . . . [and] destroyed by Suarez," the latter a seventeenth-century Spanish Jesuit theologian.[13] The idea survives in some writings, rhetorically at least, but it really isn't necessary any longer. From the time of the Peace of Westphalia of 1648 and the emergence of a still substantially intact system of nation states, the law of nations has been pretty much what contemporary nations have agreed to in writing. These principles are most visible in the Charter of the United Nations, a treaty which has been ratified by virtually every nation on earth and which provides (Article 2, Section 6): "The Organization shall ensure that states which are not members of the United Nations act in accordance with these Principles so far as may be necessary for the maintenance of international peace and security."

Even the toughest-minded "realists" such as Hans Morgenthau have taught that there was *something* there—"primitive . . . decentralized law"—which nations should and do follow.[14]

A related question is more easily answered.

What does it regulate?

Everything. Or just about. Much of the older content of international law is by now solidly agreed to and largely self-enforcing, in the manner of decentralized law. In any event, most law is now *treaty* law, which grows more, not less, ambitious, moving, for example, into areas of environmental regulation that would have been audacious for nation states less than a generation ago. Neither traditional law nor treaty law has been notably successful in controlling the use of "arrows and other missive weapons." Yet to observe a U.S./Soviet team supervising the dismantling of a Pershing II missile is, at the very least, to introduce the thought that it might be becoming more effective than it has been. It has not much improved community relations in Belfast, and to this moment "papists" will be found harassing British grenadiers in the vicinity of Flanders. Yet, as J. H. Plumb insists, the condition of man is better than it was, and the greater salience of the law of nations has contributed to this betterment.

One further event brought me back to the subject of international law. With the advent of the 101st Congress, I became chairman of the Subcommittee on Near Eastern and South Asian Affairs of the Senate Committee on Foreign Relations. This subcommittee, corresponding to a division of the Department of State, covers a vast expanse of the planet, extending from the Atlantic coast of Morocco to Sri Lanka in the Indian Ocean, but American attention has always been concentrated in the center of the "region," in the tiny state of Israel. By 1989 things were not going well there. Internal conflict, not different in its nature from that of neighboring Lebanon, was intensifying. Years earlier Nathan Glazer and I had begun our work on ethnicity. (It would be more accurate to say that years earlier I had begun to assist him in his work.) We had propounded the notion of ethnicity as a modern, even postmodern, phenomenon, the persistence of which clearly falsified the central organizing principle of Marxism. Marx forecast that a worldwide proletarian movement would emerge in the late stages of capitalism and bring about the triumph of international socialism. Wrong, said we. The workers would not unite to overthrow the system. They would fractionate to abuse one another. We anticipated a post-postcolonial world in which the satisfactions of independence from one or another European master would give way to "internal" conflict, as for example between Christian and Muslim in Lebanon.

Clearly, Israel would not escape this form of conflict; it was *born* of such conflict. In its early years it represented the triumph of the Wilsonian principle of self-determination, a people delivered from horror and degradation and putting the world to shame with the grace, idealism, generosity, valor of the nation of the Jewish diaspora now recreated. But then a Palestinian people came forward with not very different demands, and the question inevitably arose as to why these demands were not equally legitimate, and why Israel seemed to deny them. A yet more difficult question concerned the Israeli response, or rather the response of official Israelis. There was little. Few of those in office seemed to perceive the shift in Israel's circumstance, or, if they did, seemed particularly concerned. Clearly, an assumption had settled in that the relationship with the United States that had been fashioned following the Six Day War in 1967 would endure indefinitely. There was now a "strategic relationship" which depicted Israel as an essential bulwark against Soviet expansion. But by the end of the 1980s such confidence was altogether misplaced. There is a Hebrew phrase, *ha-mavin yavin*, which translates as "those who understand, will understand." For one thing the defense budget of the United States has now (1989) declined in real terms for five consecutive years, and is heading further down. This is something of a state secret, but there is reason to believe that other nations are onto it, and also that they know that the principal reason for the decline is that the United States, a debtor nation with a seemingly intractable deficit, can no longer afford a vast military establishment; nor yet the overseas alliances that have accompanied this establishment. Nor can we any longer afford foreign aid on the scale once taken for granted. Happily the Soviets appear to be in much the same position. The deputy secretary of state, Lawrence S. Eagleburger, writes that both superpowers crossed "the finish line very much out of breath" and with "a frankly diminished capacity to influence events."[15] What then of strategic relationships? Client states of *both* superpowers are likely soon to be at a discount. Those who do not know this have simply not been listening to conversations in Washington. Far more important, the symbolic status of Israel is shifting. As I write, for example, the student government at the University of Wisconsin is establishing a student-to-student relationship with An Najah University, a Palestinian institution in Nablus, in the "Israeli-occupied West Bank," as the press routinely describes the area. An Najah University has been closed since the early days of the *intifada* ("to shake off" or "shaking off"), as the Palestinians call their uprising. Does it require great foresight to sense where these trends will have taken us in twenty years? I think back to a moment described in *A Dangerous Place*. The Palestine Liberation Organization was about to be admitted to a session of the Security Council.

> In the midst of the Security Council debate I had lunch with Edouard Ghorra, the Permanent Representative of Lebanon, a man of great gentleness and transparent goodness, now in utter torment as the Russians, through the Syrians and the P.L.O., went about the destruction of Lebanese government and society . . . In October the first reports had come of significant amounts of Soviet aid to leftist forces through the Lebanese Communist Party. At the end of that month the State Department warned against outside interference in Lebanon, but the spokesman added that the United States was giving "absolutely no consideration" to military intervention. No carrier flights to Tel Aviv. No airborne troops alerted. Just a warning, which might as well have been an invitation for the Syrian invasion which would come shortly now. Ghorra asked if there was any hope of American help. I said there was none.[16]

And there was none. Why? Basically because none of the parties in Lebanon had acquired any hold on American idealism. A powerful, at times a defining force in the twentieth century, but also a waning one.

Whence we return to law. Israel is one of the states in the Middle East that emerged from the mandatory system established by the Covenant of the League of Nations at the Paris Peace Conference. It declared its own existence as a state and established itself by force of arms in 1948. But the context of international agreement persists. The United Nations voted overwhelmingly to accept the partition of the Palestine mandatory territory. It accepted Israel as a member state. During the first twenty-five years or so, Israel enthusiastically acknowledged and honored the role of the United Nations in securing its existence. The UN Security Council has been seized of Israeli affairs from the moment the state emerged. Security

Council Resolution 242, which came after the Six Day War, and Resolution 338, adopted during the Yom Kippur War, are the bedrock commitments of the international community to the legality and permanence of the Jewish state. It is not clear, to me at all events, that we could carry Resolution 242 in the present Security Council. No matter. In the celebrated exhortation of Mikhail Gorbachev to the Forty-third General Assembly (see Chapter 6), *Pacta sunt servanda*, agreements must be kept. A world in which the essential undertakings of international law, as contained in the UN Charter, are upheld will be a world in which the state of Israel is secure. Absent that, prospects are grim. And so in a sense we return to the Wilsonian project, but with a new emphasis. Great global wars seem a thing of the past. We may yet blow ourselves up, but there is not likely to be another Guadalcanal. There will, however, almost certainly be a profusion of ethnic and regional conflicts, always with a danger of escalation, but more likely to remain regional. We will now see to what extent the international community can constrain and confine such conflicts.

If there is an answer to this question, it escapes me. My purpose is merely to raise the question once again. Do we want to try again? There *will* be law. The question is what law. The law of the Charter? No? Then what law? In what follows I will have little to say on the subject of international law itself save that it exists. Those who do not think this absurd may be disposed to think it obvious, and ask, why belabor the obvious? Sidney Hook was frequently asked a similar question concerning his half-century struggle to affirm in the face of Marxist derision that democracy was both a valid and a viable form of government. He once observed by way of reply:

> My conclusions will not be startling—originality in this sphere is almost always a sign of error . . . At any rate, I console myself with Justice Holmes's observation that sometimes the vindication of the obvious is more important than the elucidation of the obscure—especially when the obvious is challenged.[17]

I could hope for no more. That challenge has gone on long enough in the case of international law, an aspect of a despairing time that may now be coming to a close. The long twilight struggle is ending;

we appear to have prevailed. It is not too soon, then, to ask by what rules we expect to conduct ourselves in the next century. Nor is it too late to recall that we began the present century and, earlier, our own national existence with firm views and, yes, great expectations on this matter.

CHAPTER ONE

Peace

In 1826 James Kent, New York lawyer, Federalist, appointed master in chancery by John Jay, and professor at Columbia College, published the first of his four-volume *Commentaries on American Law,* Part I of which was titled "Of the Law of Nations." The first lecture, "Of the Foundation and History of the Law of Nations," began:

> When the United States ceased to be a part of the British empire, and assumed the character of an independent nation, they became subject to that system of rules which reason, morality, and custom had established among the civilized nations of Europe, as their public law. During the war of the American revolution, Congress claimed cognizance of all matters arising upon the law of nations, and they professed obedience to that law, "according to the general usages of Europe." By this law we are to understand that code of public instruction, which defines the rights and prescribes the duties of nations, in their intercourse with each other. The faithful observance of this law is essential to national character, and to the happiness of mankind.[1]

Thus did the first great treatise of its kind begin by presenting the law of nations as the first principle of the American legal system. That which both set it apart from and joined it with others; that which defined its compass; its extent as well as its limitation. That such law was binding was self-evident, as the founders might say. Surely this was believed, and the Congress acted on the belief. It is in fact clear from the *Journals of the Continental Congress* that during the Revolutionary War Congress considered matters arising under the law of nations and "professed obedience to that law."[2]

It could do little else, for the Declaration of Independence had claimed independence as a right under "the Laws of Nature and of Nature's God." This in the first passage, and then this in the second:

> We hold these truths to be self-evident, that all men are created equal, that they are endowed, by their Creator, with certain unalienable rights, that among these are life, liberty, and the pursuit of happiness. That to secure these rights, governments are instituted among men . . .

The idea of a law of nature was ancient by the time of the eighteenth century, but of course men of that century, notably the men of Philadelphia, were close to ancient things. The Greek texts were readily at hand; so also the Roman practice (for it was under Rome that the effort was made to work through questions of a "world" order comprising many different jurisdictions, and not just as an exercise in reason but as a matter of practical politics and government).[3] Christianity found this a coherent notion. St. Thomas Aquinas argued that natural law was the reflection of divine wisdom in human beings, discoverable by reason. The theoretical unity of Christianity dissolved with the emergence in the seventeenth century of an international, which is to say European, order of assertible and sovereign national states. We date this from the Peace of Westphalia (1648), which brought an end to the Thirty Years' War and the secular pretensions of a Holy Roman Empire. This was not an easy moment, at all events for the clerkly class. Was mere anarchy to be loosed upon the world? The war of all against all? Enter the idea of international law, as a direct and specific derivative of natural law.

J. L. Brierly of Oxford University first published *The Law of Nations* in 1928. Through successive editions he had no reason to much revise his version of the origins of international law. European events "seemed about to justify the whole theory of sovereignty."[4] Yet there was also a mutuality of interests. The discovery of America, for one, created a shared interest in a reasonably stable division of the spoils. The Renaissance had created a heightened sense of a common European culture, while there was "the common feeling of revulsion against war" caused by the savagery of the Catholic-Protestant conflict.

All these causes co-operated to make it certain that the separate state could never be accepted as the final and perfect form of human association, and that in the modern as in the medieval world it would be necessary to recognize the existence of a wider unity. The rise of international law was the recognition of this truth. It accepted the abandonment of the medieval ideal of a world-state and took instead as its fundamental postulate the existence of a number of states, secular, national, and territorial; but it denied their absolute separateness and irresponsibility, and proclaimed that they were bound to one another by the supremacy of law. Thus it reasserted the medieval conception of unity, but in a form which took account of the new political structure of Europe.[5]

A certain duality emerged from this process. On the one hand there is asserted that which is timeless, settled, immutable. Blackstone, in his introduction to *Commentaries on the Laws of England* (1765–1769), has it thus:

> This law of nature, being co-eval with mankind and dictated by God himself, is of course superior in obligation to any other. It is binding over all the globe, in all countries, and at all times: no human laws are of any validity, if contrary to this; and such of them as are valid derive all their force, and all their authority . . . from this original.[6]

On the other hand, Brierly writes, "the law of nature stands for the existence of *purpose* in law,"[7] preeminently the purpose of world peace, beginning in northern Europe and expanding, it might be said, as northern Europe expanded. Hence Brierly's subtitle: "An Introduction to the International Law of Peace." This reflected Brierly's period. From the time of Grotius (1583–1645) the law of war has had equal rank with that setting forth rules of conduct in time of peace, and if anything has been more concrete. In either case the existence of law gave rise to contention as often as to consensus.

In addition to Grotius, Brierly discusses the writing of Emerich de Vattel (1714–1769), whom he criticizes for popularizing a distinction between "necessary" and "voluntary" international law, thereby "cutting the frail moorings which bound international law to any sound principle of obligation." He notes, however, that Vattel enjoyed "great popularity" in the United States because he recognized in certain circumstances the right of one part of a nation to separate itself from the rest.[8]

The first American edition of Blackstone was published in Philadelphia in 1771–72. We must assume it was familiar to the authors and signatories of the Declaration of Independence. But it would hardly appear that their "Laws of Nature" were the same as those of the English magistrate, a supporter of George III, by whom he was knighted in 1770. Nor yet of Samuel Johnson. "How is it," Johnson asked in *Taxation No Tyranny* (1775), "that we hear the loudest yelps for liberty among the drivers of Negroes?"[9] (The reference was to Jefferson, who owned a hundred slaves at the time he drafted the Declaration of Independence.)[10] Johnson was an abolitionist, as scornful of "the English barbarians that cultivate the southern islands of America" (the West Indies) as ever he was of the lawyers and landowners of Philadelphia.[11] He even held that Indians had rights. Donald Greene has noted that in the Seven Years' War Johnson's sympathies were entirely with the native Indians, who stood to lose no matter who won, albeit the French were to be preferred.[12] The French associated with Indians, and intermarried with them. The American colonists were the last group Johnson could have wished to succeed either the British or the French. The Declaration, for example, charged that George III had set loose upon the colonies "the merciless indian savages, whose known rule of warfare, is an undistinguished destruction of all ages, sexes, and conditions," a closer description of the behavior of the colonists than of their foes. And what of this item "submitted to a candid world" in evidence of George III's purpose to establish "an absolute tyranny" over the soon to be United States?

> . . . abolishing the free system of English laws in a neighboring prov-
> ince, establishing therein an arbitrary government, and enlarging its
> boundaries, so as to render it at once an example and fit instrument
> for introducing the same absolute rule into these colonies . . .

This is to say, the Quebec Act of 1774, which granted the province of Quebec, "the free Exercise of the Religions of the Church of *Rome*."[13] Henry Steele Commager describes the measure as "one of the most enlightened pieces of colonial administration in the history of European colonial expansion."[14] It was nothing of the sort to the orators of Boston. It was an "intolerable" act intended, as John C. Miller summarizes, "to employ the 'Popish slaves' of Quebec to establish the doctrines of royal absolutism and Roman

Catholicism throughout the American colonies."[15] So much for the then American "Laws of Nature."

The point is that international law is not higher law or better law; it is *existing* law. It is not a law that eschews force; such a view is alien to the very idea of law. Often as not it is the law of the victor; but it is law withal and does evolve. There was little that could be called human rights law in Dr. Johnson's time; there is much today. Ironically, if you like, the Battle of Saratoga hastened that evolution.

In its earlier stages it was a formidable task, for commentators no less than statesmen, to determine just what the law *was*. Some subjects were simpler than others. Brierly observes that "the international rules relating to territory are still in essentials the Roman rules of property."[16] An unproductive detour was taken with the rise of theories about a primal "state of nature" in which men once abided in obedience to a beneficent code of good conduct and unaffected affability. Even so, rules came into being; some more often acknowledged than adhered to, but rules withal. Increasingly, law corresponded to the behavior of states. Chancellor Kent fairly described the process as seen early in the nineteenth century.

> The law of nations, so far as it is founded on the principles of natural law, is equally binding in every age, and upon all mankind. But the Christian nations of Europe, and their descendants on this side of the Atlantic, by the vast superiority of their attainments in arts, and science, and commerce, as well as in policy and government; and, above all, by the brighter light, the more certain truths, and the more definite sanction, which Christianity has communicated to the ethical jurisprudence of the ancients, have established a law of nations peculiar to themselves. They form together a community of nations, united by religion, manners, morals, humanity, and science, and united also by the mutual advantages of commercial intercourse, by the habit of forming alliances and treaties with each other, of interchanging ambassadors, and of studying and recognising the same writers and systems of public law.[17]

As late as 1900 the Supreme Court in the case of the *Paquete Habana,* declaring that "International law is part of our law," could look to find it among "the customs and usages of civilized nations; and, as evidence of these . . . the works of jurists and commentators, who by years of labor, research, and experience, have made themselves peculiarly well acquainted with the subjects of which they treat."[18] But by that point such subject matter had dwindled to admiralty and prize cases. Nations were now putting it in writing.

. . . . .

Nineteen hundred. A good year for international law. The long peace of the nineteenth century seemed to have settled in as an aspect of the human condition. Evidence of this peace was, first of all, the absence, or brevity, or marginality of war. Evidence of peace was also to be found in the growing body of international agreements and arrangements designed to prevent war. The design and development of these contrivances were proving ever more congenial to American statesmen who, as from the outset, were likely also to be lawyers. If, as is frequently charged, Americans had a propensity to view the international arena as a court of law, so be it. That was a disposition, and not all that difficult to understand. Among other things, courts were cheaper than navies.[19]

The prominence of lawyers in American public life, if frequently noted, ought not on those grounds to be ignored. It approaches a national trait. Twenty-three of the fifty-six signers of the Declaration were lawyers, and they were a clear majority at the Constitutional Convention. In the nineteenth century the law all but eclipsed other professions or occupations in the Congress. In 1989, two centuries out, nearly two-thirds of the Senators are lawyers. Still. For better or worse this has made a difference. The Declaration was less a manifesto than a brief. The charge was usurpation: "[t]he establishment of an absolute tyranny over these States. To prove this, let facts be submitted to a candid world." For which read jury. Eleven years later, at the Constitutional Convention, it was readily agreed that the law of nations would be part of our law and that Congress should enact laws to punish offenses against it. Any assembly of this sort at that time would likely have done as much. But lawyerlike debate on the floor of the Convention turned to the question of whether the term *law of nations* was sufficiently precise. Vagueness is fatal in a criminal statute. Accordingly, the founders decided to give Congress the power to define as well as to punish offenses against it.

Curiously, Congress did not much pursue this matter; others did. In what was either the last of the constitutional accords of the new republic, or the first of the political bargains, Jefferson and Hamilton in 1790 agreed to move the capital from New York City to a swamp on the banks of the Potomac, the latter having the great virtue, in Jefferson's view, of being miasmic, malarial, and, best of all, nearly inaccessible. The government would move there. The culture would remain in New York.[20] One result was that much of the international affairs of the new nation continued in the hands of New York lawyers. This indeed gave a legalist cast to American foreign relations that was distinctive among nations. It was New York centered, more specifically centered on the Upper East Side of Manhattan, in Michael Barone's phrase "the heartland of the robust, confident, ruling Republican Party of the era of Theodore Roosevelt and William Howard Taft."[21] A good exemplar is William Maxwell Evarts (1818–1901), sometime president of the Association of the Bar of the City of New York, chief counsel for the Republican party, United States senator. Evarts was counsel on the American side of the *Alabama* claims arbitration that took place in Geneva in 1871–72. The success of the tribunal seemed epic at the time. The United States had all but gone to war with Britain over the construction, fitting out, and provision of Confederate ships in British ports. (The *Alabama* was a wooden steam-powered sloop built in Liverpool. She cruised from 1862 to 1864, at which point she was sunk off Cherbourg by the *Kearsarge*.) But then for most of the century the prospect of war with Britain had loomed at intervals. After Appomattox our blood was up; something was going to happen, and we were going to start it. The British sensed this and more; their relations with the United States needed to change in the context of Europe. By the Treaty of Washington of 1871, the British agreed to arbitration.

In the event, the United States was seen to have won: $15,500,000 in gold. Further, the five-person tribunal—Italian, Brazilian, and Swiss arbitrators, and one each from the United States and the United Kingdom—laid down rules relating to the conduct of neutral powers which were seen to be a large advance. The *Alabama* Tribunal was unanimous, save for the British member, in awarding damages and, in the process, invoking "principles of international law" as dispositive.[22] A jubilant editorial in the *New York Times* noted that the Treaty of Washington had agreed in advance that the arbitration should be "settled by the rules of international law long held by the American Government but rejected by the English Government."[23] Washington and Jefferson, it continued, were vindicated. The 1872 election was approaching, the parties and their partisans at full decibel. The reputation of the Grant administration was necessarily involved. The *Times* claimed victory for its candidate and his arbitration. "Crazy blatherskites ready to pick a quarrel with Great Britain on any pretense . . . and silly partisans" might cavil, but, the editorial concluded, any such would "find themselves utterly powerless to conceal the solid gains honorably won by the United States in the settlement of the *Alabama* claims." With a measure of portent, the editorialist included among the former "the ultra Fenian Press." For the moment, however, international law and the pacific settlement of disputes could be counted as solid Republican assets.

Abraham D. Sofaer, the jurist and sometime professor at Columbia Law School, suggests that this renewed enthusiasm for law owed much to "the monumental destructiveness of the Civil War," the first conflict to approach the slaughter of "industrial" warfare.[24] Matters went further, however, impelled by a growing sense of Anglo-American ties and by the expanding American empire. The time came when Frederic R. Coudert, a respectable New York attorney, might decline an offer to be chief justice of the United States Supreme Court but cheerfully go off to arbitrate dominion over fur seals in the Bering Sea, and thereafter to settle the respective claims of Britain and Venezuela in the rain forests of South America. In 1890 the First Pan-American Congress established an arbitration system which Secretary of State James G. Blaine hailed as a "new Magna Carta."[25] In 1897 Secretary of State Richard Olney negotiated a five-year arbitration agreement with Britain to resolve all differences not settled by diplomacy. The *New York Times* declared that *this* would pass into history with both the Magna Carta *and* the Declaration of Independence.

These events and the accompanying enthusiasms are not to be dismissed. By the end of the century, war with Britain, putatively the world's greatest power, was simply no longer a prospect. New York lawyers knew this; Sea Lords knew it. By the late nineteenth century, for the first time since American independence, the battle plans of the British Caribbean Squadron all but precluded any possibility of hostilities with the United States. And it did seem to work with others. In 1905 the United States for the first time emerged as a mediator in a serious war between great powers, yet brought it off in that "bully" American manner. The manner of William Maxwell Evarts, Frederic Coudert, Charles Evans Hughes, or Elihu Root. It is all nicely captured in the official history of the Lotos Club, then located at midtown on Fifth Avenue. The club had been founded in 1870 by the mayor of New York "to establish a congenial meeting place in which he could entertain distinguished visitors from Europe and other parts of the world." It now served just such a purpose.

> When President Theodore Roosevelt assembled Japanese and Russian arbitrators in America for the purpose of ending the bitter Russo-Japanese war, these dignitaries left a deadlocked conference one afternoon to retire to the Lotos bar where they miraculously found themselves talking the same language. Shortly afterwards, points of agreement reached in the clubhouse were incorporated in the Treaty of Portsmouth, which ended the war.[26]

Here was this still new nation, just setting up "a congenial meeting place" for foreign visitors, settling a portentous clash of arms between two powers that before the century was out would be successively our most wounding and our most dangerous adversaries ever. Taking an active, if innocent, part in events that would lead on to just such encounters, the while initiating a process of peacemaking that had no true precedent in history. Bright, confident morning indeed! Theodore Roosevelt received the Nobel Peace Prize, the first American to do so.

In 1899 Nicholas II, the czar of Russia, had convened a great peace conference at The Hague, with the United States in attendance. The Permanent Court of Arbitration was thereupon established. In 1904 Theodore Roosevelt proposed a second such conference, which met in 1907 with forty-four nations on hand. (That being about as many nations as there then were.) All manner of arrangements were discussed for the pacific settlement of international disputes. A draft plan was also prepared for a judicial international *court,* a court of law that is, a tribunal with jurisdiction well beyond that of an arbitration panel. Americans thrived on this. These particular Americans, at all events. Sofaer comments: "The early supporters of a world court were a special breed, successful, cultured, articulate, and above all devoted to the elevation of reason over force in human affairs."[27] It was, of course, recommended that a third peace conference be convened presently.

And of course, it never met.

CHAPTER TWO

War

In the wet spring of 1946, Evelyn Waugh in England received an invitation to attend a Pax Romana conference in Spain. It was much welcomed, for he was "stale and bored," and bitter. The Second World War had been over for a year and the aftermath was now clear to him, as politics often is clear to the apolitical. The defeat of Fascism was everywhere, seemingly, turning into a victory of Communism. A hideous modern paganism was being supplanted by a yet more hideous modern atheism; "all that seeming-solid, patiently built, gorgeously ornamented structure of Western life was to melt overnight like an ice-castle, leaving only a puddle of mud."[1] In the 1930s Waugh had seen Ethiopia overrun by Fascist troops, even as the League dithered on about sanctions against Italy. In the 1940s he had seen Tito prevail in Yugoslavia, with the non-Communist enemies of Fascism within the Yugoslav resistance now on trial and soon to die. His diary records the journey:

> London–Madrid, Saturday 15 June 1946: At Croydon we met . . . Professor Brierly of All Souls on his way to Francisco de Vitoria celebrations . . . At Madrid Professor Brierly was met by suave lawyers . . . and conducted in car to Palace Hotel . . . I by gauche Pax Romana students who took us by bus to low-class Hotel Nacional. It then became plain that Francisco de Vitoria Association was a luxury tour for international jurists . . . after dinner . . . called on Brierly . . .[2]

The professor was off to Castile; the novelist joined him.

Three years later Waugh published the novella *Scott-King's Modern Europe*. Brierly, the professor of international law, reappears as a hapless, if not in the end ignoble, classics master at an English public school; his misadventures as a guide to the new dark age. His passion was the work of a late Renaissance poet, Bellorius.

No one, except perhaps Scott-King himself, could be dimmer. When, poor and in some discredit, Bellorius died in 1646 in his native town of what was then a happy kingdom of the Habsburg Empire and is now the turbulent modern state of Neutralia, he left as his life's work a single folio volume containing a poem of some 1500 lines of Latin hexameters . . . The subject was irredeemably tedious—a visit to an imaginary island of the New World where in primitive simplicity, untainted by tyranny or dogma, there subsisted a virtuous, chaste and reasonable community.[3]

Neutralia now discovers Bellorius in its own past and, experiencing some difficulties with its reputation in the present, convenes an international conference to celebrate the tricentennial of the author. Scott-King is invited, and sets off with subdued but stirring expectations. Waugh continues.

Something must be known of this history if we are to follow Scott-King with understanding. Let us eschew detail and observe that for three hundred years since Bellorius's death his country has suffered every conceivable ill the body politic is heir to. Dynastic wars, foreign invasion, disputed successions, revolting colonies, endemic syphilis, impoverished soil, masonic intrigues, revolutions, restorations, cabals, juntas, pronunciamentos, liberations, constitutions, coups d'état, dictatorships, assassinations, agrarian reforms, popular elections, foreign intervention, repudiation of loans, inflations of currency, trades unions, massacres, arson, atheism, secret societies—make the list full, slip in as many personal foibles as you will, you will find all these in the last three centuries of Neutralian history. Out of it emerged the present republic of Neutralia, a typical modern state, governed by a single party, acclaiming a dominant Marshal, supporting a vast ill-paid bureaucracy whose work is tempered and humanised by corruption.[4]

The pilgrimage proceeds by stages from innocence to horror, ending in "No. 64 Jewish Illicit Immigrants' Camp, Palestine."[5]

In the *New York Times Book Review* George Orwell described the coda.

Back at Granchester, amid the notched desks and the draughty corridors, the headmaster informs him sadly that the number of classical scholars is falling off and suggests that he shall combine his teaching of the classics with something a little more up-to-date:

"Parents are not interested in producing the 'complete man' any more. They want to qualify their boys for jobs in the modern world. You can hardly blame them, can you?"

"Oh, yes," said Scott-King, "I can and do."

Later he adds: "I think it would be very wicked indeed to do anything to fit a boy for the modern world." And when the headmaster objects that this is a short-sighted view, Scott-King retorts, "I think it the most long-sighted view it is possible to take."

Then, with the perfect pitch that writers of great gift have for one another's work, Orwell sums up:

This last statement, it should be noted, is intended seriously. The book is very short, hardly longer than a short story, and it is written with the utmost lightness, but it has a definite political meaning. The modern world, we are meant to infer, is so unmistakably crazy, so certain to smash itself to pieces in the near future, that to attempt to understand it or come to terms with it is simply a purposeless self-corruption. In the chaos that is shortly coming, a few moral principles that one can cling to, and perhaps even a few half-remembered odes of Horace or choruses from Euripides, will be more useful than what is now called "enlightenment."[6]

Brierly had indeed begun his section "The Classical Writers on International Law" with an appreciation of Francisco de Vitoria, professor of theology at Salamanca from 1526 to 1546, one of the "Catholic" progenitors too often "neglected" by subsequent Protestant authorities. His principal work, published after his death, contained "an examination of the title of the Spaniards to exercise domination over the inhabitants of the New World which is remarkable for its courageous defence of the rights of the Indians."[7]

Well, men had thought that way. But it no longer much mattered. There was not going to be a "New World . . . untainted by tyranny or dogma." There would be nothing *save* tyranny and dogma. What was coming was Orwell's world of *1984*, which would appear in Britain four months after his review of Waugh was published in the United States.

In 1951 Hannah Arendt, a Jewish refugee, one of the lucky ones, now in New York, published *The Origins of Totalitarianism*. It began:

Two World Wars in one generation, separated by an uninterrupted chain of local wars and revolutions, followed by no peace treaty for the vanquished and no respite for the victor, have ended in the anticipation of a third World War between the two remaining world powers. This moment of anticipation is like the calm that settles after all hopes have died.[8]

This dying of the light had not come suddenly; only a certain resigned understanding had come suddenly. At dusk on August 3, 1914, the British foreign secretary, Viscount Grey, observed to a visitor to the Foreign Office, "The lamps are going out all over Europe; we shall not see them lit again in our life-time."[9] But it was not quite that. A dimming, yes, a fading until darkness came at noon, but a sequence even so. It began, of course, that August of 1914, with the First World War.

The origins of the First World War are not, on the surface, all that difficult to sort out. More easily lost to our age is the shock of the actual event. Some ten million killed, some thirty million casualties in all. At the Somme in 1916 the British would lose as many men in one day as they had lost in a near quarter-century of war with Revolutionary and Napoleonic France. Citing Montesquieu, Chancellor Kent suggested that international law was "founded on the principle, that different nations ought to do each other as much good in peace, and as little harm in war, as possible, without injury to their true interests."[10] This was not naive. Not that much harm *was* possible. (The Continental Army and its French allies lost 262 men at Yorktown.) Now a wholly different order of destructiveness made its appearance. Previously unimaginable costs became routine as they became the condition of success. Even granting vast incompetence in the ruling classes, the impact of technology seems decisive. The American Civil War had suggested as much. Inventors proclaimed as much. It is all there in the proceedings of the Hague peace conferences. No submarines; none of the new mines; no discharge of projectiles and explosives from balloons; no bombardment of towns from the sea. They missed the machine gun and mustard gas; but then the third conference never met. With the carnage came a certain coarsening. Governments were cruel in ways never before experienced. Recall the Declaration's charge against the tyrant George III: "He has called together legislative bodies at places unusual, uncomfortable, and distant from the depository of their public records, for the sole purpose of fatiguing them into compliance with his measures." Still harsher measures proved possible; these now made their appearance. Not reappearance. Not the return to barbarism on the part of nations that had taken to referring to themselves as "civilized." Something altogether new. The totalitarian state. William Pfaff has written that Leninism merged into totalitarianism in part because it emerged from the cataclysm of the Great War:

> Whatever Leninism otherwise might have become, in the actual conditions of 1918 it took for its social model what was before it in the West—the war state, "totally" mobilized, with hundreds of millions of people under arms or drafted to war production, centrally planned, directed by governments given exceptional powers over how citizens lived, where they worked, how they died.[11]

From the war on the Eastern front to the "war Communism" of the early Soviet state was a short walk indeed. Pfaff notes that Asian Communists shared this experience; Chou En-lai and Ho Chi Minh were in France at the time. Hitler was there, too. Carrying messages to the front, acquiring his wounds—psychic as well as physical—and learning firsthand how "total" war is waged.

Pfaff concludes that those who "accepted totalitarianism were in some sense retroactively justifying what they had been through in the world war. An appalling sacrifice had been demanded, and had been made. The values of the societies that enthusiastically had gone to war were the values that the war itself contradicted or discredited." Lenin, Chou, Ho, and Hitler adopted the methods, replacing the values. "Nihilism was thus the war's principal outcome."[12]

In a slightly different formulation, it might be said that nihilism was the war's principal victor, for the way had been prepared, not least in czarist Russia, where the term was first used in Turgenev's *Fathers and Sons*.[13] Leopold Labedz observes that the Nazi victory in Germany was described as a "revolution of nihilism."[14] Nazism, however, was too specifically a nationalist movement—*National Sozialistische Bewegung*—to have any universal appeal. By contrast, Italian Fascism made more general claims as a political theory and found adherents here and there, especially in Catholic polities, where corporatism had a respectable lineage. (In truth, a neocorporatism is prominent in contemporary European social theory, or, more accurately, social practice.) But for universal appeal no totalitarian doctrine equaled Marxism-Leninism as it took form in the closing days and immediate aftermath of the First World War.

In the beginning there was the scientism of Marx and Engels: the claim to knowledge of the future. Any such claim could gain a friendly hearing in nineteenth-century Europe, at times seemingly preoccupied with devising schemes for ideal societies. (Which perhaps explains why so little heed was paid the claim of the American founders to have developed a "new science of politics," on the basis of which American constitutional arrangements were founded.[15] They sought to establish a stable society, not an ideal one.) There was also, obviously, a displaced religiosity in all this. Note the persistence of Frederic Engels as a cult figure. Party theorists insisted on this with the punctilio of the strictest trinitarian. As late as 1975 four portraits hovered over Tiananmen Square atop immense flagstaffs: Mao, the Han Chinese; Stalin, with a touch of Mongol about the eyes; and two hirsute Victorian gentlemen in waistcoats, white shirts, and flowing ties: Marx, of course, but Engels also.

In the 1920s Bertrand Russell noted the parallels between Communism and organized Western religion.[16] Founders, martyrs, texts, hierarchy, faithful. (This was painfully in evidence in Russia, where in time children took to wearing lapel pins of the infant Lenin.) It was a religion of consolation and redemption; suffering now, paradise to come.

Lenin commences to seem part of a distant past. He isn't; or at least until quite recently, wasn't. In his apartment in the Kremlin, there is a bookshelf behind his desk, with a number of works in English. A visitor in the 1980s recognized books by three authors he had himself known, talked with, read. Lenin and most of his fellow Bolsheviks were intellectuals moved by a concern for the "masses"—and able in turn to mobilize them—that is mysterious to this very day. *Why* were they so concerned, and if they were so concerned, why were they so brutal to the objects of their concern? Were they, in the end, just another cadre of Western bourgeois overwhelmed by guilt, much of it associated with the First World War?

In the 1970s John Dollard at Yale addressed the subject of guilt as a political motive.[17] In his view one of the ideas man tolerates least well is the notion that a large number of hard-to-control forces and circumstances dominates the lives of individuals and societies. Religions have responded to this unease. Now a secular religion had appeared to serve something of the same purpose. In this Dollard follows Russell, but from his own Freudian perspective. Modern sensibility rejects explicitly religious explanations; life is no longer satisfactorily explained in terms of the divine. The loss of this framework left a void. "Somebody or something he feels must be to *blame*" for things that go wrong. This need to blame is rooted, says Dollard, in one's earliest days, arising from the perceived treachery of a father or faithlessness of a mother, not to mention plotting by siblings. To survive in this heaving sea of guilt and malevolence the psyche must displace responsibility, clinging to blame as would a shipwreck victim to flotsam. And because man has "been in the market for an exculpatory theory, one which would shift from him the responsibility for his miserable lot," he is easy prey for Marxism. The more wretched, the more psychologically desperate to identify the villain who has stolen mankind's "surplus."

Pressing the point, we come to the thought that while Marxism enabled some men to proclaim that they had been robbed, it enabled others to proclaim that they were—robbers! Or at all events to confess that cousins, uncles, aunts had been. In the aftermath of the First World War, guilt about the state of society was at least as prominent as anger, and with a pronounced social class distinction. Of New York in the 1930s it was correctly noted that the intelligentsia, which is to say people who had gone to college, blamed the depression on capitalism. Workers, which is to say people who had not finished high school, tended to blame it on prohibition. But it is a bit too easy at this distance to ridicule the "right left people," Orwell's term. They wanted to stand for something decent as the world, crawling out of the horror of the First World War, slouched toward the horror of the second.

The American experience of Communism was largely of this order. Nathan Glazer has recorded the extraordinary growth in the party's membership in the United States beginning in the 1930s.[18] Many, most, were but one or two generations away from Europe and were simply closer to European political ideas. Others were simply American idealists, seeing little hope with what was at hand at home. There is, heaven knows, a literature depicting both attachments; confessional in the main, for the attachments tended to be brief. And yet, as time passes and ideology fades, the intensity of expectations, its millennial immediacy, becomes difficult to construct. Richard Rovere, later of the *New Yorker* magazine, was then a young party member working on the *New Masses,* and assigned to cultivate the newest recruit, A & P heir Huntington Hartford. Then came the fateful day of the Molotov-Ribbentrop pact. Rovere, who would go on to become one of the most lucid, retentive political commentators of his age, had even so one blank spot. He could remember almost nothing of August 24, 1939. That was the end of ideology for him, of course, as for others. But the Communist idea did not die. In scarcely a half-dozen years it would seem never so ascendant in the world at large.

It was, *The Economist* would observe, an idea that threatened to take the twentieth century by storm. The century; the world. This was at first its defining feature: it was an international movement. The blood of all men is red; hence the Red Flag. Hence that doleful anthem, "The Internationale." Hence, the Communist International (or Comintern) established in March 1919 to get history's work over and done with. For this was the essential Marxist claim. International Communism was the next stage in history. It was written. It was, you could say, nothing personal. And nothing could stop its international progress. In time Brierly's international peace would come about, but not in Brierly's way. Thus, Leninist doctrine decreed that there would be one final convulsion between the "two camps." Which was Hannah Arendt's view also, save that she expected only yet greater evil to come of it.

CHAPTER THREE

Wilson

At the moment the Comintern was launched at a meeting in Moscow in March 1919, the Paris Peace Conference was drafting the Covenant of the League of Nations. Thus commenced one of the defining contests of the Twentieth Century War, that between the world visions of Vladimir Ilyich Lenin (né Ulyanov) and Woodrow Wilson. There was a Tocquevillian symmetry to the events; the emergence as he foretold of America and Russia as the great powers of the earth. The event was all the more concise given that each power, looming over a shattered Europe, set forth its version of a future world system that it would not so much dominate as define. There was ambiguity. Was it Lenin's vision or Russia's destiny? Wilson's or America's? Or both? Yes in one case, not in the other? Which case? And yet, in the end, the conceptions were elementally opposed, one to the other. They were not presented as choices; rather as alternative futures yet to be revealed. One or the other, but which? It would come down to law. Would the law of "history" prevail, or would it be the law of nations?

Two years earlier the United States had gone to war in the name of said law of nations. Wilson, who had taught the subject at Princeton, went to the Capitol on the evening of April 2, 1917, with a legal brief demonstrating that the imperial German government, in violation of the laws of neutrality, had commenced actions that constituted war against the government and people of the United States. In "unhesitating obedience to . . . constitutional duty," he advised the Congress to respond in kind.[1]

The address was quintessential Wilson. We begin with texts. The German government was denying to neutral nations "the defense of rights which no modern publicist has ever before questioned."

(Observe a president of the United States assuming, and with reason, that by "publicist" those in attendance at and those reading about the joint session of Congress would understand the reference.) He set forth the actions of the German government and expressed the revulsion that right-thinking persons and nations would experience.

> I was for a little while unable to believe that such things would in fact be done by any government that had hitherto subscribed to the humane practices of civilized nations. International law had its origin in the attempt to set up some law which would be respected and observed upon the seas, where no nation had right of dominion and where lay the free highways of the world. By painful stage after stage has that law been built up, with meagre enough results, indeed, after all was accomplished that could be accomplished, but always with a clear view, at least, of what the heart and conscience of mankind demanded. This minimum of right the German Government has swept aside under the plea of retaliation and necessity and because it had no weapons which it could use at sea except these which it is impossible to employ as it is employing them without throwing to the winds all scruples of humanity or of respect for the understandings that were supposed to underlie the intercourse of the world . . .
>
> It is a war against all nations. American ships have been sunk, American lives taken, in ways which it has stirred us very deeply to learn of, but the ships and people of other neutral and friendly nations have been sunk and overwhelmed in the waters in the same way. There has been no discrimination. The challenge is to all mankind. Each nation must decide for itself how it will meet it. The choice we make for ourselves must be made with a moderation of counsel and a temperateness of judgment befitting our character and our motives as a nation. We must put excited feeling away. Our motive will not be revenge or the victorious assertion of the physical might of the nation, but only the vindication of right, of human right, of which we are only a single champion.[2]

A century earlier the United States had gone to war over the rights of neutrals, but Madison in 1812 had not proposed that human rights were involved. The law of nations, yes.[3] This was new. Nor did he stop there.

> Our object now, as then, is to vindicate the principles of peace and justice in the life of the world as against selfish and autocratic power

and to set up amongst the really free and self-governed peoples of
the world such a concert of purpose and of action as will henceforth
ensure the observance of those principles. Neutrality is no longer
feasible or desirable where the peace of the world is involved and
the freedom of its peoples, and the menace to that peace and freedom
lies in the existence of autocratic governments backed by organized
force which is controlled wholly by their will, not by the will of their
people. We have seen the last of neutrality in such circumstances.
We are at the beginning of an age in which it will be insisted that
the same standards of conduct and of responsibility for wrong done
shall be observed among nations and their governments that are
observed among the individual citizens of civilized states.[4]

What was this all *about*? Was submarine warfare the only aspect
of the First World War that the president found himself "unable
to believe"? Was this a war between good people and bad? In what
way had Wilhelmine Germany become a significantly different
society from that, say, of Edwardian Britain? From a distance we
would recognize most of the major belligerents of 1914 as liberal
nineteenth-century societies, with some variance in political rights,
but civil societies, with extensive civil rights, these often a substitute
for political ones. To be sure, you could get yourself sent to jail for
offending an official. But it would be a five-day sentence, and it
could be arranged to turn one's self in *after* Prince Orlofsky's ball.
Czarist Russia was the least developed of the great powers, but
was even so, as the term would come to be, a developing society.
Opposition was open, save when it chose to be secret. (*Pravda,* the
Communist party paper, was routinely published and just as routinely purchased and read.) As for concentration camps, they had
last been seen in South Africa, where the British had brought civilization to the Dutch-speaking Boers in an experiment whose outcome is still unclear. Wilson's vehemence against Germany was
surely disproportionate.

There is no easy understanding of this man. In Arthur S. Link
he has had a biographer and chronicler of a genius to match his
own. But in the end it is a mystery and will remain so. Much is
made of The Presbyterian and The Professor. More might be made
of The Southerner. Link records that Wilson's earliest memory was
that of a passerby shouting news of the election of Abraham Lincoln as president. His father was then pastor in a church in

Augusta, Georgia, which became a civil war hospital. The future president became all too familiar with the details of Sherman's march through Georgia. Thus the law of war had personal immediacy for him, and his record in this regard is exemplary. (After the United States entered the war in Europe mass civilian bombing was proposed; he vetoed the idea without hesitation.) He was, however, forever going to war; or rather, sending troops. First to Nicaragua, which he sought to make a protectorate, until rebuffed by the Senate.[5] Next, Haiti. Then the Dominican Republic. And, of course, Mexico. There the dictator of the hour had arrested some American sailors on shore liberty in Tampico. Then apologized. Not good enough. Wilson demanded he go to Tampico and salute the American flag. In 1918, quite without provocation, he sent expeditionary forces to Murmansk, Archangel, and Vladivostok. The last United States troops were not withdrawn until 1920.

Is there something of the Southerner in this? The postbellum Southerner? Honor. Valor. Something. Wilson was fiercely anti-imperialist where others were concerned. He wished, if anything, to see the end of the British Empire. But it was imperial Germany that was sinking our ships, and that was enough at the end of the day. Samuel Flagg Bemis has argued that in appeasing the British who were impressing American seamen during the Napoleonic Wars, Jefferson had been frittering away the independence of the United States. This southern president—the first since Andrew Johnson—would have none of that. On the occasion of his address to the Congress calling for a declaration of war, he had driven to the Capitol with an escort of cavalry. Congress had thundered its approval. The world *would* be made safe for democracy.

The address ended on an ominous note:

It is a fearful thing to lead this great peaceful people into war, into the most terrible and disastrous of all wars, civilization itself seeming to be in the balance. But the right is more precious than peace, and we shall fight for the things which we have always carried nearest our hearts, for democracy, for the right of those who submit to authority to have a voice in their own governments, for the rights and liberties of small nations, for a universal dominion of right by such a concert of free peoples as shall bring peace and safety to all nations and make the world itself at last free. To such a task we can dedicate our lives and our fortunes, everything that we are and everything that we have, with the pride of those who know that the day has come when America is privileged to spend her blood and her might for the principles that gave her birth and happiness and the peace which she has treasured. God helping her, she can do no other.[6]

Whatever else, we may agree that it was a fearful thing to lead Woodrow Wilson to war. Recall that he had commenced his administration by choosing William Jennings Bryan, a pacifist, for secretary of state. There were political considerations. Something had had to be done about or at least offered to Bryan. Clearly the champion of the American Bimetallic League had to be kept away from the Treasury. What was there in the cabinet? He was offered State and took it on condition that he might negotiate a network of arbitration and conciliation treaties and that this be central to the administration's foreign policy. (Twenty-nine treaties for the Advancement of Peace were in fact negotiated. Twenty were ratified.)[7] Wilson took care to see that the post of counselor to the department went to John Bassett Moore, professor of international law at Columbia University. But otherwise he was tolerant of the earnest innocence Bryan brought to most matters. Bryan's biographer, Louis W. Koenig, records that when asked his views on foreign policy, the Boy Orator stated that these had been set forth in a speech in Indianapolis in 1900: He

> envisioned the ideal of the American Republic proclaiming and practicing in its relations with the world the principle that all men are created equal. He aspired to see "a republic standing erect while empires all around are bowed beneath the weight of their own armaments—a republic whose flag is loved while other flags are only feared." Let the United States hasten the coming of "universal brotherhood," let it be "the supreme moral factor in the world's progress." For Bryan the awaiting Secretaryship of State was a Promethean opportunity. In that office, as he conceived it, he could become a lasting benefactor of mankind. He could banish the scourge of war from the face of the earth.[8]

Bryan secured Wilson's further agreement that official dinners be teetotal—from London George Bernard Shaw proposed that this achievement for mankind be capped by making them vegetarian as well—and that he could continue to accept lecture fees. That done, he was on his own, determined to banish war as a curse of mankind.[9]

By 1915 war had come and Bryan had departed, succeeded by his deputy, Robert Lansing, who had previously been associate counsel for the United States in the Bering Sea arbitration and had served in similar capacities before a number of international tribunals. Lansing was a founder, in 1906, of the American Society of International Law and helped establish the *American Journal of International Law* in 1907, serving as one of the editors until his death. (He had also been Democratic chairman of Jefferson County, New York, with its rolling farmland, plunging rivers, and strategic location on the Canadian border.) His *Notes on Sovereignty from the Standpoint of the State and the World,* published by the Carnegie Endowment for International Peace, is a considerable work of jurisprudence in the field of international law. Save, possibly, Webster, no American secretary of state before and none since has been so accomplished in this specific discipline.

But even among those who put great store by international law, and we observe that there were many such at the beginning of the century in the United States, there were crucial differences as to how the law might come to be obeyed. In *Man, the State, and War,* Kenneth Waltz distinguishes among those who think wars arise from the nature of man, those who think it is driven by the internal nature of certain "aggressive" states, and those who hold that wars arise from the nature of the international system and lack of arrangements for suppressing the disorders that inevitably arise.[10] The generality of American statesmen and publicists of this period held with the last view, which of course implies that world peace is, after all, possible. Very well, what then?

How does one propose to suppress disorder? Men such as Lansing did not. Which is to say that they did not think of an enforcement system, but rather of one that was *self*-enforcing. For all the sophistication, this came close to asserting that goodwill and arbitration treaties would do the trick. Wilson himself seems to have begun there. In 1916 he addressed the first National Assembly of the League to Enforce Peace.[11] Lansing records that "after preparing his address he went over it and erased all reference to the use of

physical force in preventing wars." Lansing approved. He stressed
the point with Wilson. "In our conversations prior to 1918 I had
uniformly opposed the idea of the employment of international
force to compel a nation to respect the rights of other nations and
had repeatedly urged judicial settlement as the practical way of
composing international controversies, though I did not favor the
use of force to compel such settlement." The armistice was signed
November 11, 1918. Eleven days later, Lansing, now a peace commissioner, wrote to Wilson. He feared "a disposition to adopt physical might as the basis of the organization," which is to say the
League of Nations (the British having come up with a name).[12]

It is possible to be dissatisfied with these men, but not on grounds
of fuzziness. Lansing saw *precisely* the issue. The Europeans were
dreaming up an organization designed to keep Germany from
starting another war. The Americans were going along in the
hope—nothing more—that something grand would come of it all.
Something altogether new was of a sudden being proposed. This
was beyond international law; this was getting close to international government. Lansing's note to Wilson on November 22,
1918, is required reading. The draft Covenant proposed that the
League would "respect and preserve" the territorial integrity of
members. In which event,

> the power to act rather than the right to act, becomes the funda-
> mental principle of organization, just as it has been in all previous
> Congresses and Concerts of the European Powers.
>
> It appears to me that a positive guaranty of territorial integrity
> and political independence by the nations would have to rest upon
> an open recognition of dominant coercive power in the articles of
> agreement, the power being commercial and economic as well as
> physical. The wisdom of entering into such a guaranty is question-
> able and should be carefully considered before being adopted.
>
> In order to avoid the recognition of force as a basis and the ques-
> tion of dominant force with the unavoidable classification of nations
> into "big" and "little," "strong" and "weak," the desired result of
> a guaranty might be attained by entering into a mutual undertaking
> *not* to impair the territorial integrity or to violate the political sov-
> ereignty of any state. The breach of this undertaking would be a
> breach of the treaty and would sever the relations of the offending
> nation with all other signatories.[13]

We are now at a great transition in the history of our subject. Lansing believed in *law,* and as much on those grounds as any other was suspicious of *organization.* Waltz describes such persons as noninterventionist liberals, who called for "no special activities to bring about the widely desired goal of perpetual peace."[14] This may have been—may be—an illusion; but how much evidence have we that organizations do better? In any event, the interested reader wants to be clear that the question of international law is independent of the question of international organization. The League of Nations, like the United Nations later, was designed to enforce law, not to make it, save as a setting in which agreements might be reached. Each created or inherited political tasks that were problematic at best. Lansing did not fail to note "the perplexing and seemingly unsound system of mandates."[15]

Wilson opted for organization. In truth, he followed in Theodore Roosevelt's steps. In 1910, on the occasion of accepting his Nobel Peace Prize, the sometime Roughrider took muscular internationalism to new heights.

> . . . it would be a master stroke if those great powers honestly bent on peace would form a League of Peace, not only to keep the peace among themselves, but to prevent, by force if necessary, its being broken by others. The supreme difficulty in connection with developing the peace work of The Hague arises from the lack of any executive power, of any police power to enforce the decrees of the court. In any community of any size the authority of the courts rests upon actual or potential force; on the existence of a police, or on the knowledge that the able-bodied men of the country are both ready and willing to see that the decrees of judicial and legislative bodies are put into effect. In new and wild communities where there is violence, an honest man must protect himself; and until other means of securing his safety are devised, it is both foolish and wicked to persuade him to surrender his arms while the men who are dangerous to the community retain theirs. He should not renounce the right to protect himself by his own efforts until the community is so organized that it can effectively relieve the individual of the duty of putting down violence. So it is with nations. Each nation must keep well prepared to defend itself until the establishment of some form of international police power, competent and willing to prevent violence as between nations. As things are now, such power to command peace throughout the world could best be assured by some

combination between those great nations which sincerely desire peace and have no thought themselves of committing aggressions.[16]

In this perspective Wilson becomes more representative, more an amalgam of his time as against the singular man. The war would be a war to end war. On January 8, 1918, the president addressed a joint session of Congress and set forth the nation's war and peace aims in the Fourteen Points. The first of these was a pledge to openness in diplomacy. (The Bolsheviks were publishing secret treaties.) Next came the law of the sea: "Absolute freedom of navigation upon the seas, outside territorial waters, alike in peace and in war, except as the seas may be closed in whole or in part by international action for the enforcement of international covenants." Lastly, "A general association of nations must be formed under specific covenants for the purpose of affording mutual guarantees of political independence and territorial integrity to great and small states alike."[17]

The rest is ruin. Wilson went in person to Europe—an event without precedent—and brought back a treaty with Germany that included a League of Nations. The Senate attached reservations that Wilson refused to accept. The Republican candidate, Warren G. Harding, was elected president in 1920, and the United States went its own way. This history is now twice told and need hardly be repeated. Still, somehow, nothing is settled as to what really did or could have happened. The issues are still with us, and the possibilities may usefully be recounted. There are, at least, two.

· · · · ·

It was not possible.

It was indeed "a fearful thing" to lead the American people into that "most terrible and disastrous of all wars."[18] The United States was then, as now, a multiethnic polity. But then, unlike now, there was an unchallenged assumption that the nation was basically "Anglo-Saxon" in its leadership and its ethos. The long quarrel with Great Britain was past. There *was* an American establishment, and by 1915 it was solidly on the side of Britain and the Allies, as they had come to be called, who stood for democracy and freedom. The Central *Powers*—the choice of terms is suggestive—stood, as Koenig writes, for "imperial militaristic autocracy."[19] The great

German-American community was now subjected to mortification approaching that of Japanese-Americans in the Second World War. It was vulgar, no less than scandalous. Sauerkraut became Liberty Cabbage. It was villainous, as in the increasing celebration of race. (In our day the treatment of German-Americans in that day would be called racist.) Imperial Germany was not above meddling with American ethnic groups. German agents were involved with an armed expedition of California Sikhs which actually made its way to the Punjab in British India. Irish Americans were involved with the 1916 nationalist uprising in Dublin, and German agents were active thereafter. Wilson probably never learned of the California incident, but he was indignant and disdainful of the Irish, who after all had only got him elected governor of New Jersey.

The painful truth is that American neutrality in the European war was something of a lie. Wilson was an anglophile, but many of his principal aides were much more. They were pro-Allied. Koenig writes that Bryan's early strictures on neutrality were simply ignored.

> At London the American ambassador, Walter Hines Page, like Wilson, was an admirer of British society and culture, possibly even more so than the President. Thanking "heaven I'm of their race and blood," Page was easily amenable to the thesis advanced by the captivating British Foreign Minister, Sir Edward Grey, that the Allies were fighting America's battle for democracy. Time and again, Page toned down his instructions and presented American protests in ways that left the British impressed that the United States was not serious. "I have now read the despatch," Page said one day in handing Grey a document signed by Bryan, "but I do not agree with it; let us consider how it should be answered!"[20]

Most potent of all those with an Allied bias was none other than Lansing, the stickler for the rules. On one important matter after another, he enveloped neutrality in a fog of legal technicalities and manipulated argument freely in favor of the Allies and against Germany.

> I saw with apprehension the tide of resentment against Great Britain rising higher and higher in this country . . . I did all that I could to prolong the disputes by preparing . . . long and detailed replies, and introducing technical and controversial matters in the hope that

before the extended interchange of arguments came to an end something would happen to change the current of American public opinion or to make the American people perceive that German absolutism was a menace to their liberties and to democratic institutions everywhere.[21]

Lawyerlike, as you might say.

If the secretary of state took liberties with the law of nations, both Congress and the executive were soon taking liberties with the Constitution. The Espionage Act was followed by the Sedition Act. American society became less free. The historian Alvin M. Josephy, Jr., writes of the transformation. First, the mobilization of industry and labor. Then taxes, the War Revenue Act. Then surveillance, the Trading with the Enemy Act. He continues:

At the same time several acts, urged by the administration and supported by the fervent patriotism and anti-German feeling of a great majority of the American people and their representatives' in Congress, broke sharply with the benign atmosphere of political tolerance and freedom of dissent of the progressive period. Paralleling the emergency controls on business, they seriously abridged civil liberties and traditional American rights.[22]

The Bolsheviks appeared on cue; the response was savage. For the first time since the Alien and Sedition Acts the American national government began the legal persecution of dissenting opinion. Hence Oliver Wendell Holmes in his dissent in *Abrams v. United States,* 1919:

In this case sentences of twenty years imprisonment have been imposed for the publishing of two [pro-Bolshevik] leaflets that I believe the defendants had as much right to publish as the Government has to publish the Constitution . . . I think that we should be eternally vigilant against attempts to check the expression of opinions that we loathe and believe to be fraught with death, unless they so imminently threaten immediate interference with the lawful and pressing purposes of the law that an immediate check is required to save the country.[23]

Distinctions were lost: pacifists, conscientious objectors, anarchists, Eugene V. Debs. Trunch, trunch, truncheon did the trick. Writing of the period, Byrd uses the term "hysteria."[24] It reached its peak in 1920 when Wilson's attorney general Alexander

Mitchell Palmer deployed federal agents to arrest "reds" from coast to coast. Universal dominion of the right, indeed.

The nation changed and Wilson changed but in opposite directions. What the estimable Link has called Wilson's "missionary diplomacy" now became messianic.[25] He would have followers around him now, fewer and fewer advisers. And he, of all people, began to forget that ours was a government of divided and shared powers, most especially in the area of foreign policy, and most specifically in the matter of treaties. The framers had not the least doubt as to the intermixture of power here. The president would negotiate but the Senate must approve. If treaties are to be "the supreme Law of the Land," then the making of treaties is a legislative function, no matter how negotiated. Hamilton lays this out in *Federalist* No. 75. "It must indeed be clear to a demonstration that the joint possession of the power in question, by the President and the Senate, would afford a greater prospect of security than the separate possession of it by either of them."[26] In his great work on the presidency Edward S. Corwin sets forth the matter with perfect authority.

> Where does the Constitution vest authority to determine the course of the United States as a sovereign entity at international law with respect to matters in which other similar entities may choose to take an interest? Many persons are inclined to answer offhand "in the President"; but they would be hard-put to it, if challenged to point out any definite statement to this effect in the Constitution itself. What the Constitution does, and *all that it does,* is to confer on the President certain powers capable of affecting our foreign relations, and certain other powers of the same general kind on the Senate, and still other such powers on Congress; but which of these organs shall have the decisive and final voice in determining the course of the American Nation is left for events to resolve.
>
> All of which amounts to saying that the Constitution, considered only for its affirmative grants of powers capable of affecting the issue, is an invitation to struggle for the privilege of directing American foreign policy.[27]

It is a cautionary tale. Wilson was the first political scientist ever to become president. (And the last.) His most original work, *Congressional Government* (1884), demonstrated the effective supremacy in that time of the Congress over the executive departments, to use his term. (The office of the president rarely enters his calculation.) Another essay, also written in 1884 while Wilson was still a graduate student, posed the question "Committee or Cabinet Government?" Here we learn that the Speaker of the House is "the most powerful functionary in the government of the United States," and that "legislation is altogether in the hands of the Standing Committees." Thus,

> The Secretary of the Treasury must heed the commands of the Finance Committee of the Senate and the Ways and Means Committee of the House; the Secretary of State must in all things regard the will of the Foreign Affairs Committees of both Houses; the Secretary of the Interior must suffer himself to be bidden, now by the Committees on Indian Affairs, now by those on the Public Lands, and again by those on Patents. The Secretary of War must assiduously do service to the Committees on Military Affairs; to still other committees the Postmaster-General must render homage; the Secretary of the Navy must wear the livery of the Committees on Naval Affairs; and the Attorney-General must not forget that one or more of these eyes of the Houses are upon him. There are Committees on Appropriations, Committees on the Judiciary, Committees on Banking and Currency, Committees on Manufactures, Committees on Railways and Canals, Committees on Pensions and on Claims, Committees on Expenditures in the several Departments, and on the Expenditures on Public Buildings, committees on this and committees on that, committees on every conceivable subject of legislation.[28]

On the other hand, the youthful Wilson made it clear that he deplored this arrangement. It was "idle to talk of steadying or cleansing our politics" without change. He proposed to emulate the British. "English precedent and the world's fashion must be followed in the institution of Cabinet Government in the United States."[29] Had wishes given way to realism? We will never know. But certainly power gained a purchase for Thomas Woodrow Wilson.

In 1915 when German submarine warfare commenced, Wilson had responded to the warhawks with the celebrated pronouncement, "There is such a thing as a man being too proud to fight. There is such a thing as a nation being so right that it does not need to convince others by force that it is right."[30] And there is, alas, such a thing as a president's being too proud to struggle for the privilege of directing American foreign policy. He had come to the presidency with no very conspicuous views on foreign policy, and had remarked beforehand to a Princeton friend, "It would be the irony of fate if my administration had to deal chiefly with foreign affairs."[31] No chief magistrate expecting otherwise would have given the State Department to Bryan. And so it may be that Woodrow Wilson—again of all people—was not prepared for the tasks of an administration dealing chiefly with foreign affairs. On January 31, 1917, Germany announced the resumption of unrestricted submarine warfare. Wilson asked Congress for authority to arm merchant ships. A filibuster led by Robert La Follette and George Norris killed the measure. The president was incensed. (He demanded that the Senate change its rules. Which it did, establishing cloture under the new Rule 22!) But soon Lansing showed him how the merchant fleet could be armed by executive order.

Congress, especially the Senate, can be defied. But defiance had better succeed. The 1918 midterm congressional elections came along. Breaking a wartime "truce" on partisan politics, Wilson appealed for Democratic majorities. He got instead Republican majorities. They took the Senate by only two seats, but enough to organize the body, and more, much more, than enough to block the ratification of any treaty. *This* was the moment of decision. He had gambled; he had lost. Now was the time to conciliate. Something similar happened to Franklin D. Roosevelt in the midterm elections of 1938 when he sought to "purge" the Senate of a number of southern obstructionists, as he saw them. He, too, lost, but immediately set about making up. (A mutual friend called on Senator Walter George of Georgia. Senate lore has it that the conversation began with the president's emissary saying, "You know Franklin. He's his own worst enemy." "No he isn't," George replied.) Wilson proved there is such a thing as a man too proud to conciliate. Given the absolute certainty that he would bring back a treaty to a Republican Senate, he went off to Paris a month later without a single senator, and with but one nominal Republican. In such circumstances, the issue "What happened?" does not really arise. The Treaty of Versailles was defeated before it was negotiated.

As noted, he opted for a League to Enforce Peace. Abraham D. Sofaer writes of Wilson in Paris that "he had no faith in law or legal reasoning as an effective solution to the problems of world peace, for the attainment of which he had an even more visionary plan of international government."[32] The first part of this statement may be disputed. Wilson had immense, even unreasoning faith in the potential of international law to provide a structure for world peace. He believed, however, that this could happen only in the aftermath of the establishment of a world order in which there was something like the monopoly on the use of force that characterizes other legal societies. In that respect the second part of the statement is entirely correct. He did opt for "an even more visionary plan for international government." The essence of the League as it emerged in Paris was the pledge by member nations to preserve the independence and territorial integrity of all other members from attack by any other nation, member or not. In Wilson's view, war would continue so long as each nation had to be responsible for its own defense. Each would arm in anticipation of others' arming; attack in the anticipation of others' attacking. There was much prescience in this. The First World War had not ended war, but it had pretty much ended the idea that there was money to be made by it or glory to be got from it. Well, no. In 1939 Nazi Germany and then in 1941 imperial Japan went to war for a bit of both. But the Second World War settled the point. War, to the extent there is war, has become a reluctant, reactive affair. Wilson was not wrong in thinking that a League of Nations that would actually defend the territory and independence of any member attacked might indeed put an end to war.

He was not, however, under the illusion that any of the other heads of government at the peace conference thought this. This only strengthened his conviction of American exceptionality and mission. Speaking on behalf of the treaty in St. Paul, Minnesota, the following September, he grew rapturous.

> Every other nation has certain prepossessions which run back through all the ramifications of an ancient history. We have nothing of the kind. We know what all peoples are thinking, and yet we by a fine alchemy of our own combine that thinking into an American

plan and American purpose. America is the only Nation which can sympathetically lead the world in organizing peace.[33]

What is to be said?

· · · · ·

It would have been so easy! Easy, that is, to bring about American membership in a world organization with large ambitions but limited means. To learn if the powers could get the hang of the thing.

In 1876, having graduated from the Law School, and having received the first Ph.D. in political science to be granted by Harvard University, Henry Cabot Lodge thereupon became a lecturer in American history at Harvard, and editor of the *International Review,* in which capacity he accepted an article from a Princeton undergraduate, Woodrow Wilson, who would not earn his doctorate from Johns Hopkins until 1886. Thus began a relationship that was to culminate in the fateful days of 1919.

When the Republicans achieved a majority in the Senate in the midterm elections of 1918, Lodge, by now the senior senator from Massachusetts, became both floor leader and chairman of the Committee on Foreign Relations. In today's Senate this would be thought too much authority for any one senator. Floor leader *and* committee chairman. But there he was, and in the one country on earth that could be said to have in some meaningful sense a legislative as well as an executive branch. This is a curiously obscure fact of American government; we seem hardly to know it ourselves, and foreigners seem in the main to be not aware of it at all. Either there is an executive and no legislature, which is to say a President for Life or a *maximo lider* (Fidel Castro Ruz, Presidente del Consejo del Estado y del Consejo de Ministros, y Premier Secretario del Partido Comunista de Cuba), or else the executive has moved into the legislature, effectively abolishing its independence. This is best observed in the British Parliament, where, even by 1919, the prime minister had almost total power until replaced by another prime minister, who in turn succeeded to almost total power. A treaty negotiated by "the Crown," for which read the foreign secretary, at the behest of first lord of the Treasury (as the brass plate on the door of Ten Downing Street reads) is ratified without a comma's being changed, or for that matter, the details' necessarily being known to the House. This is not, or not yet, the case in the United States. American presidents, dealing with other heads of governments situated so differently, can bring themselves to think otherwise. No one suggests that this happened to Wilson. But had it done, he could hardly have behaved more ineptly than he behaved in 1919.

The peace conference commenced, and before long the main elements of the proposed League of Nations were reported in the press. Lodge, something of an anglophobe, had a problem: a *routine* problem. The Republican side of the aisle was divided. There were those who would accept anything Wilson brought home; those who would accept nothing Wilson brought home; those who would want to make some changes, if only to establish their role in the process. (Bear in mind that the peace treaty itself was becoming something of a victor's orgy, and Wilson was going along with the likes of David Lloyd George and Georges Clemenceau. Why not with the likes of Lodge?)

Nicholas Murray Butler, president of Columbia University, an eminent New York Republican committed to internationalism and legalism, wanted a League of Nations—with some changes. Bryan wanted a League of Nations—with some "improvement." Even the League to Enforce Peace was divided. A third of the Executive Committee wanted *only* the League Wilson had brought back from Paris; two-thirds were willing to see some changes.

In light of subsequent stereotypes, let us note some who did *not* want a League of Nations. The American Peace Society did not want a League of Nations, noting that its lack of provision for "judicial processes" would make it "Prussian in its conception." In his masterly survey, *Seeking World Order: The United States and International Organization to 1920,* Warren F. Kuehl reports from another familiar precinct. "The liberals, best illustrated by the editors of the *New Republic,* labeled the Covenant unjust. With its authoritarian overtones and emphasis on coercion, they found the price of membership too high and turned away."[34] There were others.

Again, this history is at once too familiar and too little understood. This was a moment when academics, intellectuals, editors, and public spirited, and the spirited public were exceptionally busy.

We ought not to wonder that they and their assigns thereafter wrote a very great deal about what they said to whom and when and why and where. But it really doesn't matter.

What matters is that the chairman of the Committee on Foreign Relations wanted changes. In his foreword to Robert C. Byrd's magisterial *The Senate: 1789–1989*, William E. Leuchtenburg observes that the neglect of congressional history is something of a scandal of American scholarship.[35] This is nowhere more flagrant than in the common understanding that a seesawing armageddonic battle for the League went on through all of 1919. In point of fact, it was all over in two days in March. On March 3, Lodge and three like-minded colleagues collected thirty-nine Republican signatures on a resolution stating that there would have to be changes. Byrd recounts the scene in the Senate the following day.

> At two minutes past midnight on March 4, 1919, just prior to the adjournment of the Sixty-fifth Congress, Lodge arose in the Senate. One reporter claimed that Lodge's hand was shaking as he held the "Round Robin" resolution he wished to offer. "Mr. President," he said, "I desire to take only a moment of the time of the Senate. I wish to offer the resolution which I hold in my hand, a very brief one." While brief, the resolution was a remarkable slap in Wilson's face. It called the League, "in the form now proposed," unacceptable to the United States and urged that it be separated from the peace treaty and carefully reconsidered after "negotiating peace terms with Germany." The purpose of the Round Robin was twofold: Lodge intended the resolution to signal the President that the League and the peace treaty must be separated if the latter were ever to be approved by the Senate; and, secondly, to let the peace conference in Europe know that "the President was not the only part of the government necessary to the making of a treaty."[36]

Wilson promptly declared that the senators would have no other choice, and for good measure insulted them. Byrd continues:

President Wilson was unmoved. On the eve of his departure for Paris, he boasted to the world that, when the treaty was brought back, the "gentlemen on this side will find the Covenant not only tied in it, but so many threads on the Treaty tied to the Covenant that you cannot dissect the Covenant from the Treaty without destroying the whole vital structure." He declared the senators opposing him, particularly Lodge, to be "contemptible . . . narrow

... selfish ... poor little minds that never get anywhere but run round in a circle and think they are going somewhere ... I cannot express my contempt ... If I said what I think about those fellows in Congress, it would take a piece of asbestos two inches thick to hold it."[37]

And there was the end of it.

Parliamentary procedure provides a useful analogy. The Senate is a body, generally speaking, unencumbered by rules and much dependent on comity. It normally operates by "unanimous consent" and moves along nicely. But at other times proceedings can be tedious and dilatory and it often appears that nothing is ever going to be decided, when suddenly a procedural motion is adopted and one side has won and the other side has lost and the matter is concluded. So it was when thirty-nine Republican senators stated that Wilson's treaty would require changes. (Lest they be placed in an awkward position, no Democratic senators were asked to sign Lodge's letter. It was well understood that a number would have done so.) When Wilson said no to them, it meant there would be no treaty.

The text was laid before the Senate July 10. It was referred to the Committee on Foreign Relations, where Lodge personally read the entire 268-page text plus that of the Covenant into the record. He brought the measure to the floor on September 10, noting that deducting Sundays and a holiday it had been before the committee for forty-five days, of which the committee met on thirty-six. "In view of the fact that six months were consumed by the peace conference in making the treaty ... the period of six weeks consumed by the committee in considering it does not seem excessive."[38] *And* the treaty was reported *favorably*. There were four reservations, only one of consequence affecting the Covenant.

> The United States declines to assume, under the provisions of article 10, or under any other article, any obligation to preserve the territorial integrity or political independence of any other country, or to interfere in controversies between other nations, members of the league or not, or to employ the military or naval forces of the United States in such controversies, or to adopt economic measures for the protection of any other country, whether a member of the league or not, against external aggression or for the purpose of coercing any

other country, or for the purpose of intervention in the internal conflicts or other controversies which may arise in any other country, and no mandate shall be accepted by the United States under article 22, Part I, of the treaty of peace with Germany, except by action of the Congress of the United States.

Under no circumstances, the reservation continued, was the treaty to impose "any legal or moral obligation upon the United States to enter into war or to send its Army and Navy abroad" without action of the Congress. "Under the Constitution . . . the Congress alone has the power to declare war."[39] Was this not elementally the law of the land? Was it not, further, the secretary of state's own view of what was wise? More. Had not Wilson been reelected president because he'd "kept us out of war"? Certainly he was given no mandate to enter into a treaty providing that American forces could be committed to battle all over the world on the basis of the decision of the Council of the League of Nations. True, it would presumably require the president's consent through his representative on the council, but then where did the Congress come in? Article I, Section 8, immediately after the power "to define and punish . . . Offenses against the Law of Nations," gives Congress the power "to declare War."

Wilson was crossing the country campaigning for the Covenant as it was. His last speech, given extemporaneously at Pueblo, Colorado, on September 25, is as moving as anything in the language of the American presidency:

Again and again, my fellow citizens, mothers who lost their sons in France have come to me, and taking my hand, have shed tears upon it not only, but they have added, "God bless you, Mr. President!" Why, my fellow citizens, should they pray God to bless me? I advised the Congress of the United States to create the situation that led to the death of their sons, I ordered their sons oversea, I consented to their sons being put in the most difficult parts of the battle line, where death was certain, as in the impenetrable difficulties of the forest of Argonne. Why should they weep upon my hand and call down the blessings of God upon me? Because they believe that their boys died for something that vastly transcends any of the immediate and palpable objects of the war. They believe, and they rightly believe, that their sons saved the liberty of the world. They believe that wrapped up with the liberty of the world is the continuous protection of that liberty by the concerted powers of all civilized people. They believe that this sacrifice was made in order that other sons should not be called upon for a similar gift—the gift of life, the gift of all that died—and if we did not see this thing through, if we fulfilled the dearest present wish of Germany and now dissociated ourselves from those alongside whom we fought in the war, would not something of the halo go away from the gun over the mantel-piece, or the sword? Would not the old uniform lose something of its significance? These men were crusaders. They were not going forth to prove the might of the United States. They were going forth to prove the might of justice and right, and all the world accepted them as crusaders, and their transcendent achievement has made all the world believe in America as it believes in no other nation orga-nized in the modern world. There seems to me to stand between us and the rejection or qualification of this treaty the serried ranks of those boys in khaki, not only these boys who came home, but those dear ghosts that still deploy upon the fields of France.

Wilson also spoke of his visit to a cemetery in France filled with American graves:

... France was free and the world was free because America had come! I wish some men in public life who are now opposing the settlement for which these men died could visit such a spot as that. I wish that the thought that comes out of those graves could pene-trate their consciousness. I wish that they could feel the moral obli-gation that rests upon us not to go back on those boys, but to see the thing through, to see it through to the end and make good their redemption of the world. For nothing less depends upon this deci-sion, nothing less than the liberation and salvation of the world.[40]

A speech from the cross. Hours later he collapsed. By October 2 he was an invalid. The Democratic floor leader visited his bedside, the president looking awful with a long white beard. There would have to be some reservations, some compromise. "Let Lodge com-promise!" came the reply.[41]

· · · · ·

And so the age of Wilson passed. Or did it? Recall once again the assessment by Herbert Hoover in *The Ordeal of Woodrow Wilson*. "For a moment at the time of the Armistice, Mr. Wilson rose to intellectual domination of most of the civilized world. With his courage and eloquence, he carried a message of hope for the independence of nations, the freedom of men and lasting peace. Never since his time has any man risen to the political and spiritual heights that came to him."[42] Such a man casts a shadow. In his time, and through his vocation, he transformed the standards of legitimacy in government throughout the world. We are perhaps only beginning to see this. After Wilson, governments became legitimate only as they could show that they were democratic. This was a religious vision. The architectural critics Colin Rowe and Fred Koetter liken the vision to that of the redemptive architecture and city planning of Le Corbusier and others of this time. "The ex-president of Princeton's dream, the pathetic by-product of a liberal Presbyterian faith which was both too good for this world and not good enough, which was only to be honoured in the breach, created its own portentous vacuum and devastation."[43]

Yes, yes . . . And yet. He spoke one last time, on Armistice Day, 1923, to a group of friends outside his house on S Street.

> I cannot refrain from saying it: I am not one of those who have the least anxiety about the triumph of the principles I have stood for. I have seen fools resist Providence before and I have seen their destruction, as will come upon these again—utter destruction and contempt. That we shall prevail is as sure as that God reigns.[44]

And what does modern sensibility have to say of this?

CHAPTER FOUR

Roosevelt

The Treaty of Versailles came into force January 10, 1920. As
provided in the text, the United States thereupon convened the
Council of the League of Nations, which came somewhat furtively
to life in the Clock Room of the Quai d'Orsay six days later. It was
not a promising beginning for the new world order, but then it was
not a beginning at all. The International Labor Organization had
found its way into the world four months earlier and was already
busy with the large undertakings of a major organization of the
League system. It had held a conference of thirty-five nations at
which, for the first time in history, representatives of employers
and employees sat and voted independently of their national governments. It had admitted Germany and Austria to the international society of the postwar world. It had welcomed the British
dominions and the other new nations into that world. It had drawn
up and put into practice the first rules of procedure for the assem-
blies of the new international system. It had adopted six items of
international labor legislation, chosen a director, and begun its
permanent establishment. All this was accomplished at a conference in Washington in November 1919.

The history of the ILO and of American relations with it is generally passed over because it is so difficult to explain. Of the three
principal institutions established by the treaty, the League of
Nations, the Permanent Court of International Justice, and the
ILO, the last was the one the United States was surely least likely
to join. It is, however, the only one we did. Of the three organizations, it was arguably the least likely to survive the next quarter-
century; it is the only one that did. Of the three, it was the least

likely to achieve anything of consequence; it may be the only one that did.

With the ILO and the labor treaty, we move to a further stage of international lawmaking. To say this, of course, is to accept an evolutionary construct; or linear, as some like. Legal theorists must attend to such questions; they are clearly legitimate. For our purposes it is enough to observe that domestic law in Western societies has followed a pattern that begins with restraints and moves on to rights. Thereafter to entitlements. At an early stage restraints were seen to codify what already *was* law. This pattern is to be found in the development of international law. Chancellor Kent sought to divine the rights of American merchant ships from the practice of the Amphictyonic Council of Greek city-states during the Peloponnesian War in the fifth century B.C. Only with time do we come to legislation that sets forth principles or practices that are avowedly new.

All of which is familiar. It is, however, worth pausing to observe that the League system established an institutional arrangement for enacting social legislation at the international level, at a time when the United States was still not certain this was a legitimate activity for even the national government. Moreover, the issues involved were hardly peripheral or easily resolved. These were not treaties concerning Canadian geese, or for that matter Arctic fur seals. The International Labor Organization dealt with *the* issue of the time, "the social question," as it was called. The politics of almost every industrial nation in the world was organizing around this issue. The British party system, for example, underwent its first change in two centuries, with a Labour party becoming the alternative government. Something approaching this realignment would come about in America in the 1930s. But this was a long way off when the United States, even so, began to be involved in labor legislation on an international level. It is difficult for an essay on international law not to take on a deterministic cast: beginning, middle, end. Low, middle, high. Whatever. And yet, as we have seen in the ordeal of Woodrow Wilson, individual behavior also shapes history. (What would Leninism be without Lenin?) Historical forces dispatched the ILO to our shores, but particular men and women saved it from foundering, indeed, fitted it out and sent it off again under full sail. A nautical image is in order, for the person most involved was Franklin D. Roosevelt.

The idea of international labor treaties was a by-product of the general movement for labor legislation in nineteenth-century Europe. Legislated improvements in the terms and conditions of employment were thought to impose a competitive disadvantage in world markets. This obstacle could be overcome by international agreements that raised standards simultaneously.

The idea was reformist. It assumed the legitimacy of the capitalist concern with competition. In the beginnings it was almost exclusively an idea of reform-minded businessmen. It was subsequently taken up by academic and social reformers but retained its establishment aura. By the time of the First World War, international labor legislation was on the agenda of the career secretaries of the most important European ministries concerned with labor and social legislation. Time and again when the governments of Europe found themselves faced with the threat of international socialism, they turned to international labor legislation as an alternative. Typically, socialists agreed.

A fair statement of the case was made by Bismarck in a note inviting nations to attend the first international labor conference in 1890.

> The competition of nations in the trade of the world, and the community of interests proceeding therefrom, makes it impossible to create successful institutions for the benefit of working men of one country without entailing that country's power of competing with other countries. Such institutions can only be established on a basis adopted in common in all countries concerned. The Working classes of the different countries have, in due appreciation of this fact, established international relations aiming at the improvement of their conditions. But efforts in this direction cannot meet with success unless the governments interested endeavor to come to an agreement on the more important questions concerning the welfare of the working classes by means of international discussion.[1]

The German-sponsored conference met in March 1890. The results, though limited, did include the proclamation of standards for the employment of women and children and the statement that "the deliberations of the States taking part in the Conference should be renewed."[2] Of most importance, the idea of internationally agreed-upon labor standards was no longer the property of reformers and enthusiasts. A British participant later declared that the conference "placed international cooperation in regard to labor questions definitely in the field of practical statesmanship."[3] This, to say again, at a time when "the social question" was *the* question.

In 1900 an International Association for Labor Legislation was organized at a conference in Paris presided over by the then-socialist minister of commerce. Economists of considerable distinction, including Richard T. Ely of the University of Wisconsin, a founder of the American Economic Association, were present, as were government officials. As a compromise between those who wanted a strictly intergovernmental organization and those who wished a purely private one, it was decided that the IALL should be both. Individuals could join; trade unions could join; governments could join; all could join directly or through national sections. An unlikely arrangement, but one which worked. Thus from the very beginning the institutions around which the movement for international labor legislation were organized assumed a pluralist character which made them unique and which almost certainly contributed to their success.

In 1906 the American Association for Labor Legislation was established as a national section of the international body. It thereafter convened at the annual meeting of the American Economic Association. The AALL was, for the most part, an association of officials and professors, but in either case they tended to be men of affairs also accustomed to influencing events and much concerned to do so. Among the officials was Charles Patrick Neill, U.S. commissioner of labor and a confidant of Theodore Roosevelt. Among the professors was Woodrow Wilson, who became a vice-president of the AALL in 1911 and remained so throughout his term as president of the United States. A similarly active member was a Princeton professor of politics, Royal Meeker, whom Wilson appointed commissioner of labor statistics.

The labor movement was in the AALL, if not necessarily of it. The American Federation of Labor was one of the corporate bodies included. Both Samuel Gompers, president of the AFL, and John Mitchell of the United Mine Workers were vice-presidents.

The details are many; suffice that what began with Plimsoll marks and phosphorous matches and Sunday labor went on to become the first systematic effort to establish an international code of human rights. In the 1980s the survival of the Solidarity movement in Communist Poland would very much turn on the state's obligations under the ILO conventions on freedom of association and on the right to organize and bargain collectively.

By 1918 labor movements in most or all of the Allied nations had put international labor legislation high on their lists of "war aims." By 1919, with Bolshevism in the air, the Allied governments were scarcely disinclined. Certainly not Wilson. He was a friend of organized labor and, rather in contrast to the labor movement of that time, an advocate of labor legislation. "Legislation in regard to International Labor" was on the agenda of the first session of the peace conference. A commission headed by Gompers expeditiously and knowledgeably drafted the ILO Charter, which became Part XIII of the treaty.

This was not well received in the Senate. No one knew enough about the subject. Even Porter J. McCumber of North Dakota, the president's strongest Republican ally, could not bring himself to accept Part XIII. In November he introduced and carried a reservation to the treaty withholding American membership for the time being. Others went further. Henry L. Myers, Democrat of Montana, solidly with Wilson on the issue of the Lodge reservations, wanted no part of an international labor organization. The ILO, he told the Senate, "would afford an opportunity for the international industrial boycott and would enable the freaks, lunatics, and Bolshevists of Europe to make all sorts of demands upon and complaints against the stable governments of the earth." They might even interfere in the case of "the infamous, red-handed murderer, assassin, anarchist, Tom Mooney." Hiram Johnson, Republican of California, followed Myers:

Mr. President, I want no international banker control in this country. I want no international labor control in this country. I want no international imperialistic control in this country. I want to preserve the promise of American life, preserve it in its pristine purity, because of all that it has done in the past and all of its promise for the future.

I want no international control of America. I want to be just American again.[4]

Even so, the foreigners were coming. The peace conference plenary session of April 11, 1919, provided that the first annual Labor Conference would convene in Washington at noon on October 29. An Organizing Committee met in London. The United States now had a Department of Labor, which joined in the enterprise. James T. Shotwell of Columbia University was the American representative on the Organizing Committee. In June he asked that someone be sent to help him provide the committee with the data being assembled. The secretary of labor, William B. Wilson, a Scots immigrant, former secretary-treasurer of the United Mine Workers, and from 1907 to 1913 a representative from Pennsylvania, promptly sent Meeker. In this the president was more than well served by his appointees, who grasped what he wanted and set out to get it for him. This attitude of cooperation was sustained by Wilson's own enthusiasm. On returning from London, Meeker wrote to his former colleague, stating that the Department of Labor was doing all it could to prepare for the coming conference. He then asked whether it would be appropriate for him, as a government official, to participate publicly in the event. By all means, replied the president: "I need not tell you that I am intensely interested in seeing that the first International Labor Conference under the League shall be a complete success . . . The Labor Conference is in the nature of the first breath of this new born babe."[5]

On July 31 Senator William S. Kenyon, Republican of Iowa, introduced at Secretary of Labor Wilson's behest a joint resolution authorizing the president "to convene the first meeting of the international labor conference in Washington." This was referred to the Foreign Relations Committee, promptly reported by Lodge, and just as promptly passed in the Senate. In the House a member from Texas wanted to know whether Lenin and "Trotski" would appear as delegates from Russia. The House sponsor, a Republican member from Wyoming, replied that he didn't know, and the resolution passed. Elapsed time, three days. Almost wistfully Wilson sent a note congratulating his secretary of labor, adding, "I wish I could learn your skill in such matters."[6]

Early in August the American ambassador to Britain, in the name of the president, had invited the Organizing Committee to transfer its activities to Washington in September and set up offices in the Department of Labor. Thereupon Harold Butler, a former British civil servant, now provisional secretary-general of the conference, sailed for the United States, arriving in New York September 13, 1919. Before he left the ship he received a message from Wilson, then on his western tour. The president stated that when he got back to Washington in a fortnight's time, he intended to assume personal direction of the preparations for the International Labor Conference.[7]

Wilson spoke repeatedly of the conference on his western tour. Repeatedly he pointed to the incongruousness of the American situation. He said in Des Moines, "The confidence of the men who sat at Paris was such that they put it in the document that the first meeting of the labor conference . . . should take place in Washington. I am going to issue that invitation, whether we can attend the conference or not. But think of the mortification! The thing is inconceivable, but it is true."[8] In Oakland: "And now we are waiting on the Senate to tell us whether we can have a part in the conference. At any rate we can sit by and watch."[9] And there were shouts of protest.

On September 23, acting Secretary of State Phillips telegraphed the president in Reno reporting that there was sentiment in Europe for postponing the conference in view of the situation in the United States. Wilson's reply from Ogden, Utah, was immediate. "With regard to the date of the International Labor Conference that is entirely in our hands and can be postponed only by us, I beg that you will give every assurance that we will lend our cooperation in the most effective way, whether we can at the time of the meeting actually participate officially or not."[10]

The conference was only weeks away, and practically no arrangements had been made. The AFL had set up a committee that secured the use of the Pan American Building at Constitution Avenue and 12th Street. But beyond that, almost nothing had been done. The president had personally instructed his secretary of labor to "take entire charge of all arrangements." When Butler arrived, however, the secretary offered him a cordial welcome, but little else. He told Butler nothing could be done until the president returned.[11] Then the president returned stricken.

Butler recalled: "From that moment everything fell into confusion . . . There was no one at the helm in Washington, a fact which quickly began to make the prospects of the Conference exceedingly dark. There was no money, no offices, no typists, no messengers, no machines, only a hall in the Pan American Building."[12] The president's telegram from Utah precluded the idea of postponing the conference so far as the cabinet was concerned, but on the other hand, they would do nothing to make it possible to hold it.

Butler appealed to London which sent money. But this left the problem of finding office space, that most indispensable of organizational imperatives. Butler again:

[A] god had appeared out of an unlooked for machine, who had lavishly provided us with office-accommodation. One night my wife and I were invited to dine with Mr. Franklin D. Roosevelt, Assistant Secretary of the Navy. It was a delightful dinner in a room filled with a wonderful collection of prints of famous American frigates and yachts, which betrayed Mr. Roosevelt's passion for the sea. He himself was a fine figure of a man, tall, handsome, abounding in vitality. At the other end of the table was Mrs. Roosevelt with her broad and generous mind, as sensitive to the currents of home politics and world-affairs as her husband. They were both intensely interested in the Conference, but even if they had been totally indifferent to it, we should have surrendered to their charm none the less readily. After dinner Mr. Roosevelt took me aside and asked how I was getting on. I replied "Not at all," and poured out my troubles into his sympathetic ear. When I had finished, he broke into one of his jovial laughs, which I came to know so well in after years, and said: "Well, we have to do something about this. I think I can find you some offices at any rate. Look in at the Navy Building tomorrow morning and I will see about it in the meanwhile." This first ray of hope was tremendously cheering, but much more the feeling that I had found a real friend at court, whose whole personality plainly suggested that he certainly would do something.

Next morning I duly turned up in the long, low temporary building, which housed the staff of the United States Navy, . . . The Assistant Secretary received me as if he had known me all his life and with that characteristic snap of the jaw told me that a set of forty rooms would be put at my disposal. With a broad grin he added that he would have to eject a number of Admirals and Captains, who were using the most nautical language about him, but if I called on the Chief Clerk next day, everything would be ready. And so it was. In due course we moved in, and the language of the naval officers—"turned out to camp in the park," as Tom Grant my American establishment officer shocked me by gleefully explaining—did not become less lurid when they found that some of the offices were actually occupied by the Japanese delegation. The whole episode revealed the qualities which afterwards made F.D.R. one of the great Presidents of the United States. But my mind instinctively switched back to Whitehall. I could not help gasping at the thought of what would have happened if the Parliamentary Secretary had made similar proposals to the Admiralty. I tried to imagine the Olympian wrath of the Sea-Lords and felt sure that his life would have been neither long nor merry.[13]

The conference accordingly met. The League system began.

·   ·   ·   ·   ·

In 1921 Warren Gamaliel Harding succeeded to the presidency, and a kind of regression took place. Successive Republican secretaries of state did not disown the Wilsonian interval; they simply picked up where William Howard Taft had left off. There was much internationalism, but little of international organization.

Disarmament conferences convened, arbitration treaties were negotiated. In 1928 Calvin Coolidge's secretary of state, Frank B. Kellogg (who as a senator from Minnesota had voted with Lodge in 1919), joined his French counterpart, Aristide Briand, in the Pact of Paris renouncing war and extolling the peaceful settlement of disputes. All the nations of the earth in existence at that time, save only Argentina, Bolivia, El Salvador, and Yemen, joined the pact, many, however, reserving the right of self-defense. (Which Japan invoked when it invaded China in 1931.) Kellogg went on to become a member of the Permanent Court of International Justice, the third body the League system had established and which Harding, Calvin Coolidge, and Herbert Hoover each in turn proposed that the United States should join. But the League, no; and the ILO, never.

It was just one decade from the opening of the Washington conference of the ILO, October 29, 1919, to the stock market crash of October 29, 1929. If no one in the United States was fully prepared for the depression that followed, the person least unprepared was Frances Perkins, industrial commissioner of the state of New York, first under Governor Alfred E. Smith and now under Franklin D. Roosevelt. Then, as now, social legislation in the United States was largely based on European models. Perkins was much aware of the International Labor Office, now headed by Butler, as a kind of clearinghouse for new thinking on such matters. In February 1933 Roosevelt asked her to become his secretary of labor. She had a list of things to be done; joining the ILO was one. Roosevelt was all for it. On May 19 the subject was discussed at a cabinet meeting; the United States would send observers to the International Labor Conference in Geneva that June. Secretary of State Cordell Hull much agreed. The Wilsonians were back.

With a difference: Wilsonians after Wilson. If one thing had been learned, it was that Congress was necessarily involved in foreign affairs. The following year the decision was made to join the ILO. It was proposed to do this by joint resolution, requiring simple majorities in both houses rather than a two-thirds majority in the Senate, as is required for a treaty. In the event, it was carried in the Senate by unanimous consent on June 13, 1934. The next day it was reported from the House Committee on Foreign Affairs and that evening called up by the Speaker, Samuel D. McReynolds of Tennessee. The State Department sent a representative to the Hill. Evidently, Roosevelt got on the telephone. For certain a White House view was made known. Finally the *New York Times* noticed that something was up. So did George Holden Tinkham, another Bostonian of pedigree. The resolution was brought up under suspension of the rules. Tinkham rose, incensed at what he regarded as a dishonest attempt to slip into the League by a side door.

> Mr. Speaker, this is the hour and this is the time, as we near adjournment in confusion, when legislation is reported to this House which never would be reported if due deliberation could be given it. It is the spawning hour for the propagation of proposals fostered by corruption, by special interests, by foreign intrigue, and by conspirators against the public weal.

... this resolution is not before the House in accordance with a fair interpretation of the rules; in accordance with honest procedure. There was no notification to the members of the Committee on Foreign Affairs that the resolution was to be considered, a quorum was not present when the resolution was reported, and no witnesses appeared before the committee.

Referring to Miss Perkins' statement in a letter to McReynolds that "the Organization is not even now an integral part of the League of Nations," he cited articles 387, 391, and 392 of the ILO constitution and concluded: "This statement of the Secretary is wholly false. It was made to deceive and to mislead the Committee on Foreign Affairs of the House and the House itself." He continued:

> Let me explain what the real intent of this proposal is. The League of Nations is a part of the Versailles Treaty. The Covenant of the League of Nations is the center; its two wings, affiliates, or branches are the Permanent Court of International Justice and the International Labor Organization. Both are bureaus, instrumentalities, or agents of the League of Nations. This set-up can be compared with the Capitol in which we are sitting. There is a center and there are two wings. Any entry to either wing is an entry into the building itself. An entry into either wing of the League of Nations is an entry into the League of Nations itself. If you vote for this resolution you vote to enter the League of Nations . . .
>
> The intent of those who are opposed to American nationalism is first to have the United States become a member of the International Labor Organization, then adhere to the Permanent Court of International Justice, and finally become signatories of the Covenant.[14]

Tinkham went on, perhaps too much so, to denounce the dangers of the League and internationalism in language not many people really believed fifteen years after the peace conference. Nonetheless, he was making his point about the procedure whereby the resolution had come before the House. Republican John G. Cooper of Ohio rose

> to ask the gentleman from Massachusetts what prompted the bringing in of this resolution. It is something new to me. It comes in here at the last minute. None of us has had an opportunity to study it, and I would like to know if labor of the United States is in favor

of joining an international labor organization which in the European countries today is controlled chiefly by Communists.[15]

McReynolds had stated that the resolution was "endorsed by labor organizations throughout this country,"[16] but Cooper's remarks were applauded.

Emanuel Celler of Brooklyn saved the resolution. He got Tinkham to admit there might be no harm in joining the ILO if it did not involve us with the League, whereupon Celler said: "I have listened with interest many times to the gentleman from Massachusetts; I have the greatest respect for him and admire his intellectual ability, but with his conclusions in this instance I must emphatically disagree. The gentleman is wrenching this bill out of its proper content, design and its implication."[17]

Tinkham, his time having expired, was gaveled down in his final plea:

> If the House wishes eventually to enter the League of Nations, which would mean the destruction of the United States in the next war, then let the House pass this resolution . . . But if the House is for American independence, for American ideals, for American nationality untarnished, then let the House vote against this resolution.[18]

It was late. The Speaker had the votes. The yeas and nays were ordered: 222 Democrats and 11 Republicans voted for the resolution; 81 Republicans and 28 Democrats voted against.

On Tuesday, June 19, 1934, the president signed "S.J. Res. 131. Joint Resolution providing for membership of the United States in the International Labor Organization."

On June 22 Butler, who had been in on the planning from the outset, laid the text of the Senate resolution before the annual labor conference meeting in Geneva. There was no precedent for a nation's joining the ILO and not the League, but the Japanese government delegation proposed immediate acceptance. Whereupon a tripartite American delegation, happily on hand and complete with John L. Lewis, entered the conference hall to much cheering.

In Europe the American move was hailed, both for itself and for what it seemed to foretell. The United States was moving closer and closer to the League, or at least to an active internationalism.

The *Manchester Guardian* especially welcomed the event: "So ends one more chapter of the decline and fall of the isolationism which began in 1920 as a reaction from American intervention in the war."[19]

In the United States there was a warm response from pro-League circles, and little reaction from those opposed. A *New York Times* editorial asserted that

> Congress in authorizing the United States to enter the ILO, took a far more important step, practically and psychologically, toward the League than entering the World Court would have been, in the view of observers well acquainted with the Geneva situation . . . What makes the ILO much closer to the League than is the court is that it is essentially a means of getting international legislation, or treaties, negotiated, as is the League itself. The heart of the League System is its permanent mechanism for continuous international negotiation, and the ILO parallels this machinery throughout in its limited field of social questions.

By opposing the move on these grounds, Tinkham had emphasized this aspect: "The fact that, thanks to Rep. Tinkham's vigorous opposition, the Congress acted with its eyes open and made a roll-call vote, seems likely to make its action much more effective in strengthening the authority of the League and bringing Germany and Japan back."[20]

Not three weeks later, in a conversation in Moscow, William C. Bullitt, the first American ambassador to the Soviet Union, objected to a proposal by the people's commissar for foreign affairs, Maxim Litvinov, saying it would be getting the United States into the League by the back door. He reported to Hull in Washington that Litvinov replied the United States had already done that when it had joined the ILO. Germany had left the League; the Soviets, anxious, had just joined. They longed for company.

However, whatever was gained in June was lost in January. Roosevelt moved to join the Court. Harding, Coolidge, and Hoover had all recommended this, and the Senate had agreed in 1926, but with reservations the existing members could not accept. This was in any event a great enthusiasm of Eleanor Roosevelt, as well as of Hull, and the Democratic platform had pledged it. The measure was reported from Foreign Relations January 9, 1935, but by only a 14-to-7 vote. Debate began. Hiram Johnson of California rose to proclaim himself a citizen of the United States and not a "citizen of the world" and to renounce any truck with "the League of Nations Court." On January 29 the measure failed, 52 to 36, seven votes short of the required two-thirds.[21] There was a new opposition now, populist; even plebeian. No longer Henry Cabot Lodge, great-grandson of one senator and grandfather of another, Harvard men from colonial times, insisting on senatorial prerogatives. Now it was Huey Long on the floor going on about Japs; Father Charles E. Coughlin on the radio hinting about Jews; and "the Hearst press," as Mrs. Roosevelt's friends called it, hinting about Roosevelt. They were not well-mannered. Friends of the Court, friends of the League were no match for them at this low point of what Auden called that "low, dishonest decade."

·   ·   ·   ·   ·

In any event, war was five years away. Joining a failed League of Nations would have been futile. The Soviets soon enough figured this out. In 1939 they joined the Nazis instead, with the Molotov-Ribbentrop agreement. (Litvinov, né Wallach, a great negotiator of nonaggression pacts and the advocate at Geneva of "collective security" by the "peace-loving nations," was a Polish Jew and as a matter of delicacy had to be replaced by Molotov before the two parties reached agreement to invade, conquer, and partition Poland. Whereupon that "grotesque" product of the Versailles Peace Treaty, as Molotov described it to the Supreme Soviet in October 1939, disappeared from the map. With it, for the moment, went number thirteen of the Fourteen Points, the establishment of "an independent Polish state" in territory "inhabited by indisputably Polish populations.")

By degrees Roosevelt opted for an alliance with Britain. Barely perceptible degrees. Congress was not disposed to international involvements. The enthusiasms of the Theodore Roosevelt–Taft era had quite vanished, as had the idealism of the Wilson period. There were saving remnants of both periods dispersed across the nation, but here and there organized, and most conspicuously in the Council on Foreign Relations in Manhattan.

Elihu Root, B.A. Hamilton College, teacher at Rome Academy

(the Rome on the Mohawk), New York University Law School, member of the Alaskan Boundary Tribunal in 1903, counsel for the United States in the North Atlantic Fisheries Arbitration in 1910, member of the Permanent Court of Arbitration at The Hague, secretary of war, secretary of state, United States senator from 1909 to 1915, became honorary chairman of the council. He was of that generation of New York international lawyers who, as Robert D. Schulzinger writes, "argued the identity of interests between American actions and expectations of international law."[22] He received the first Woodrow Wilson Foundation medal and prize for championing the "Court of International Justice." The prize helped to get *Foreign Affairs* going. In 1915 the League to Enforce Peace, with former president Taft as its head, set out to be, and more or less became, a mass movement. The Council on Foreign Relations was a club, and a hard one to get into. In his wonderful romp on *The American Establishment,* published in 1962, Richard Rovere wrote that "the directors of the Council on Foreign Relations make up a sort of Presidium for that part of the Establishment that guides our destiny as a nation."[23] But this was after the Second World War. Before that the political agenda and the imaginative range of the council were pretty much those of New York investment bankers. The "old" American internationalism might well have been judged to have simply faded away.

But that would have been wrong. Franklin D. Roosevelt remained. Wilson's heir, and, like Wilson, able to summon great commitment from the American people. He had served Wilson, had taken risks for him then, and had brought to his own presidency a sense of accounts still to be settled. This would not be easy. The Republican internationalist tradition in particular had faltered to the point of inertness. There were a few left of the New York school. There was, for example, Charles Evans Hughes. Born farther up the Hudson than Roosevelt; Columbia Law School; governor of New York; resigned to be named an associate justice of the Supreme Court by President Taft; resigned to run against Wilson for president (almost won, didn't promise as Wilson did that the United States would never go to war); secretary of state under Harding; arbitrator in the Andes; member of the Permanent Court of International Justice; and then, on the nomination of

Herbert Hoover, back to the Court as Chief Justice. But he was now at the end of his career with no successor in sight. President Hoover was surely part of the Wilsonian tradition, but he was, for the moment, in political disgrace. (Roosevelt would have nothing to do with him.) There was no League to Enforce Peace. There was instead the America First movement, organized in 1940, militantly isolationist, and more than passing popular with young Republicans on Ivy League campuses.

Off campus there was the American Legion, founded also in Paris at the end of the Great War and, if not a mass movement, at very least a formidable political institution. The Yanks who'd gone off to save the world for democracy had come back little disposed ever to go off again, at least on that quest. What popular internationalism did exist was to be found on the far left in Communist or Communist-influenced environs. But its adherents were hardly disposed to take up arms to save a dying capitalism. The Communist left was quite prepared to see Britain go under, and totally opposed to any American involvement until June 22, 1941, when Hitler turned on Stalin and invaded the Soviet Union. Apart from more or less avowedly pro-British groups such as Union Now and the Committee to Defend America by Aiding the Allies, there was little on the American political scene to suggest anything like a return to the Wilsonian enterprise. Yet we were about to do just that.

A particular irony is that Roosevelt took America into the war as if the United States *had* joined the League. He could hardly have done so in the name of a preexisting principle of the rights of neutral nations and of freedom of the seas, which were Wilson's grounds, whatever else may have been Wilson's purposes. To the contrary, the United States under Roosevelt became anything but neutral. In 1939 war materials were made available to belligerents on a cash-and-carry basis, but only the Allies were buying. In 1940 Britain was given fifty "over-age" destroyers in return for ninety-nine-year leases on naval and air bases in Newfoundland, Bermuda, the Bahamas, Jamaica, St. Lucia, Trinidad, and British Guiana. On March 11, 1941, Congress enacted the Lend-Lease Act, and with it began the open supply of armaments to Britain and Russia. What could this be but adherence to Article 10 of the Covenant: "The Members of the League undertake to respect and preserve as against external aggression the territorial integrity and existing political independence of all members of the League . . ." Which is precisely what the Senate in 1919 would not have. We got it anyway.

Now to the great difference between the two presidents. There were the great similarities, not least that each would be stricken in the climactic hours of his presidency as he sought to put in place a new international system. But Wilson insisted on doing this alone. Roosevelt took Congress along every step of the way. The Congress was no more "enlightened" in 1944 than it had been in 1919. If anything, less so. It is one thing to reserve the right of the United States to decide when and where and whether to commit its armed forces to battle. It is another thing to pass the better part of a decade holding hearings to demonstrate that it was the Morgan banks or the munitions manufacturers that had got the United States into the First World War, or enacting neutrality acts that would keep us out of the next.[24] These were not Congresses to be reasoned with; they had to be manipulated. At some points Roosevelt went past any line of propriety. When the destroyer–naval base deal was consummated by executive agreement, Attorney General Robert H. Jackson gave out a legal opinion that found everything in order. He cited the relevant statute, the Neutrality Act of 1917. In his version of the text, however, a comma was inserted that completely changed the effect of the statute. Section 3 of the act stated that it was

> unlawful to send out of the jurisdiction of the United States any vessel built, armed or equipped as a vessel of war, or converted from a private vessel into a vessel of war, with any intent or under any agreement or contract, written or oral, that such vessel shall be delivered to a belligerent nation . . .

As adopted by Congress the clause had three basic operative parts: (1) sending out of the jurisdiction of the United States, (2) any vessel equipped for war, (3) with the intention that "such vessel" be delivered to a nation at war.

The attorney general's version of the law was something altogether different. With a new comma between "vessel" and "built" he attempted to argue that there were two basic operative parts: (1) sending a vessel out of the United States, which was (2) built with the specific intent that it would be delivered to a belligerent state. Delivery of a warship to a belligerent nation after it was built for the purpose of defending the United States was quite a different matter.[25]

It may be asked, was Roosevelt violating the very laws he claimed, or at least was presumed, to be upholding? An answer must be twofold. As regards the Neutrality Act, he not only failed to "take Care that the Laws be faithfully executed"; he actually subverted the law. He was clearly subject to impeachment. Yet, no impeachment was proposed. His presidential opponent in 1940 supported the deal. Congress either didn't mind or didn't know. He ought not to have done it. He probably could have got the law changed. But there it is. Whatever else he did, Roosevelt did not *conceal* his behavior. (At the close of the war, he *with* Churchill reached an agreement with Stalin at Yalta that reflected nothing more than the facts on the ground; military facts that the United States had no capacity to change. Yet this agreement was widely depicted in the United States as a betrayal of American principle; possibly as a violation of international law.)

As for aiding Britain, no issue of neutrality arose. Neutrality is not an obligation under international law. A president would have been blind who did not see the threat to the United States from a Nazi-dominated Europe. A nation, threatened, has every right to defend itself, and woe to those that do not. Germany could well have argued that the United States was now a belligerent state under international law, despite its declared neutrality, and would be treated as such; it chose not to do so for the sound reason of hoping to keep the United States from fully entering the war. In the first war, Germany violated American neutrality. In the second, it threatened our national security. In each case, the United States acted in more than sufficient compliance with the law of nations.

In the event the Japanese imperial navy resolved the issue. The effect of Pearl Harbor was more than that of taking the nation into war. It was to bring a concise end to the notion of American exceptionalism with respect to the prospect of war. For as long as anyone could remember, war had been *our* choice. *We* attacked. Now it appeared that others could make that decision and attack us. Nothing has since been the same. (If anything, events have repeated the experience. As in the 1940s, in the 1950s and the 1960s the

United States went to war in response to an attack by others. The Korean experience was as concise as Pearl Harbor, the Vietnam experience more problematic; yet even there our view was that Communist forces had begun the conflict, as indeed they had.)

· · · · ·

Even before America entered the Second World War, the planning for peace had begun. This time it would be done better. In Cordell Hull Roosevelt had a superbly adept secretary of state. His entry in the *Biographical Directory of the United States Congress, 1774–1989* records that he is "known as 'the Father of the United Nations,'" which is sufficiently near the truth. Hull had been in the House of Representatives in 1919–1920 and needed no instructions on how not to get a treaty through the Senate.

In his State of the Union address on January 6, 1941, Roosevelt set out the Four Freedoms, which purported to describe the goals of the democratic countries then at war. "Freedom from want" and "freedom from fear" were new to the vocabulary of war aims. Soft notions, maybe, but compelling. The Atlantic Charter that followed in August was more traditional, beginning with the familiar pledge against territorial aggrandizement, and anticipating a new world organization along the lines of the League. When war did come, the papers were ready. On January 1, 1942, twenty-six nations fighting the Axis powers signed the Declaration by the United Nations, which accepted the Atlantic Charter. The basic outlines of the UN Charter were agreed to by the United States, Britain, Russia, and China at a conference at Dumbarton Oaks in Washington, which met from August 21 to October 7, 1944.

Two weeks later, on October 21, the president rode fifty miles in an open car in the rain through four boroughs of New York City. Ebbets Field, the Grand Concourse, the World's Fair site in Queens, Harlem, Greenwich Village, and the apartment the Roosevelts maintained at 29 Washington Square. Crowds all along the route. Despite an exhausting day, and an earlier speech on behalf of Senator Robert F. Wagner, Roosevelt went that evening to address the Foreign Policy Association accompanied by James Forrestal, Henry Stimson, and Herbert Lehman. (Catholic, Protestant, Jew: nothing left to chance.)

The president's address was surprisingly partisan. The 1944 election was two weeks away; he would do well enough, that should have been clear. But the speech was an appeal not so much for his own reelection as for the continuation of a Democratic Congress and most especially a Democratic Senate. A Republican Senate would mean that his "old friend," Hiram Johnson of California, "still a friend," would be chairman of the Senate Foreign Relations Committee. Did the American voters want the "heavy hand" of Republican "isolationism" to control the Senate just as the United Nations project was bearing fruit? The speech ranged across the previous quarter-century. Harding had said "he favored with all his heart an Association of Nations 'so organized and so partici- pated in as to make the actual attainment of peace a reasonable possibility.'" However "—and this is history, too—after President Harding's election, the Association of Nations was never heard of again." Isolationism took hold. "All petitions that this Nation join the World Court were rejected or ignored." He had done his best in 1935. Now was another chance. "Never again, after cooperating with other Nations in a world war to save our way of life, can we wash our hands of maintaining the peace for which we fought." The way had been prepared.

> The Dumbarton Oaks Conference did not spring up over night. It was called by Secretary Hull and me after years of thought, discus- sion, preparation, and consultation with our allies. Our State Department did a grand job in preparing for the Conference and leading it to a successful termination. It was just another chapter in the long process of cooperation with other peace-loving Nations— beginning with the Atlantic Charter Conference—that's a long time ago—and continuing through Conferences at Casablanca, Moscow, Cairo, Teheran and Quebec and Washington. It is my profound conviction that the American people as a whole have a very real understanding of these things.
>
> The American people know that Cordell Hull and I are thoroughly conversant with the Constitution of the United States—and know that we cannot commit this Nation to any secret treaties or any secret guarantees that are in violation of that Constitution.

But the people must understand. They *did* understand! "For this generation must act not only for itself, but as a trustee for all those who fell in the last war—a part of their mission unfulfilled."[26] Roosevelt might have used to good effect Wilson's phrase from the

Pueblo, Colorado, speech: "Those dear ghosts that still deploy upon the fields of France."

This, too, was a speech from the cross. Roosevelt was dying. It is a wonder the day had not killed him; in the event he would be dead by April. The passion is there, not to be mistaken. He now took on the issue that had brought Wilson down.

> Peace, like war, can succeed only where there is a will to enforce it, and where there is available power to enforce it.
>
> The Council of the United Nations must have the power to act quickly and decisively to keep the peace by force, if necessary. A policeman would not be a very effective policeman if, when he saw a felon break into a house, he had to go to the Town Hall and call a town meeting to issue a warrant before the felon could be arrested.
>
> So to my simple mind it is clear that, if the world organization is to have any reality at all, our American representative must be endowed in advance by the people themselves, by constitutional means through their representatives in the Congress, with authority to act.
>
> If we do not catch the international felon when we have our hands on him, if we let him get away with his loot because the Town Council has not passed an ordinance authorizing his arrest, then we are *not* doing our share to prevent another world war. I think, and I have had some experience, that the people of this Nation want their Government to work, they want their Government to act, and not merely to talk, whenever and wherever there is a threat to world peace.[27]

He had worked at this speech, which went through four drafts. In the fourth he had added the passage about the Town Council, and quite specifically had crossed out the Lodge reservation, a sentence which ran: "We shall enter a peace organization as a sovereign power, and therefore our representative in that organization cannot legislate for us."[28]

Public opinion was now once again fiercely internationalist, and Roosevelt knew it. Edward R. Stettinius, Jr., as under secretary of state, had sent him a memorandum reporting a "confidential public opinion survey conducted by the Office of Public Research, Princeton University" just before the Dumbarton Oaks proposals were made public. Nine out of ten persons favored the United States' joining an international organization "in an effort to prevent future wars." (These are the State Department's words.) Eight in ten favored the use of force, if necessary to prevent war. Stettinius made another notable point:

> *Congressional approval before use of American armed forces.* Opinion is at present about evenly divided on the question of whether Congress should, in each case, before American armed force is used, approve of action recommended by the organization in which the American representative acting on Presidential authority concurs.[29]

Pause a moment. A president of the United States, with, as we will see, solid support from Congress, was proposing that an American representative be given the power to commit American forces to battle *on his own*. Or on the instructions of the White House. Or both; it is never clear in the documents. On July 15, from aboard the Presidential Special, Roosevelt sent word to Hull approving—"Good luck!"—the United States Tentative Proposals for a General International Organization, which were then directly sent to the United Kingdom, the Soviet Union, and China and were thereafter the principal documents in the Dumbarton Oaks discussions. This included "Measures Involving the Use of Armed Force":

> 1. In the event that other measures prove to be inadequate, the executive council should be authorized to provide for the use of armed force to assure the maintenance of security and peace.
> 2. The member states should undertake to furnish forces and facilities when needed for this purpose at the call of the executive council and in accordance with a general agreement governing the number and type of forces and the kind and extent of facilities to be provided.[30]

Hull had already convened a senatorial "Committee of Eight" to discuss such matters. In May he had told his former colleagues that he thought the president should have power to deal with minor conflicts, the while keeping the Congress informed. He writes in his memoirs that no other course seemed practical "because there were threatened breaches of the peace almost every week of the year in some part of the world or other." Major breaches of the peace "meant war rather than police action, in which event the prerogative of Congress to declare war would be completely safeguarded."[31] Ruth B. Russell records that "the Senators seemed satisfied when Hull assured them that the proposed treaty allocating forces would be submitted to the Senate."[32]

Roosevelt's speech was partisan, but it would seem that his purpose was less to confront the Republicans than to divide them. Soon a Republican senator demanded to know of the presidential candidates whether they would support such a provision, fearing that the Republican candidate, Thomas E. Dewey, would not. This was Joseph H. Ball of Minnesota. On September 19 he had spoken in the Senate on the subject of Dumbarton Oaks. He was not sure the delegates had gone far enough. His fear was not that the proposed world organization would have too much power, but that it would have too little. The League had had too little. "The Kellogg-Briand pact outlawed war as an instrument of national policy but provided no means of enforcing that international law. It proved to be an empty gesture. The League of Nations left the decision as to whether force would be used to stop aggression up to each individual nation. It also failed. Millions have died because of those failures." Surely, there would be a standing peacekeeping force, and just as surely the United States would contribute its share. "This time let us keep faith with those who are fighting and dying to make this second chance for a lasting peace possible. Let the United States shoulder, without fear or equivocation, its share of the job of maintaining peace in the world." Thence to a notable view of the war powers provision.

> The question raised here by several Senators is whether even such a United States quota force should be used to stop aggression at the direction of the council [of the United Nations], our representative agreeing, unless Congress had formally declared war . . . I cannot see how the Constitutional authority of Congress to declare war is concerned in the slightest. The world security organization would not be making war, but preserving the peace. Its whole purpose is to eliminate war from the world, not make it. It appears to me that either under the general welfare or the national defense clause, the Congress has full constitutional authority, in the light of the world situation today, to provide in advance for whatever world policing is considered necessary to prevent another great war.[33]

Extraordinary times. In 1919 the American Peace Society, founded in 1828, had turned against the Covenant on grounds that it lacked a "judicial process," hence was "Prussian in its conception and in its dangers." Now, in the October 1944 issue of its journal, *World Affairs,* the same society reported with "great satisfaction" that there seemed to be bipartisan agreement on the use of force to put down threats to world peace. The journal published articles by Senator Thomas Connally, chairman of the Committee on Foreign Relations, and Senator Warren Austin, author of the international plank in the 1944 Republican platform. In his contribution, Senator Austin disclosed that the international planks of both the Republican and Democratic platforms were written to conform to the American plan being offered at the Dumbarton Oaks conference. The troublesome issue was whether the U.S. representative to the reconstituted League could commit United States troops to a peacekeeping mission without specific recourse to Congress. The senators agreed that as the U.S. representative would have veto power over the use of force, the United States could not be committed to a war without its consent. And no matter what the treaty provided, the U.S. representative would be acting pursuant to U.S. legislation. He could not act outside the boundaries established by Congress. The message was clear. As summarized in the *New York Times* by Arthur Krock, this "thorn[y] issue . . . can and will be solved legislatively."[34]

Two days after Krock reported the Connally-Austin accords, the White House staff was considering how to make use of Senator Ball's challenge to embarrass Dewey. On October 13 Stettinius reported to Roosevelt, in a memorandum approved by his legal advisers, that the Security Council of the United Nations would indeed have the power to order the use of force and the United States would thereby be committed. Stettinius was unequivocal: "there is no question so far as the Charter itself is concerned that a vote of the Council to use force, in which the American delegate concurs, would commit our Government to fulfil its treaty obligations with respect to the supplying of forces." A vote by the council to send troops, absent a veto, and the United States was treaty-bound to take up arms. And yet, as did Connally and Austin, the under secretary resolved the problem thus: "The relation of the American delegate to his government is not a matter which can properly be dealt with in the treaty. It is a matter to be determined by the Constitution and statutes.[35] The United States would retain full rights to instruct its delegate and, therefore, to choose for itself when and where to engage its forces.

Near to half a century has passed; this delegation of power, or, if you like, arrogation, seems quite extraordinary. But it wasn't really. The institutional setting was to be an organization enforcing international law. Clearly this made a claim then that it does not now. After war broke out in 1939 Duff Cooper, the British parliamentarian and diplomat, came to the United States on a lecture tour. He had resigned as a minister at the time of Munich; had fully expected war with Hitler; had almost wanted it after the humiliations of the 1930s. For some reason the Chamberlain government, still in office, was concerned that his lectures might call for the United States to join in, and would be labeled British propaganda. Cooper later recalled that he had no such disposition.

> I could see no reason whatever why America should come into the war at that date . . . If we had fought a year before, we could have said with truth that we were fighting for a great principle, the observance of international law, and for the existence of a small country which had come into being in accordance with President Wilson's doctrine of self-determination. We had not been willing to fight then . . . We were fighting now neither for a principle nor for others. We were fighting for our lives. It might become an American interest to save our lives, but until it plainly was so I could see no reason for their intervention.[36]

There was a sense in 1944 that war need not have come, had only the former allies stuck to their principles, insisted on the observance of law. Woodrow Wilson had been right! Almost a quarter-century to the day after Wilson collapsed in Pueblo, his then—assistant secretary of the navy was redeeming his pledge, and this time the Congress was with him.

CHAPTER FIVE

"Big White Space"

On December 8, 1988, an editorial in the *New York Times* offered a novel thought. "Perhaps not since Woodrow Wilson presented his Fourteen Points in 1918 or since Franklin Roosevelt and Winston Churchill promulgated the Atlantic Charter in 1941 has a world figure demonstrated the vision Mikhail Gorbachev displayed yesterday at the United Nations." And, indeed, allusions to both Wilson and Roosevelt could be found in the general secretary's text.[1] We must "make the world a safer place for all of us." There must be an end to "the terror of hunger and poverty and political terrorism." The text was openly allusive, harkening back to a period in which the United States and the Soviets had common enemies. "Let me be somewhat more specific on this subject. To paraphrase the words of an English poet, which Hemingway used for the epigraph to one of his famous novels, I will put it as follows: the bell of each regional conflict tolls for all of us."

The "news" of the speech was arms reduction. The Soviet Union would cut its forces by 500,000 men, would withdraw six tank divisions from Central Europe. It would go further: prepare an "internal conversion plan as part of its economic reform effort," beginning with "two or three defense plants"; and "make public its experience in re-employing defense personnel and using defense facilities and equipment in civilian production." (This later proposal tracked with the Intermediate Nuclear Forces Treaty, signed in Washington the previous December. Each side was to *watch* the other side dismantle and destroy its Pershing IIs or SS2os. By now the respective teams were wearing Latin/Cyrillic name tags in the spirit of a shared enterprise.) The Soviets looked for "consistent movement" toward a treaty on a 50 percent reduction in strategic offensive arms.

The address celebrated the United Nations, its newfound effectiveness in peacekeeping operations, its enduring precept of legality.

The world was on the edge of an extraordinary transformation. Much as the British, French, and Dutch colonial empires were dismantled following the Second World War, the Soviet empire in Central Europe was about to be dissolved without any significant Soviet resistance. Not a Soviet round would be fired. People in Moscow had changed their minds. Almost certainly the failure of the economy was the compelling concern; proof of the failure of theory; proof of the need for change. *Possibly* the new theoreticians in the Kremlin saw international law and international human rights procedures as a way of opening a closed system to a free flow of information for lack of which the system was failing. It would not exactly be market information—prices, quantities—but it would be information associated with the liberal culture of markets. Free men, free markets, as the phrase went. Whatever, this is the banner he raised: "As the awareness of our common fate grows, every state would be genuinely interested in confining itself within the limits of international law."

The Soviet leader proposed an end to the cold war. As if to anticipate suspicions in Washington, he allowed that there were those in his own capital who thought his views "overly idealistic, overestimating the maturity and potential of the thinking of the world public." He allowed that the Soviets had started a lot of it. "It is regrettable that immediately after its foundation the United Nations was subjected to the onslaught of the Cold War. For many years it was a propaganda battlefield and a scene of political confrontation."

The world had entered a new stage. "Some former disagreements and disputes are losing their importance." Two great revolutions —"the French Revolution of 1789 and the Russian Revolution of 1917"—had had a powerful impact "on the very nature of the historic process." But "today a new world is emerging, and we must look for new ways." That was then, now was different. "This new stage requires the freeing of international relations from ideology." The world should seek "unity through diversity." And then this: "We in no way aspire to be the bearer of the ultimate truth."

Just one month earlier the Soviet foreign minister, Eduard Shevardnadze, had allowed at a UNESCO meeting in Paris that the Soviets had "submitted to the influence of confrontation and adopted its spirit," which helped to disrupt that body.[2] (Readers of Soviet texts are expected to pick up what, in Hemingway's Spain, was described as the *linea politica*.) It was not, William Pfaff would write, that the cold war was over. "Marxism-Leninism was over." The totalitarian pretense was over; the claim to have spoken for history and to be the next stage in history was over. Thus, Pfaff: "Whatever happens now in the Soviet Union's competition with the Western powers, there is no connection with that 'struggle for the world' which both East and West conceived it to be from 1918 to the mid-1980s."[3] The revolutions of 1989 now commenced. Before the summer was out, Francis Fukuyama published a celebrated essay in the *National Interest* introducing the question "The End of History?" More than the cold war was over; more than the claims on the future of the Marxist totalitarians, there was "a larger process at work" more startling yet:

> The twentieth century saw the developed world descend into a paroxysm of ideological violence, as liberalism contended first with the remnants of absolutism, then bolshevism and fascism, and finally an updated Marxism that threatened to lead to the ultimate apocalypse of nuclear war. But the century that began full of self-confidence in the ultimate triumph of Western liberal democracy seems at its close to be returning full circle to where it started: not to an "end of ideology" or a convergence between capitalism and socialism, as earlier predicted, but to an unabashed victory of economic and political liberalism.

At the end of history it was "not necessary that all societies become successful liberal societies, merely that they end their ideological pretensions of representing different and higher forms of human society."[4]

The scientist and philosopher Michael Polanyi had a saying: People change their minds. This was not offered as a scientific proposition, nor yet as a philosophical one. Merely as an observation, but of more than passing interest. His thought was that the large movements of belief in the world take place somewhat out of sight until a sudden moment of recognition. He and Arthur Koestler would discuss this, using the homely image of construction workers in Britain preparing sand for mortar. Rough gravel is thrown against a propped-up screen. Sand goes through and sand goes through and nothing seems to change when of a sudden there is no space behind the screen and sand no longer goes through. Whereupon everything has changed. This would seem an application of Polanyi's widely influential idea of tacit knowledge in science. In any event, something such happened in 1989. When the year was over, peoples throughout the world who had not known that Communism was over of a sudden did know. When asked "What do you still find useful in the works of Marx?" Soviet officials would answer, "Nothing." If not the end of history it was surely the end of ideology.

This, curiously, was a phrase of Friedrich Engels, from his 1886 essay, "Ludwig Feuerbach and the End of Classical German Philosophy." (The concept was embodied in the Marxist term *demystification*.) When men—for which read the masses—become aware of their true interest they shed their false consciousness, as, for example, patriotic nationalism, and proceed promptly to the ranks of United Workers of the World. Victorian Marxism was stuffed with such notions, not all wrong, but none quite right. More powerful analyses came along. Max Weber, especially in the works published in the 1920s, got closer to the truth with the proposition that under conditions of universal suffrage ideological differences between political parties would become *less* not more pronounced. This would be termed a shift to functional rationality. Karl Mannheim's *Ideology and Utopia*, which appeared in Germany in 1929, brought this analysis to a nice edge. The logic of politics weakens ideological commitment.[5]

In 1949 T. H. Marshall, in Britain, propounded a general explanation of the rise and decline of total ideologies. They emerge with the rise of a new social group, such as industrial owners or industrial workers. Each seeks rights of citizenship in various manifestations. When such rights are denied, ideologies are advanced which depict the glories that will follow their attainment. When such rights are attained both the arguments and the vision fade. "The source of the decline of such ideologies in democratic countries . . . lies in the eventual integration of these groups in society and polity."[6] The history of 1989 is yet to be written, but we can state that the necessary precondition—the loss of faith in totalitarian systems—was foreseen. From Weber to Mannheim to Marshall a kind of Second Law of Thermodynamics was developed. These systems cool off.

Two events slowed this perception in the West. The Chinese Communists came to power in 1949, and Communist movements had some successes in the Third World. The regimes that followed, however, were invariably grim and, as with China in the 1960s, frequently ghastly. Refugees from Communist states became a fixture of the second half of the century, much as refugees from fascist regimes had been earlier. Nevertheless, there was some evidence of a still vital movement. There were those for whom the very brutality of the Communist regimes was a sign of vigor, which the West was said to lack. A familiar formulation; as in the "better red than dead" disposition of the 1950s. Bertrand Russell was not above such silliness. And then there were the leftist outbreaks of the 1930s and then the 1960s in the West. The New Left of the 1960s in the United States had at times the appearance of a mass movement. It was as much as anything a demographic phenomenon—the baby boom—with a dynamic that would make the cohort as "conservative" in middle years as it was "radical" in youth. But again this was not clear.[7] Marxism continued to win recruits among intellectuals, especially in Europe. Not untypically those involved passed through a period of Marxism which persisted in the form of anti-Marxism. (Ignazio Silone wrote repeatedly in the 1940s that the final battle would be between Communists and ex-Communists.) Frequently, this began as a schism within the Marxist camp—Trotskyites as never-yielding foes of Stalinists, a preoccupation that would persist long after their renunciation of Trotsky. Less frequently, there were to be encountered those who got it all straight from the outset. In a 1947 article in *Commentary*, Robert Warshow wrote:

> For most American intellectuals [*read* New Yorkers], the Communist movement of the 1930s was a crucial experience . . . there was a time when virtually all intellectual vitality was derived in one way

or another from the Communist party. If you were not somewhere within the party's wide orbit, then you were likely to be in the opposition, which meant that much of your thought and energy had to be devoted to maintaining yourself in opposition.[8]

Those who did, and those they taught, were ready when the second wave of the 1960s came along. (Norman Podhoretz records that William Phillips of the *Partisan Review* once told English critic Kenneth Tynan that he "could not argue with him about politics, because Tynan's arguments were so old that he, Phillips, could no longer remember the answers.")[9] As if by arrangement, in 1960 Daniel Bell first published *The End of Ideology*. It would be an interesting decade, he appeared to say, but it would come to nothing.

> The new generation [of intellectuals] ... finds itself seeking new purposes within a framework of political society that has rejected, intellectually speaking, the old apocalyptic and chiliastic visions. In the search for a "cause," there is a deep, desperate, almost pathetic anger ... In the U.S. .... there is a restless search for a new intellectual radicalism ... The irony ... for those who seek "causes" is that the workers, whose grievances were once the driving energy for social change, are more satisfied with the society than the intellectuals. The workers have not achieved utopia, but their expectations were less than those of the intellectuals, and the gains correspondingly larger.[10]

This was more now than argument in the abstract. A century after Engels, social science had become somewhat quantitative. It could attempt assessments of theory. The facts seemed to fit with Weber and Mannheim. One such survey found a "negative correlation between the degree of economic development and the intensity of ideological politics within a given country."[11] Seweryn Bialer holds that in all probability the theoretician Mikhail Suslov, who died in 1982, "was the last Politburo member to have read even the first volume of Karl Marx's *Capital* or some of the more complex works of Lenin."[12] In the end, however, economics settled the matter. (A nice Marxist irony.)

In economics not everything is relative. After the Second World War, the economies of the West experienced extraordinary, ahistorical growth. But so did the Soviet Union. Things seemed to be working for them also. Life was better than it had been. Expectations were greater. In 1961, comparing the Soviet economy with the U.S. economy, Nikita Khrushchev declared that by 1970 the U.S.S.R. "will not only catch up with you, it will outstrip you!"[13] Every indication is that he was not lying. Boasting perhaps, but no more than that. This was the information which he and the party leadership had. When Khrushchev was ousted in 1964, it was not on the basis of any doubts about the Soviet experiment as such. Directly thereafter a *Pravda* editorial was triumphal on the subject.

> Undeviatingly pursuing this [Leninist] line, the Party and the Soviet people are gaining victories in accomplishing the chief economic task—creating the material and technical base of communism.
> . . . there is a swelling torrent of joyous tidings of new enterprises being opened, of the mastering of production of progressive types of goods, of glorious labor achievements by our working class, collective farm peasantry, state farm workers and specialists in all branches of the national economy. Millions of Soviet people by their creative labor in plants and factories, at construction projects, on collective farm and state farm fields, in scientific institutes and laboratories and in cultural, educational and public health institutions are implementing in practice the Program of the C.P.S.U. [Communist Party of the Soviet Union], advancing the great cause of communist construction, which has become the dear cause of the millions, of the entire Soviet people.[14]

At just that moment, the new leader, Leonid I. Brezhnev, began eighteen years in power, which in time would be known as "the period of stagnation." American wheat began arriving. The Pacific Rim took off. In 1987 in Moscow, officials would speak of the "widening gulf between the Soviet Union and the advanced capitalist countries."[15] They were not talking of Holland. Peter the Great had figured out Holland. They were talking of Korea—South Korea—Taiwan, Hong Kong, Singapore. The proverbial Asian coolies suddenly sweeping world markets with electronic circuitry, while all the Soviets could sell abroad were natural resources, principally oil and gas, much like Saudi Arabia or, more aptly, Colonel Khadafy's Libya.

Yet the delusion persisted. The United States surely had something to do with this. Early in the cold war the U.S.S.R. was declared to be a "superpower"; one of two. The world moves by metaphor, and none is more satisfying than the opposition of two equal forces. Interaction among more than two forces introduces what scientists call the "many body problem." This is intractable to all save theoretical physicists. Once the notion of developed and underdeveloped economies emerged in postwar discourse, there were economists who toyed with the thought that the Soviet Union might be one of the latter, but this remained something of an eccentricity. For one thing, Russia was so large; how could its economy not be equally large? It had been doing well at the beginning of the century; any normal progression would have brought it much further along. (True; but also true of Argentina, another large place. In 1908 per capita income there was $1,018, almost equal the $1,129 of the United States. Yet it commenced to misgovern itself.) And then there was the matter of weaponry. They had a bomb, we had a bomb. They had missiles, we had missiles. In reality these were never shared monopolies, but seemed such. A genuine puzzle involved the Central Intelligence Agency. It began reporting on the size of the Soviet economy to the Joint Economic Committee in 1959, and five years later it began to publish its findings. Still later a side-by-side comparison of the U.S. and Soviet economies appeared. From the first, the Directorate of Intelligence has regularly reported that the Soviet Union possesses the second-largest economy in the world. The *Handbook of Economic Statistics, 1989* put U.S. total output in 1988 at $4.8 trillion; Soviet total output at $2.5 trillion; Japan a distant third at $1.7 trillion. Just as this was being published Secretary of State James A. Baker gave the Senate Finance Committee his opinion that there was "serious doubt" that the Soviet Union was even the third-ranking economy in the world. In 1985, by the estimate of the Central Intelligence Agency, Soviet GNP per capita was 46 percent that of the United States. Given the pattern of Soviet expenditure, principally the heavy cost of weaponry, Soviet per capita consumption stood at 32 percent of the American level, barely above Mexico and Argentina. Something happened in the 1980s. Soviet GNP reached 59 percent that of the United States in 1982; then declined steadily to 52 percent in 1988.[16]

There had been signs. The most powerful, or at all events the one that most impressed me, came in 1983 when Murray Feshbach testified before the Joint Economic Committee of the Congress that life expectancy for males in the Soviet Union was declining.[17] Vital statistics usually tell more about reality than economic data; everything comes together in births and deaths and family relations in between. Life expectancy "cannot" decline in a developed economy. Of late it has rarely if ever declined in an underdeveloped economy. Accidents happen. A new strain of malaria, or whatever. But it takes a lot of explaining if the virus attacks only males. No one seems to know just what happened in the Soviet Union. Male alcoholism is the most favored hypothesis. In any event, not exactly "a swelling torrent of joyous tidings."

Pfaff writes: "The Soviet experiment is ending as the victim not of Bolshevism's enemies but of the movement's own contradictions." This is more than just a play on Marxist babble about the contradictions of capitalism. They were there for all to see in what computer buffs call real time. Rhetorical rights; actual repression. Rhetorical progress; actual regression. Rhetorical paradise; actual hell. The moment came when this *was* seen. We have no notion why. As a working hypothesis Polanyi's principle seems best: Russians woke up one morning and found they had changed their minds. Pfaff is almost certainly right in locating the event in the persons of a newly emerged Russian intelligentsia, educated and *traveled*. (Gorbachev had been a regular visitor to Western Europe before becoming general secretary.) "In contrast to the peasant/ worker semi-illiterate aparatchiks who preceded them, they learned the truth about the world and the U.S.S.R.'s position, understanding that instead of overtaking and surpassing the West the U.S.S.R. actually was being overtaken and surpassed by Pakistan."[18] And, if not by Pakistan, then surely by South Korea and a host of others.

Simultaneously, to continue with Weber's theorem, the routine of management wore away at ideology. In 1987 Boris Yeltsin, still outwardly the orthodox party leader of Moscow, would tell visitors that his housing problem was impossible with rents frozen at 1929 levels. A senator from New York was assured that Manhattan realtors would find ready opportunity and assured profits in the capital of the Soviet Union, and were not to worry about idiot regulations that permitted foreigners only minority participation in joint ventures.

But it took more than economic problems to bring down what Leon Wieseltier has called "so powerful a lie." The loss of faith in totalitarianism involved in at least some measure the recognition of a more powerful set of ideas, those of political liberalism. "The Leninist soteriology, its ideals of social perfection and human happiness, are being discarded everywhere, especially by Leninists, as are its ideals of economic organization."[19] As much or more. The great event of modernity was the *American* revolution. It may be more prudent to describe it as the revolution of modernity that happened to take place in America. Either way, it is the case that the framers set out to shape a government according to the principles of the "new science of politics" which they insistently claimed to possess—not to have discovered, mind, merely to have put to proper use. It was a mechanistic science—all that was available from the natural sciences—and limited. Still, as noted, there was a psychological realism that far more deserved the claim of objectivity and replication than the high Victorian vapors of Marx and Engels.[20] The essence of the American revolution was to establish a contractual relationship between a government and its people. Two centuries passed and this became, in the observation of Bert Horwitz, the great issue of the world.[21] In the totalitarian world, the issue erupted first in the satellite nations that had had the more extended experience of nineteenth-century political liberalism. Hannah Arendt did not miss this. In 1958 she published a new edition of *The Origins of Totalitarianism*, wherein, as we recall, she had first taught that nothing could change such a system. Now she added a chapter titled "Epilogue: Reflections on the Hungarian Revolution." Could it be, she asked, that the system *can* change? *Be* changed? This became the last thought in her epic work: "The danger signs of 1956 were real enough, and although today they are overshadowed by . . . the fact that the [totalitarian] system was able to survive, it would not be wise to forget them. If they promise anything at all, it is much rather a sudden and dramatic collapse of the whole regime than a gradual normalization."[22]

· · · · ·

A half-century of conditioning teaches us not to believe Soviet leaders. After all, even the word *soviet* is a lie. Workers' councils first emerged during the 1905 revolution. Grassroots democracy.

The Bolshevik battle cry "All power to the Soviets!" meant *no* power to the soviets or any representative body, informal or otherwise. Yet, Gorbachev at the U.N. in December 1988 had stated that "with the recent introduction of constitutional amendments by the U.S.S.R. Supreme Soviet and the adoption of a new electoral law, we have completed the first stage of the political reform . . . Soviet democracy will then develop on a sound legal basis."[23] Words? Yes. But such words can in themselves be deeds. They are not readily withdrawn in societies that are no longer closed. The following spring, elections *were* held. Party leaders were defeated. Yeltsin, in disgrace, now returned in opposition. The Supreme Soviet convened; television covered the proceedings in the manner of C-SPAN, with an audience across eleven time zones estimated at 100 million people. Ministers were rejected; the head of the KGB questioned.

"Bourgeois legality" became a preoccupation of nations Lenin had hoped to deliver from such false consciousness. Again, this appeared in its most developed form in the most politically developed of the satellite states. In Hungary in the spring of 1989, the minister of justice, Kalman Kulscar, charged with drafting a new constitution, presented a visitor with a background paper replete with references to American books and scholars. The English-language title: "Rule of law state, constitutionalism, human rights in the transformation of the Hungarian political system." Interviewed on Radio Free Europe, Imre Pozsgay, a member of the Politburo of the Hungarian Socialist Workers party, asserted that it was impossible to reform the Stalinist system then in place in the Soviet Union and Eastern Europe. It would have to be replaced. The Budapest press reported this, noting that Pozsgay was an official of a party that had routinely denounced Radio Free Europe as a "tool of the most reactionary imperialist circles." On March 15, 1989, he had written the inaugural manifesto for the Movement for a Democratic Hungary. A graduate of the Lenin Institute of Budapest, he had gone on to become a party theoretician, the clerisy of Leninist regimes, finally to the presidium of the ruling party. He now, however, was of the view that "the proper subject of political freedom is the citizen, its framework is the nation, and its tool is the State."[24]

The distinguishing feature of a civil society is that its proceedings are open and its records are kept intact. Historical truth was the first victim of totalitarianism; suppression, distortion, rewriting became institutionalized, as Orwell had described. The struggle against this seemed hopeless; the single person against the state. In the end you would love Big Brother regardless of how you got there. And yet, the struggle went on. Sidney Hook and John Dewey could organize a commission to inquire into the guilt of Trotsky and the authenticity of the Moscow treason trials. But nothing could ever be resolved. Men of great tenacity set out to compile and publish the record, but almost all of them were in the West. Robert Conquest, such a man, has written of the struggle for the minds of men and women living under Communism that "it would be incorrect to call this merely a struggle of ideas, for it has often been a struggle over the mere facts."[25] But now, of a sudden, the facts came rushing forward. As if exhumed. Who killed Trotsky? Stalin obviously, but now that the subject had been raised, here was the name of the KGB colonel who was sent to Mexico City, and this was the amount of money he brought for the Spanish Communist who was the designated assassin. Nikolai Bukharin? Innocent, of course, as Koestler surmised. But would anyone care to know more of the pledge he extracted of his wife on the day he was taken off to what he knew would be his doom? Trotsky himself reappeared in photographs with Lenin in which Stalin had airbrushed him into presumed oblivion.

The "secret" was that there had been two revolutions, not one. On March 12, 1917 (by the modern calendar), there had been a substantially democratic Russian revolution, which overthrew the czar and established a provisional government headed by Prince Lvov. Then it in turn was overthrown by Lenin and Trotsky. When the Constituent Assembly took its place in 1918, Bolsheviks were in a minority. It was dispersed by Lenin. Aleksandr Kerenski, at first minister of justice in the provisional government, then prime minister from July to November, would thereafter wander the high school corridors of Manhattan insisting that there had been two revolutions, the first democratic, the second totalitarian. A foreigner with a hard-luck story. At the New Leader he was understood; it was founded by exiles such as he. But elsewhere? No single totalitarian myth was more powerful than that of the single, redemptive, irreversible October revolution (October 25 by the old calendar). The popular version: John Reed's *Ten Days That Shook the World*. Sailors from Kronstadt and the Red Guards advance through Petrograd. The cruiser *Aurora* guards the vital bridge over the River Neva and signals the attack. Storm the Winter Palace!

As late as 1987 a visitor could remark to the mayor of Leningrad that with Peter the Great's city lovingly restored, including Lenin's quarters at the Smolny shrine, his statue everywhere, and now the *Aurora* refurbished, could there not be some small notice taken of Kerenski? Silence. On July 6, 1989, an editorial writer of the *New York Times* suggested that while the first elected Russian assembly in seventy years was now meeting in Moscow, "silence persists about how the old Assembly was killed." Glasnost, he continued, obviously had its limits. It was surely the right question to put. For if it were known that the old assembly had been killed, it would follow that there had been not one but two revolutions. Whereupon a political columnist for the official Soviet journal *Izvestia*, at the time a senior associate at the Carnegie Endowment for International Peace, responded.

> To the Editor:
> The postman delivered two newspapers to my door July 6, the *New York Times* of that day and [*Nedelia,*] a weekly supplement of *Izvestia* published June 12 . . .
> In *Nedelia* . . . appears "Once More about 'Blank Spots,'" by a well-known Russian historian, Vladlen Sirotkin, who teaches at the Diplomatic Academy of the Soviet Foreign Ministry.
> Professor Sirotkin writes about "blank spots" in the history of the Soviet Union, events that were concealed from the Soviet public before glasnost. He deals precisely with Mr. Meyer's litmus test—the dispersal of the First Constituent Assembly of Russia on January 18, 1918.

The writer claimed that "there is nothing new in this horrible story. It has been described many times by our historians and writers." Apparently Professor Sirotkin discussed the incident in detail, acknowledging that the Bolsheviks and other "left-wing parties" represented in the soviets deserved criticism for their role. The reason for dispersing the assembly? No longer any need to mince words. Marx considered violence the "midwife of history." Violent suppression of democratic trappings "was an implementation of [his] theory of how to create a new mechanism of the people's power."[26]

Recall that not six months earlier Gorbachev was still speaking of "the Russian Revolution of 1917" in strict conformity to the untruth that there had been but one. In fairness Russian Communists may be allowed the view that their revolution was the only one that mattered. But Russian society now required more; the restoration of history had been institutionalized in a column in the official government newspaper.

An epic event now occurred. At the end of May 1989 *Trybuna Ludu,* the official organ of the Polish United Workers' party, and *Pravda,* the Russian party paper, simultaneously published the report of a Polish-Russian commission that had been set up to inquire into the existence of a secret protocol to the Molotov-Ribbentrop pact of 1939 providing for the partition of Poland. The British had obtained a German microfilm of the nonaggression pact between Germany and the U.S.S.R. in 1945, and the fact of the collusion was known in the West. But West is West; now the fact was acknowledged in the East. And more. The Polish-Russian commission determined that "the Soviet government committed serious violations of international legal norms." The pact was signed in Moscow on August 23, 1939. The Second World War began on September 1, with the Nazi invasion of Poland. Russia invaded on September 17. Six weeks later, the report continued, Molotov told a session of the Supreme Soviet that "a short blow by the German army, and subsequently by the Red Army, was enough for nothing to be left of this ugly creature of the Treaty of Versailles, which lived off the oppression of non-Polish nationalities."[27]

It is a bizarre document. Stalingrad not four years away, and here were Russian diplomats negotiating a restoration of czarist boundaries in the manner of the old regime. A supplementary, secret protocol disposes of territories with the flourish of the Congress of Vienna and the tallying up of the Fuggers.

> 1. The government of the German Reich renounces its claims to the portion of the territory of Lithuania mentioned in the September 28, 1939, Secret Protocol and shown on the included map.
> 2. The Government of the Union of Soviet Socialist Republics is prepared to compensate the Government of the German Reich for

the territory mentioned in Point 1 of this protocol by payment of the sum of 7,500,000 gold dollars = 31 million 500 thousand reichsmarks to Germany.

Payment of the sum of 31.5 million reichsmarks will be accomplished by the U.S.S.R. in the following way: one eighth, i.e., 3,937,500 reichsmarks, in shipments of non-ferrous metal within three months of ratification of this treaty, and the remaining seven eighths, 27,562,500 reichsmarks, in gold by a deduction from the German payments in gold which the German side was to bring up by February 11, 1941.[28]

On August 24, 1989, the Polish Sejm elected Tadeusz Mazowiecki of the Solidarity movement to be the nation's first non-Communist prime minister since 1945. There were four dissenting votes. In an interview in *Izvestia* Mazowiecki described himself as "a Christian, a Catholic who follows the social teachings of the Catholic church."[29] He was content with the Warsaw Pact. From Moscow, the Soviet Council of Ministers sent a message of friendship and cooperation. From Washington, Zbigniew Brzezinski declared, "We are dealing with an epochal event . . . For once . . . words like 'watershed' and 'turning point' are no overstatement."[30] In Estonia posters appeared in Russian and English saying "U.S.S.R. Go Home." There was no stopping it now. One after another, the Communist regimes of Central Europe collapsed in the face of nothing more than street rallies.

In Roosevelt's 1944 address to the Foreign Policy Association he recounted how in 1933 "a certain lady—who sits at this table in front of me" had come back from a trip on which she attended the opening of a schoolhouse where she had seen "a map of the world with a great big white space upon it."[31] The schoolteacher had explained that the school board wouldn't let her say anything about that space, not even to give it a name. Well, he, the president, had reestablished ties with the Soviet Union. True enough, an understanding of Communist Russia was slow in coming. Yet is it so much to be wondered at that a relatively isolated United States should be uncomprehending of something as distant and as different as Stalin's Russia? It was one thing for Sidney Hook at New York University to master the subject. But others? Elsewhere? The cosmopolitan cultures of Elihu Root and Sidney Hook—the references to "New York" in this essay are only to that—made little impression beyond Manhattan. Generally speaking, the "big white space" stayed red and that was all there was to say. For almost half a century following Roosevelt the United States would be dealing with another society which it really didn't know. Dealing with a society whose "images of the world," Weber's term, were almost inaccessible to our own thinking. An ironic inversion occurred. The more sophisticated presidents, and by extension the statesmen of the postwar era, who had sufficiently sympathetic imaginations to grasp something of the Soviet reality, were often the most hostile. (Walter Lippmann was able to persuade John F. Kennedy to change his characterization of the Soviets as "enemy" to "adversary" in his inaugural address. The Bay of Pigs invasion went ahead withal.) The more experienced and educated statesmen of the cold war era generally kept their heads, and hewed to a fairly steady, continuous doctrine of containment, much as set forth in George F. Kennan's "long telegram" from Moscow sent in 1946.[32] But political figures in Washington, notably presidents, were often plainly confused when not actually befuddled. Following the invasion of Afghanistan in 1979, Jimmy Carter acknowledged that his "opinion of the Russians has changed more drastically in the last week than even the previous two-and-a-half years."[33] When Lou Cannon asked Ronald Reagan whether he thought Gorbachev was "a different kind of leader than the Soviets have had before," we learned this:

> Yes, I do . . . I think that one difference is that he is the first leader that has come along who has gone back before Stalin and that he is trying to do what Lenin was teaching . . . I think that this, in *glasnost* and *perestroika* is much more smacking of Lenin than [of] Stalin. And I think that this is what he is trying to do.[34]

Is it the case that the United States would never attain to an adequate understanding of the Soviet Union so long as it *was* so different, but that it might do now that it is less so? Fukuyama argued that in no way could the Soviet Union of the late 1980s be described as a liberal or a democratic country, nor is it yet likely that it will soon, if ever, become one. "But at the end of history it is not necessary that all societies become successful liberal societies, merely that they end their ideological pretensions of representing different and higher forms of human society."[35] Has that now happened?

It has. Gorbachev at the U.N. asserted: "We in no way aspire to be the bearer of ultimate truth."[36] That is all that matters.

CHAPTER SIX

"Pacta Sunt Servanda!"

Abraham Sofaer comments that in 1922 Maxim Litvinov "summed up the view that has long dominated Soviet legal thinking about dispute settlement—that in an ideologically divided world, no judge can be neutral. 'It was necessary to face the fact,' he had said, 'that there was not one world but two—a Soviet world and a non-Soviet world . . . there was no third world to arbitrate . . .'"[1] The initial Soviet reaction to the League of Nations was as to an imperialist fraud, war being inevitable among capitalist nations. Thereafter, in one or another mode, conflict would be inevitable between the capitalist and the socialist "camps." Yet now, sixty-six years later, the general secretary of the Communist Party of the Soviet Union (CPSU) was evidently proposing that the "law of class struggle" be supplanted by the law of nations. This was to extend to previously sacrosanct internal affairs. "We intend," Gorbachev told the General Assembly, "to expand the Soviet Union's participation in the controlling mechanisms of human rights under the aegis of the U.N., and within the framework of the European process. We think that the jurisdiction of the International Court in the Hague with regard to the interpretation and application of agreements on human rights must be binding on all states." Lest an iron curtain intervene: "We also see an end to the jamming of broadcasts by all foreign radio stations that transmit programmes to the Soviet Union, within the context of the Helsinki process."[2]

What was to be made of this? An earlier age would have reverted to Metternich's rule. Informed of the sudden demise of the Russian ambassador, he asked: "What can have been his motive?" Litvinov would go on forever about "collective security." But he had scarcely proposed that the hearings of the American commission on the Moscow trials be broadcast in Moscow. Such measures bring down regimes. At an earlier time a proposal by a general secretary of the CPSU to allow complaints about human rights within the Soviet Union to be adjudicated at The Hague would have defied analysis. And what is to be made of the Soviet leader's reminding the General Assembly of "the political, juridical and moral importance of the ancient Roman maxim: *Pacta sunt servanda!—agreements must be honoured!*"[3]

It did not stop there:

> While championing demilitarization of international relations, we would like political and legal methods to reign supreme in all attempts to solve the arising problems.
>
> Our ideal is a world community of states with political systems and foreign policies based on law.
>
> This could be achieved with the help of an accord within the framework of the U.N. on a uniform understanding of the principles and norms of international law; their codification with new conditions taken into consideration; and the elaboration of legislation for new areas of cooperation.
>
> In the nuclear era, the effectiveness of international law must be based on norms reflecting a balance of interests of states, rather than on coercion.
>
> As the awareness of our common fate grows, every state would be genuinely interested in confining itself within the limits of international law.[4]

Nor was this to be a one-time speech crafted for the particular setting of the United Nations. Richard Gardner, sometime deputy assistant secretary of state for international organization affairs, and professor of law and international organization at Columbia University, soon noted that Gorbachev repeatedly spoke of the "primacy of international law in politics."[5] Gardner was prepared to take this seriously, noting among other things that Gorbachev was a law graduate from Moscow State University, the first lawyer since Lenin to head the CPSU (Lenin was expelled from Kazan University Law School in 1887 for political activities, but finally did receive his degree from St. Petersburg University in 1891.) But Gardner was pretty much alone.

No one in official Washington seemed to have any idea how to respond. The insistent emphasis on international law, international adjudication, simply did not resonate. It would once have done. It did no longer. Consider Judge Sofaer, legal adviser to the Department of State and sometime professor at Columbia. Descended, in that regard, from John Basset Moore, and collaterally from James T. Shotwell. A man of honor as well as of high scholarship, he had made it known he would resign his post as legal adviser if Central Intelligence Agency director William Casey gave false testimony to Congress in an effort to cover up the Iran-Contra diversion. His Coudert Lecture (named for the celebrated international lawyer) was given at the House of the Association of the Bar of the City of New York on 44th Street, some seven blocks from the hall of the General Assembly at United Nations Plaza. It was given just eight days after Gorbachev had spoken. Sofaer's topic was "Adjudication in the International Court of Justice: Progress through Realism." Any discussion of that subject from the point of view of the United States necessarily involved consideration of the views of the Soviet Union. The chairman of the Presidium of the Supreme Soviet had just given an exceptional address, very much dwelling on this matter. The *New York Times,* on 43rd Street, had just compared Gorbachev's speech to the great pronouncements of Wilson and Roosevelt. An extraordinary conjunction, worthy at very least of acknowledgment, clearances or no. Yet whom did the legal adviser cite regarding Soviet views of international law? Maxim Litvinov.

In the annals of forgetfulness there is nothing quite to compare with the fading from the American mind of the idea of the law of nations. In the beginning this law was set forth as the foundation of our national existence. By all means wash this proposition with cynical acid and see how it shrinks. Granted, the repeated invocation of international law partook of the formalism of eighteenth-century thought. Everything was to be derived from first principles, self-evident truths. Granted, it partook of the dottiness of nineteenth-century enthusiasms, and the sanctimoniousness. Granted, it was an owners' creed as well. The law of property; the position of the status quo. And yet, was it wrong for these Americans to approach the twentieth century concerned to uphold these standards which might be lost? Was Woodrow Wilson wrong to think there might be something better ahead than Auschwitz and Hiroshima? Absurd? Yes, at times absurd. Wilson spoke of exotic encounters at Paris: "one day there came in a very dignified and interesting group of gentlemen from Adjur-Badjan [*sic*]. I did not have time until they were gone to find out where they came from, but I did find this out immediately, that I was talking to men who talked the same language that I did in respect of ideas, in respect of conceptions of liberty, in respect of conceptions of right and justice."[6] Flawed. He could have *had* the League; we have seen that. But wrong?

The idea of law in the relations of states was hardly confined to cosmopolitan easterners. In his celebrated 1920 speech on "Normalcy," Warren G. Harding surely wanted to get the nation back to where it had been, but with no apologies for where Wilson had led it. The law had so decreed: "the supremacy of law. That is a thing surpassing and eternal. A contempt for international law wrought the supreme tragedy."[7] Both the Covenant of the League of Nations and the Charter of the United Nations were decisively American documents. The Covenant was more an agreement of nations: "The High Contracting Parties" ordained and established. But the Charter might have been written in Philadelphia: "WE THE PEOPLES OF THE UNITED NATIONS . . ." The preamble to each sets forth international law as a first principle. The Covenant: "by the firm establishment of the understandings of international law as the actual rule of conduct among Governments." The Charter: "to establish conditions under which justice and respect for the obligations arising from treaties and other sources of international law can be maintained." The British have no written constitution. The Soviet constitution of 1936 made no reference to international law. Americans wrote these passages.

What happened? How did a subject once so central to our thinking about world affairs become seemingly so peripheral? Paradoxically, as regards the settlement of disputes, that is to say violent disputes, the spread of democracy has removed the urgency with which the idea of law was once advanced. Consider the world wars that, in a sense, produced first the Covenant, then the Charter. Each began as a European war. The Japanese and the Chinese come to be involved in both, but largely derivatively, the Japanese being first on one side and then on the other. This, then, is a clue. There were *sides*. The first and second wars were principally the result of

Germany's having grown too large to be restrained by the balance of the remaining powers of Europe. Austria-Hungary may have declared war four days earlier than Germany in 1914, but had the Germans not come in we would have seen a Balkan war over Serbian autonomy or whatever. When the Germans did come in, the war went round the world. War came in 1939 because Germany wanted war. Germans no longer do. Therefore, there is no longer much in the way of wars arising from the ambitions of Germans. Still fewer from the predatory dispositions of Britons.

One of the grandest, largest military engineering feats of the British Empire is the Rideau Canal, which connects the portion of the lower St. Lawrence River that is entirely within Canada with Lake Ontario via inland waterways. It was finished in 1832. Two decades later it was further improved. The canal would enable British naval forces to debouch directly onto Lake Ontario, without having to run the nearly 130-mile stretch of river from Cape Vincent to Cornwall, where the river is the boundary. It could be argued that the canal effectively put an end to the prospect of war and saved both Toronto and Washington, D.C., from being burned yet again. And yet this would not be convincing. The fact is that people along the St. Lawrence changed their minds.

Among small nations and weak nations warfare continues; sporadic for the most part, though protracted in some instances. By one account, in the first thirty-five years following the Second World War there were at least thirty serious armed conflicts.[8] The 1980s added several more, including the Falklands conflict. Several were quite bloody, including the India-Pakistan conflicts, Vietnam, and the Iran-Iraq war of 1980–1988. But none has had the scope and severity of 1914–1918 or 1939–1945. None has been nuclear, the previous outbreaks having been characterized by the rapid development of new weapons and their immediate use. None has seriously threatened to spread along the detonating cord of an alliance system, as in 1914 and 1939. Ironically, it is not for lack of alliances that the postwar period has been essentially stable. A better argument can be made that it is because alliances have been broad-based, stable, and public. The North Atlantic Treaty Organization, established in 1949, has proved the most enduring relationship of its kind since American independence.

The great fact of NATO is that from the first it was an alliance of democracies. This was something wholly new, just as the available number of democracies was wholly new, and it was to prove something wholly different.[9] Democracies do go to war. As Michael Doyle has noted, liberal states are as aggressive as any form of government in their relations with nonliberal states.[10] But rarely with each other.

Did Wilson and his cohort understand this? Probably not; the experience of a democratic Europe was still ahead. It might have seemed *too* idealistic. Professor Warner Schilling of the Institute of War and Peace Studies at Columbia University has noted that Wilson felt that "the spread of democratic influence around the globe" would make a great difference, but believed nonetheless that "the European balance of power system would spin off war after war" unless it was replaced by a system of collective security.[11] In any event, in setting forth democratic principles as a world norm, Wilson was clearly onto something as regards world peace.

In *Retreat from Doomsday: The Obsolescence of Major War,* John Mueller observes how "nonmilitary elements play an important role in decisions about war." The First World War put an end to romantic notions of combat; something such is putting an end to romantic notions of world revolution. In this view war has become obsolescent as much because of changing values as because of technological change such as the advent of nuclear weapons. Mueller feels the cold war with the Soviet bloc was never close to hot war, and by the late 1980s is nearing "terminal remission as the Soviet Union's enthusiasm for widespread revolution wanes."[12] The onset of stability is not unknown to history. Peace came to the highlands. "Rob Roy's Grave" was simply a poetic restatement of the Athenian side of the Melian Dialogue, as set forth by Thucydides: "The strong do what they can and the weak suffer what they must." Interestingly, the Athenians argued from precedent: "It is not as if we were the first to make this law, or to act upon it when made: we found it existing before us, and shall leave it to exist forever after us."[13]

Rules change. Is it too much to suppose that the principal canons of international law, of the Covenant, of the Charter, are beginning to be observed because they are thought to be normal and necessary and, well, satisfactory?

Apart from the renunciation of violence as an instrument of statecraft, the largest claim international law now makes on the world community is that it shall be a community of self-defined societies. This is to say that there may be no more colonies. It is *not* to say that there will be no more multiethnic nations whose origins lie in conquest or premodern consolidation. The Scots and the English and the Welsh and some of the Irish get on tolerably; as do the French-speaking and English-speaking Canadians; and so across a variety of arrangements. But beginning in 1919 something of a norm commenced which held that distinctive peoples are entitled to separate and independent statehood as a matter of principle, which is more or less to say a matter of law. This was a new idea and not necessarily a good one, of which more later. But it became the most powerful idea of the century.

It was there in the Fourteen Points: "x. The peoples of Austria-Hungary, whose place among the nations we wish to see safeguarded and assured, should be accorded the freest opportunity of autonomous development . . . xii. The Turkish portions of the present Ottoman Empire should be assured a secure sovereignty . . ." And such like. In the large this can be seen as the extension of the principles of nineteenth-century European nationalism to the rest of the world, along with their application in Central Europe. But in the context of the League, this became institutionalized in a manner without precedent. (The emergence of the British Commonwealth was something similar; but even so, different. Autonomous development envisaged the *severing* of ties of citizenship and loyalty, as against redefining the terms.) A cynic might have seen the mandatory system of the League as simply another mode of conquest, but the principles laid out in the Covenant effectively undermined the legitimacy of any such intentions, and yet more powerfully established the legitimacy of resistance. Development of a territory under the mandatory system was to be "a sacred trust," and "securities for the performance of this trust should be embodied in this Covenant." The nature of the mandate would vary depending upon the degree of development within the territory; more developed territories were entitled to a greater degree of self-administration. Indeed, Article 22 stated that certain of the territories had "reached a stage of development where their

existence as independent nations can be provisionally recognized."
Seven decades later the mandatory territories are without exception independent states. (Some mandatory territories were divided
into more than one state. For example, General Henri Gouraud
divided France's Levantine mandate into Lebanon and Syria in
1920.)

Where the Covenant implied self-determination, the Charter
specifies it. The "purposes" of the United Nations are to maintain
international peace and security and "to develop friendly relations
among nations based on respect for the principle of equal rights
and self-determination of peoples." And for the first time in the
history of nations, something approaching this has come to pass.
By the ninth decade of the twentieth century, most people in the
world live in independent states demarcated along lines of hoped-
for ethnic legitimacy.[14] The geographer of the Department of State
now counts 171 nations in the world. Of the 98 that have emerged
since 1943, by far the greatest number were parts of the British or
French empires or were mandatory territories, again principally
British or French. (In all, 67 of the world's nations were once
British possessions.) There have been some mergers. Egypt and
Syria at one point, assorted African states, but none seems to have
succeeded save that of Tanganyika and Zanzibar, which joined
to become Tanzania. The rule is otherwise. From 1918 to 1989 few
of the world's nations disappeared. There is the continuing agony
of Tibet, and the Department of State does not list Estonia, Latvia,
and Lithuania as sovereign nations, although the geographer has-
tens to note that the United States continues to accredit the diplomatic representatives of the last "free governments" of those lands.
There continue to be "dependent areas," islands mostly, scattered
about, odd lots of the age of discovery. The status of Antarctica is
in abeyance under terms of the Antarctic Treaty. But the world
norm, now world law, the Charter being for practical purposes
universal, is the "autonomous development" envisioned by the
Fourteen Points.

Samuel P. Huntington has noted that the second half of the
twentieth century has given rise to forms of empire that are not
necessarily territorial. Commerce once decreed the acquisition of
colonies and the control of strategic straits; it no longer does.

Armies once went abroad to conquer and garrison. Again no longer. At the close of the 1980s the United States had military installations in twenty-one countries around the world, but in friendly enough circumstances (save Guantánamo Bay), with no question of infringing territorial integrity.[15] To the contrary, we pay rent. Which is regularly raised.

Independence has not always meant democracy. Of the ninety-eight nations that have come into being since the Second World War, only some twenty-six are reckoned to be "free" in the Freedom House annual survey for 1988–89.[16] But this number includes India, the world's second most populous nation. It does not include China, not a new nation; and it does not include, as a geographic generalization, Africa. But the democracies that do exist hang on. The movement of "West" Germany and Japan into the democratic ranks established a clear preponderance of economic power on this side. Democratic states today account for roughly three-quarters of the world economy.[17] This in turn provided a test of a further Wilsonian hypothesis. He believed that democratic nations, reflecting the interests of their peoples, would avoid conflict with one another, and that together they would indeed "undertake to respect and preserve as against external aggression the territorial integrity and existing political independence of all Members," as the Covenant provides.

· · · · ·

On September 5, 1919, Wilson arrived in St. Louis on his "little expedition," as he playfully described his campaign for the Treaty that would come to its grim end twenty days later. Again he spoke of the League, "A covenant of arbitration and discussion." Of war deferred during discussion: "any nation that is in the wrong and waits nine months before it goes to war never will go to war." But then this. What if we chose not to join?

> Very well, then, if we must stand apart and be the hostile rivals of the rest of the world, then we must do something else. We must be physically ready for anything to come. We must have a great standing army. We must see to it that every man in America is trained to arms. We must see to it that there are munitions and guns enough for an army that means a mobilized nation; that they are not only

laid up in store, but that they are kept up to date; that they are ready to use tomorrow; that we are a nation in arms; because you can't be unfriendly to everybody without being ready that everybody shall be unfriendly to you.[18]

Wilson took this premise and extrapolated its consequences. No postwar reduction of taxes; an increase. "Prussian" government, for, say what one will about the defeated German enemy, they had "the only sort of government that [can] handle an armed nation." A president who is, on a daily basis, and in an active sense, a military chief.

You have got to think of the President of the United States, not as the chief counselor of the Nation, elected for a little while, but as the man meant constantly and every day to be commander in chief of the armies and navy of the United States, ready to order it to any part of the world where the threat of war is a menace to his own people. And you can't do that under free debate. You can't do that under public counsel. Plans must be kept secret. Knowledge must be accumulated by a system which we have condemned, because we have called it a spying system. The more polite call it a system of intelligence and you can't watch other nations with your unassisted eye. You have got to watch them by secret agencies planted everywhere. Let me testify to this, my fellow citizens. I not only did not know it until we got into this war, but I did not believe it when I was told that it was true, that Germany was not the only country that maintained a secret service. Every country in Europe maintained it, because they had to be ready for Germany's spring upon them, and the only difference between the German secret service and the other secret services was that the German secret service found out more than the others did. And therefore Germany sprang upon the other nations unawares, and they were not ready for it.

And you know what the effect of a military nation is upon social questions. You know how impossible it is to effect social reform if everybody must be under orders from the government. You know how impossible it is, in short, to have a free nation if it is a military nation and under military orders.[19]

A transcript of Wilson's address records that there was "laughter" when he said of spying: "The more polite call it a system of intelligence." "Applause and laughter" when he allowed that the German secret service had found out more than the rival secret services had. But could anyone in St. Louis, including the president, have ever imagined the shape of American government seventy years later when the American "secret service," now the "intelligence community," would have come to an often dominant, always significant role in the shaping of American foreign policy, including military policy? This was not the work of "bad" men, as Wilson would have judged them. Just the contrary. But the system consumes the men. Decision making becomes "threat analysis under worst-possible-case conditions." The analyses are stamped "CODE WORD" or some other such stratospheric classification. The institutions, arrangements, attitudes, assumptions that Wilson depicted as a dread possibility came to be seen as normal and necessary. The thought that there might be other possibilities came to be looked upon as innocent at best. Scott-King slipping away to be with Bellorius.

Does this seem lugubrious? Possibly. But ask what Wilson would have thought of the institution of the American presidency toward the end of the twentieth century. A president who wrote and typed his own speeches is now at some removes succeeded by presidents who do not know the names of most of their speechwriters, much less of their lawyers, economists, statisticians, strategists, and yes, as of 1989 the White House demographer. First the president got staff, then the staff got staff. In 1981 a chief of staff. In 1989 an Office of the Chief of Staff with a deputy to the chief of staff and an executive assistant to the chief of staff and a personal assistant to the chief of staff and assorted special assistants to the chief of staff. A Situation Room in the White House basement, ninety seconds from the Oval Office, ready for war at any time. An assistant to the president for national security affairs with fifty-odd staff subordinates, more and more of them military officers. A military aide carrying the briefcase with the codes for setting off nuclear war. Across the river a war room the size of the old St. Louis auditorium. A protective service grown to the size and sometimes the pretension of a praetorian guard. (The annual budget of the U.S. Secret Service under Wilson was $21,220. That much was required to protect the president's person. The budget is now $367,000,000.) A standing army, navy, air force of vast size deployed around the globe, geared to instant conflict. But above all else, the spy system. The Central Intelligence Agency, sprung from a brief section of the National Security Act of 1947; now a vast labyrinthine secret world, watching, deceiving, manipulating. On occasion some of its principals watching, deceiving, manipulating at home, in turn watched by the Defense Intelligence Agency and monitored by the National Security Agency. The State Department often a weak fourth, manipulative only to the extent that it can blame others when things go wrong, even if the usual consequence is that the others' budgets grow even larger. Secret budgets, of course. And the Treasury agents. And the FBI agents.

True, Wilson should not have been in St. Louis on September 5, 1919. He should have been in Washington arranging some great triumph for Henry Cabot Lodge, perhaps some affront to British royalty to satisfy the anglophobe brahmin, and possibly to rouse a cheer in South Boston, where another form of ancestral belligerence could be encountered. Wilson wasn't well enough to be in St. Louis. Joseph Tumulty should have seen this. Dr. Grayson should have seen this. *He* should have! Things might have gone differently. But he was not in Washington, he was in St. Louis, and he left us a premonition of things to come. He also bequeathed us a braver vision.

· · · · ·

On a winter morning early in 1941 Harry S Truman of Missouri stepped into the Senate corridor outside S-224 where he had been having his morning bourbon in the then-honored tradition of the body. He ran into Claude Pepper, his colleague from Florida, and told, as the Floridian later recalled, of a plan to investigate defense manufacturing, then booming once more. "If we don't, the Republicans will."[20] Thus came about the Special Committee to Investigate the National Defense Program, and for Truman, four years later, the vice-presidency, which office he held eighty-two days before becoming president. He was a man of his time and place. He had heard about munitions makers and no doubt about the Morgan banks. But he also shared an untroubled attachment to the principles of international conduct which Franklin D. Roosevelt was determined to put in place. These were once again accepted beliefs. The Senate of 1944 was completely behind the idea of a United Nations, and prepared to give extraordinary powers to the Security Council in the event of any "threat to the peace, breach of the peace, or act of aggression."[21] In a sequence much like that of the previous world conflict, the national mood had swung from isolationist to internationalist and would soon swing back to a distrustful, sometimes aggressive nationalism. But for the moment, all was harmony. The conversion of Arthur H. Vandenberg of Grand Rapids, Michigan, who had been a fierce isolationist, embodied this shift and ensured the first working "bipartisan" foreign policy ever. (Walter Lippmann, who had drafted most of the Fourteen Points, now took to revising Senate speeches for this ranking Republican member of the Committee on Foreign Relations, as did James Reston of the *New York Times*. Senators were still without staff; the Foreign Relations Committee had nine employees.) In the early months of his presidency, Truman had a solid working relationship with a huge bipartisan majority in the Senate. On July 28, 1945, his 107th day as president, the Senate approved the United Nations Charter eighty-nine to two.

Trouble came soon enough, and in the form of Stalin's aggression in Eastern Europe. Kennan sent his long telegram and published a version of it in *Foreign Affairs*. Lippmann responded with his book *The Cold War,* which rejected containment as globalism gone manic, an invitation to send troops everywhere to support anyone. There was to be no peace. Yet, given the tumult that followed, with politics becoming increasingly personal, frequently bitter, at times a clash of cultures more than of policies, the continuity of foreign policy is striking, as is the steady guidance provided by the canons of liberal internationalism. Men in their brief authority observed events, consulted their principles, and knew what to do. Whereupon, similarly to a striking degree, whatever that was, was done. First, aid to Greece and Turkey, next the Marshall Plan, then NATO. Vandenberg, now chairman of Foreign Relations, with perhaps more coaching from the executive than was normal then, but which could be normal now, offered a resolution declaring the North Atlantic Treaty, the republic's first ever permanent entangling alliance, to be nothing more than the "progressive development of regional and other collective arrangements for individual and collective self-defense in accordance with the purposes, principles, and provisions of the United Nations Charter."[22] The resolution passed sixty-four to six. The North Atlantic Treaty itself was adopted eighty-two to thirteen by the Senate. (Byrd records that history ought to treat Vandenberg with greater attention. He cites Dean Acheson's description: "a large mass of cumulonimbus cloud, often called Arthur Vandenberg, producing heavy word fall."[23] Anyone can make fun. But getting such a resolution through the Eightieth Congress by such a margin is something which very few people could have done and which in the event only one person did do. This is the accidental in the life of the nation.)

Next Korea. It was said that Acheson invited the invasion in a speech at the National Press Club on January 12, 1950, in which he listed strategic interests in the Far East but left out South Korea.[24] This is still asserted whenever the Congress debates removing some of the U.S. troops from there. Conceivably speeches have such consequences, but this could only have hastened events that were already in the offing. Is it too deterministic to assert that some test of arms with Marxism was coming in the postwar world? Stymied in the West, pressure shifted to the East. Marxism was still a powerful expectation; and never more fanatic than when melded with nationalism: Korea had been a colony. Now it was independent, but divided. The side with the ascendant expectations moved first.

Here in its most elemental, unambiguous form was the type of aggression which the Covenant and the Charter had envisioned. Armies crossed borders. This was precisely the kind of emergency Roosevelt had in mind in his address to the Foreign Policy Association. Article 39 of the Charter stated: "The Security Council shall determine the existence of any threat to the peace, breach of the peace, or act of aggression and shall make recommendations, or decide what measures shall be taken . . . to maintain or restore international peace and security . . ." Truman performed precisely as Roosevelt had contemplated. The United States called for an emergency meeting of the Security Council; the Russians were absent, a resolution passed. American troops went into battle under the flag of the United Nations. In time sixteen nations would join in the "police action."

Congress was not asked to declare war. Presidents had dispatched troops before; but this was an army, commanded by a general, and not just any general. Arthur M. Schlesinger, Jr., sees in this sequence a giant step toward his "imperial presidency," the power of presidents to take the nation into war. This is not all self-evident. Wilson had described an imperial presidency, but as one that would come about in the *absence* of United States membership in the League. Now that had been remedied and a test had come. Truman and Acheson acted from principle, and according to plan. Nothing could have been more explicit than those principles and that plan, repeatedly endorsed by the Congress for the better part of a decade. What was imperious in that?

By its stated terms the United Nations "police action" in Korea achieved its goal. The aggression was repulsed; the previous border, if that is how the 38th parallel is to be described, was restored; hostilities ceased. It was not enough, however. We had not "won." What winning would have been was never clear. But we did move north of the border and were thrown back in an unnerving reversal. This was, apart from 1812, a wholly new national experience. *Why* had we not won? At the time of the Soviet pressure on Greece and Turkey, Vandenberg is supposed to have told Truman that Congress would support him, but that he would have to get the public to support Congress, and to do that he had to come "before Congress and scare hell out of the country."[25] The United States of America commenced to act alarmed, yet even so with extraordinary staying powers. The American Expeditionary Force arrived in Europe in June 1917 and was there just seventeen months before the Armistice came. American forces have now been deployed in South Korea for forty years. Not as an occupation force, but as a combat force guarding another country's border, temporary or otherwise. This is the stuff of Roman legions.

At the level of national policy the momentum of the Charter era continued. The great test came at Suez in 1956. Following the nationalization of the canal, first Israel, on October 29, then Britain and France, NATO allies, on October 31, invaded Egypt. Dwight D. Eisenhower would have none of it. The Security Council convened but could not act in the face of Anglo-French vetoes. The Security Council could, and did, call upon the General Assembly to take up the issue. On November 5 the General Assembly, acting under the "Uniting for Peace" procedure adopted in 1950 to deal with the Soviet veto, established a United Nations command to "secure and supervise the cessation of hostilities." The resolution passed by a vote of fifty-seven to zero, with nineteen abstentions.[26] Fighting ended on November 6, and a UN peacekeeping force comprised of 6,000 troops from Brazil, Canada, Colombia, Denmark, Finland, Indonesia, Norway, Sweden, and Yugoslavia was sent to the area.

The founders had hoped the United Nations would have on permanent call "air, sea or land forces" for immediate deployment in situations such as arose in Korea and in Egypt. We have seen how central such an arrangement was to Roosevelt's conception of a world organization. The United Nations Participation Act of 1945 provided:

> The President is authorized to negotiate a special agreement or agreements with the Security Council which shall be subject to the approval of the Congress by appropriate Act or joint resolution, providing for the numbers and types of armed forces, the degree of readiness and general locations, and the nature of facilities and assistance, including rights of passage, to be made available to the Security Council on its call for the purpose of maintaining international peace and security in accordance with article 43 of said Charter. The President shall not be deemed to require the authorization of the Congress to make available to the Security Council on its call in order to take action under article 42 of said Charter and pursuant to such special agreement or agreements the armed forces, facilities, or assistance provided for therein . . .[27]

"*The President shall not be deemed to require the authorization of the Congress* . . ." Efforts to organize Article 43 forces began in the earnestness of the years that immediately followed. In the summer of 1947 a supplement to the *Department of State Bulletin* was issued, titled "Arming the United Nations." It opened:

> On April 30, 1947, Lieutenant General A. Ph. Vasiliev, of the Red Army, chairman of the Military Staff Committee of the United Nations, forwarded to Trygve Lie, Secretary-General, for transmission to the Security Council, a report of the Military Staff Committee containing recommendations of the general principles governing the

organization of the armed forces made available to the Security Council by member Nations of the United Nations. Thus the Security Council received the report which it had requested from the Military Staff Committee on February 13, 1947. On April 30 Herschel V. Johnson, Deputy Representative of the United States in the Security Council, requested the Secretary-General to place on the Council's provisional agenda the item, "Discussion of the best means of arriving at the conclusion of the special agreements referred to in article 43 of the Charter." Consideration of this item had been deferred since February 1946. On June 3 the Security Council began its formal study of this subject.[28]

The account went on and . . . on. In the end we learn that the Soviet "Principle of Equality" precluded any agreement.

We may never know what exactly the Soviets were up to with the "Principle of Equality." They had at that time a great enthusiasm for principles of this order. They had made much of the prospect of being outvoted in the General Assembly by the British Empire, and so at Yalta obtained an additional two seats, Byelorussia and the Ukraine. (The British Empire issue had been raised during the American debate in 1919 over the Covenant. Note also that the 1936 Soviet Constitution gave each soviet republic the "right to enter into direct relations with foreign states.")[29] But the cold war settled in, and none of the powers great or small entered into an Article 43 agreement with the UN in those early days, and none has done since. Under the prodigious leadership of Brian Urquhart, UN peacekeeping and observation forces made their first large-scale appearance in Palestine in 1948.

Perhaps the most profound expression of the willingness of the United States to vest genuine authority in the United Nations was the Baruch Plan. In 1946, following the recommendations of the Acheson-Lilienthal Report, Bernard Baruch proposed to the United Nations Atomic Energy Commission on behalf of the United States that nuclear weapons be permanently abolished. The United Nations would create an agency to control all aspects of the use of nuclear power. It would have the exclusive right to own fissionable material and would have the right to conduct whatever inspections were necessary to police the plan. There would be strong penalties for violations. Moreover, the Charter would be amended to prevent any nation from using the veto to frustrate these sanctions. All existing nuclear weapons would be destroyed once the international control agency was established and functioning.

The Soviet Union rejected the proposal, assuming, ironically, that the United States and Great Britain would continue to dominate the United Nations and its specialized agencies. It was unwilling to limit its veto power in any way. It was also unwilling to abandon its own nuclear program, already proceeding at a great pace in the effort to break the U.S. monopoly. The U.S. plan said in essence: We will maintain our nuclear monopoly while the UN establishes control; then we will destroy our weapons. The Soviet delegation at the United Nations replied: Destroy your weapons first (within three months no less); then we will create an agency to police compliance. The United States would not disarm until it had first been assured that no one else would get the bomb. Impasse. It was not resolved. But it should not be forgotten that in 1946 the United States offered in good faith to surrender the greatest unilateral military advantage ever possessed by a nation.[30]

Through the 1950s, into the 1960s, the United States kept to its professions. Our delegations deplored the "indirect aggression" by the Soviets against their satellites, notably the bloody suppression in Hungary in 1956. When former colonies commenced colonizing we were adamant, as in the 1961 Indian invasion of Goa.[31] But then there came a time of forgetting, until it would seem that all was forgotten.

The "superpower" conflict simply took precedence. Even where the Court was involved, as in the case of Western Sahara, what mattered was Moscow. Whose client state gained what? Hideous mistakes were made in Southeast Asia, not least from the assumption that Beijing was an active agent of Moscow. Serious men went mad; possessed with the delusion that only they grasped reality.

The increasing indifference to the Charter that could be detected in American conduct in the 1970s may be read as a form of withdrawal, even exhaustion. For a quarter-century the United States had been rushing about the globe preserving other peoples' freedoms, or improving their agriculture, or raising their aspirations, or what you like. We had little to show for it if gratitude is to be counted a good. To the contrary, as membership in the United Nations first doubled then tripled the new nations were anything but friendly. They were frequently explicitly hostile. Further, with but few exceptions, they corrupted the language of the Charter. Each in turn joined the family of nations as a putative constitutional democracy; with too few exceptions each in turn broke its vows. One man, one vote, one election, as the saying went. At least in Article 2 of the 1936 Soviet Constitution one read of the glorious "attainment of the dictatorship of the proletariat" and could grapple with the thought that constitutions which celebrate dictatorships of whatever kind are not likely to provide great security for whatever liberties are listed thereafter. But the "new" nations? In his Godkin Lectures at Harvard in 1955, Justice Robert H. Jackson pointed to the gathering gloom.

> Our forefathers' conception of a liberal legal order had been the dynamic ideology of most of the nineteenth century. But the twentieth century has seen the depressed masses in nearly all backward countries abandon it as their hope and turn to a militant Communism radiating from the Soviet Union, which Clement Attlee once described as merely "an inverted czardom." . . . Revolutions in our time, whether by Communists, Fascists, or Nazis, have not pretended to overthrow or moderate the power of the state over the individual, but, instead, have each aspired to concentrate in the state a more absolute power over every activity of life and leave nothing but tatters of the "rights of man." Paradoxical as it may seem, we are in an age of rebellion against liberty . . . Civilization is still threatened by forces generated within and perhaps by itself.[32]

And yet in 1956 when the Soviet Union sent its forces into Hungary, the General Assembly voted to condemn "the violation of the Charter . . . by the Government of the Union of Soviet Socialist Republics in depriving Hungary of its liberty and independence and the Hungarian people of the exercise of their fundamental rights."[33] Two decades later Soviet-backed Vietnamese forces invaded "Democratic Kampuchea." The Security Council met; the Soviet and Czech representatives in effect denied that there had been any such invasion, and the Soviets vetoed an already inconclusive resolution prepared by the Non-Aligned bloc. The General Assembly adopted a relatively mild resolution that failed even to mention Vietnam by name.

The Non-Aligned nations, two-thirds of the General Assembly, had in fact aligned themselves with the Soviet Union, and with the totalitarian world generally. (The sixth triennial meeting of the Non-Aligned nations' heads of state in 1979 was held in Havana.) This came about either through a massive miscalculation—the U.S.S.R. could provide them little save bad example and good light weaponry—or just as possibly a half-concealed acknowledgment that they were not exactly fulfilling the high hopes proclaimed at their independence. The Soviet model provided a retroactive justification for what they had done with their own countries. Some Third World nations did in fact produce Marxist regimes, notably Ethiopia, not of course a "new" nation. Most, however, remained eclectic tyrannies, usually contriving to get the worst of both worlds.

American allies were of little help; the British subdued; the French superior. (Observing that their *mission civilizatrice* had not worked out quite as hoped for, they consoled themselves that they didn't have to care any longer.) The Vietnam War had turned solid democracies solidly anti-American at the level of official pronouncement. Vietnam: as William Pfaff calls it, "liberalism's war." But liberalism had little to show for it. The United Nations became just another of our problems; international law the last place to look for support.

In November 1979 Iranian "students" seized the American embassy in Teheran and took the embassy staff hostage. The Iranian government did nothing to protect or to restore American rights. The most elemental rule of international law, the immunity of envoys, was thus challenged. The response of the United States was wholly tactical. Emissaries were sent, intermediaries sought out. There was no lack of energy in the face of an extraordinary international event which immediately became a domestic crisis, but the State Department turned every which way save toward law.

On November 20, some sixteen days after the embassy had been seized, this senator went to the floor to ask why we had not gone to the Court:

> I suppose there will be those who ask, what can the International Court of Justice do? I can answer that with, I think, some precision. The International Court of Justice can say what is law and which party has violated it. The U.S. Government has put too much of its

hopes and efforts into the rule of law to ignore the institution of the Court at this moment.[34]

Almost as an afterthought we thereupon did so. Within the executive branch there was no confidence in the Court. Surely a Soviet bloc judge would assert that we had provoked the students; a South American judge would require more submissions; an African judge would wish to conduct a parallel inquiry into human rights violations in South Africa. The Iranians wouldn't respond. Etc. Yet, two weeks later, December 15, 1979, a unanimous court handed down its provisional order, which clearly established that the rights of the United States were being violated, that the government of Iran was obliged to restore the embassy to United States control and release the hostages. In the manner of such rulings, it was further ordered that neither party take any action to exacerbate the situation, pending a final judgment.

On April 24, 1980, one month before the Court issued its final judgment, the United States launched a rescue operation that failed. The world had then to endure a televised display of the charred remains of eight American servicemen. Had the United States awaited the final ruling of the Court, delivered on May 24, 1980, we could thereafter have proceeded in a much more public and far more punitive mode and without the risk of the kind of failure we encountered. The rescue operation was not amateurish; to the contrary, it was, if anything, too sophisticated. Four decades of military hardware, spy networks, imaging satellites went into the mix. Everything money could buy, save common sense, or rather, common ciphering (as against the other kind). The operation was to proceed in five stages: an eight-hour, 600-mile helicopter flight from the aircraft carrier *Nimitz* to Desert One; refueling at Desert One; the rescue mission in Teheran; escape launch; return flight. Give each stage a nine-in-ten chance of success, you have not much more than a fifty-fifty prospect of ultimate success.[35]

This was in fact a weak policy. A strong policy would have awaited the decision of the Court, hurrying it a bit if necessary. Inevitably, unquestionably, the decision would be handed down in our favor. It was. By thirteen votes to two the Court held "that the Islamic Republic of Iran, by the conduct which the Court has set out in this Judgment, has violated in several respects, and is still violating, obligations owed by it to the United States of America under international convention in force between the two countries, as well as under long-established rules of general international law." (The dissenting judges were Syrian and Soviet. The Soviet judge had a certain argument. The United States had clear treaty rights, but the "military invasion of the territory of Iran" deprived it of them.) In any event, a unanimous Court stated that Iran "must immediately terminate the unlawful detention" of the hostages, return the Embassy and Consulates, and such like measures.[36]

Here is the moment of truth for international law. Who will enforce it? The same question arises with respect to domestic law, and the same answer is to be given. The political system enforces it. This routinely happens within a settled polity such as the United States. (Even so, recall the celebrated, though probably apocryphal, comment by Andrew Jackson concerning the Supreme Court's decision in *Worcester v. Georgia* [1832]: "John Marshall has made his decision. Now let him enforce it.") It is not routine at the international level, but neither is it unattainable. Article 94 of the Charter is clear enough.

> 1. Each Member of the United Nations undertakes to comply with the decision of the International Court of Justice in any case to which it is a party.
> 2. If any party to a case fails to perform the obligations incumbent upon it under a judgment rendered by the court, the other party may have recourse to the Security Council, which may, if it deems necessary, make recommendations or decide upon measures to be taken to give effect to the judgment.

The obvious course for the United States was to wait another three to four weeks and the decision in hand, go to the Security Council and demand that "measures be taken to give effect to the judgment." Making clear that either the council would take them or we would take them. The Seventh Fleet being headed for the Gulf. It is entirely likely that the council would have agreed. No nation favors the seizure of embassies. In the first instance the council would most likely have called for embargoes and the freezing of assets. Possibly the closing of all embassies in Teheran that were still open. This *might* have worked. Probably not, though. Whereupon the United States could have offered its services to the council to *enforce* the decision. Whereupon, with or without the Security Council's blessing—there would have been no legal difference—the United States would have commenced the high-level bombing of Kharg Island. Or whatever measures *we* thought necessary. Quite possibly some or all of the hostages would have died. Vastly greater numbers died to put in place the principles we would now be defending. But the Vienna Convention of 1961 on diplomatic relations was to be upheld at whatever the cost. If need be, fire and sword to the gates of Teheran. What was the matter with that? "The firm foundation of government," Woodrow Wilson often said, "is not pity but justice." On the wall of the 1837 Chenango County Courthouse in Cortland, New York, there is inscribed in large Roman letters the plain proposition: FIAT JUSTITIA RUAT CAELUM. Let justice be done though the heavens fall. Be assured that no one in the American government ever for one brief moment considered that we might resort to this "legalistic" device.

The irony is that the Carter administration genuinely believed in the United Nations. But knew nothing about it. I attest that the principals involved with the hostage rescue had barely heard of the Court, and did not at all appreciate our rights under Article 94. Had they done, Jimmy Carter might well have been reelected. Instead, at noon on January 20, 1981, Republican senators on the West Front of the Capitol stood fiddling with transistor radios, catching the news that Iran had released the hostages the moment Ronald Reagan became president.

CHAPTER SEVEN

A Normless Normalcy?

Until now we have attempted little more than to establish that for the longest while the United States professed a strong attachment to the idea of law in the relations of states. This profession was not always to be observed in practice, but neither was it routinely ignored. Adherence to law was thought to be expedient and practical. In any event it was thought, with varying degrees of conviction, to be obligatory. A further subject now engages us. Somewhere along the line this conviction faltered. People no longer thought what they had once thought. We now ask whether this has been good for the United States.

It will be argued that it has not. In the 1980s, indifference, on occasion hostility, to international law led the executive branch of the national government to take significant risks with our position in the world and, far more important, to put in jeopardy our own constitutional arrangements. In particular, the mining of Nicaraguan harbors early in 1984 set in motion a chain of events, the Iran-Contra Affair, that brought us to the verge of a crisis of the regime. Theodore Draper has written: "If ever the constitutional democracy of the United States is overthrown, we now have a better idea of how this is likely to be done."[1]

These are not the words of an excitable man, nor yet of an inexperienced one. Consider. What *if* the Beirut weekly *al-Shiraa* had not in November 1986 reported American arms sales to Iran? Where would events have taken us after a year, or two years, had passed? As it was, the political crisis that followed came near to destroying the administration then in office. On Saturday, November 29, it fell to me, giving the "Democratic Response" to

President Reagan's weekly Saturday radio broadcast, to warn in pleading terms:

> Mr. President, I listened to you at noon. I pray you are listening to me now. Your Presidency, sir, is tottering. It can be saved. But only you can save it, and only if you will talk to us, the Congress . . . We gave you the staff to help you direct the other departments, not to evade or undermine them; not to roam about the world setting off wars, revolutions, panic, pandemonium. And most emphatically and fundamentally, Mr. President, not to break the laws which the Congress has enacted.[2]

These remarks were the subject of some merriment aboard Air Force One returning the following day from the Thanksgiving holiday in California. The day after that, however, reality sank in in Washington. And the very next day the president came to the White House Press Office and announced the first of a long sequence of investigations into what had gone wrong. The object of this final chapter is to argue that one of the things that had gone wrong was that men and women responsible for national security affairs were either ignorant or contemptuous of international law, including treaties that are explicitly under the Constitution "the supreme Law of the Land."

In 1989 the Council on Foreign Relations issued a small, bright paperback titled *Right v. Might: International Law and the Use of Force,* in which lawyers and diplomats assessed the principal events of the 1980s from the perspective indicated by the title. For purposes of argument let us take as given the position set forth by Louis Henkin, sometime Hamilton Fish Professor of International Law and Diplomacy at Columbia University, and co-editor-in-chief of the *American Journal of International Law.* Professor Henkin's views are not dispositive. International law is not codified. (Albeit the UN Charter sums up most that is essential.) Nor is there a judicial system in place that hands down decisions in sufficient number that something like a common law can be said to have emerged, although something like it may be emerging. In this situation, writers on international law continue to serve a useful role and are still routinely cited. Professor Henkin reviews postwar history, as we have done, and concludes that if the United States had not escaped criticism altogether—the Bay of Pigs (1961), the

Dominican Republic (1965)—"there were no compelling grounds for questioning the commitment of the United States to the law forbidding the use of force."[3] In the 1980s, however, that commitment has come into "serious question" not only because of U.S. actions, but because of the justification the United States claimed for them. Thus:

> In 1983, the United States invaded Grenada. The invasion was variously justified—as necessary to save lives of U.S. nationals; as responding to an invitation by the governor-general; as urged by Grenada's small neighbors; as required to restore to the people the right of self-determination and democracy. The alleged grounds have been widely challenged as spurious or as not justifying the action.
>
> The United States mined Nicaraguan harbors and supported rebellion by the contras. It claimed that its actions were legally justified on the grounds that Nicaragua was guilty of aggression against El Salvador and that the United States was acting in collective self-defense with El Salvador. Many, including numerous members of Congress, questioned the U.S. version, interpretation, and characterization of the facts. The International Court of Justice, several governments, and most lawyers (including, it appeared, most American lawyers) rejected justifications claimed by the United States.

It is commonly accepted, he continues, "that U.S. action in Grenada and support for the contras are manifestations of the 'Reagan Doctrine.'"[4]

In an address given at Fort McNair in the final months of his administration, President Reagan offered a summary. "Around the world, in Afghanistan, Angola, Cambodia, and, yes, Central America, the United States stands today with those who would fight for freedom. We stand with ordinary people who have had the courage to take up arms against Communist tyranny. This stand is at the core of what some have called the Reagan Doctrine."[5] The position was never set forth as formal United States policy in the manner of the Monroe Doctrine or the Truman Doctrine. There was no address to a joint session of the Congress, no pronouncement from the quarterdeck of the *Prince of Wales*, no treaty. Still, this was a forceful point of view in its time, and men have died of it.

Curiously, it was a view with origins more on the left than on the right of American politics. The 1970s were difficult times for persons whose foreign policy views were informed by a close acquaintance with and intense hostility to the various manifestations of Marxist totalitarianism in the twentieth century. This world view—it was that—was very different and apart from the common varieties of American anti-Communism. Its origins were on the left rather than the right, if such terms may be used in the general understanding of the times. In the 1940s its theoreticians were far more likely to be addressing trade union audiences than chambers of commerce (and more likely to be employed by unions). If labor rank and file tended to be Catholic, the theoreticians were more likely to be Protestant or Jewish. White but not always. Eastern, with the epicenter in, of course, New York. Intensely pro-Israel. In politics, if not Socialist, then at minimum Democratic. In the 1970s this circle felt forsaken, as indeed it was. Cold war activists received little hearing in those years. The political fortunes of Senator Henry M. "Scoop" Jackson are a good indicator. An accomplished senator; his position was worth votes on almost any roll-call vote of consequence, certainly in the areas in which he specialized. A primitive New Dealer in the sense in which we speak of primitive Christians; unspoiled by power, immune to temptation. A man of singular personal qualities. He ran for the Democratic party nomination in 1972, and again in 1976. He had considerable labor support, was near to being the unofficial candidate of the AFL-CIO. He had a nationwide network of Jewish activists at a time when the condition of Israel was of great moment. A decent, good man whose views of the world were seared into him by the experience of his all but native Norway during the Second World War. This must never happen again to the democracies; the only possibility that it might do so now came from Moscow. Jackson ran twice, and was defeated twice. More, he was rejected largely because of what he stood for. In 1976 Jimmy Carter was elected and in terms of appointments all but expelled the Jacksonians from the Democratic party.

In 1980 Ronald Reagan was elected and all but welcomed them into the Republican party. This oversimplifies, as capsule history must, but the heart of the matter is that the new president had also made the journey from left to right—imprecise terms but not without content. From the *anti-Communist* left. Other elements joined in the new Reagan coalition, notably a generation of young conservatives trained on the *National Review* and the mutated historicism of the *Wall Street Journal* editorial page. In plain fact, by the 1970s Republicans had quite displaced Democrats as a party of ideas, complete with a party journal, *Common Sense,* for which Jeane Kirkpatrick, an eminent Jacksonian, wrote a celebrated article, "Why We Don't Become Republicans."[6] Which, however, she soon did, having in the interval become Mr. Reagan's permanent representative at the United Nations.

In these circles ideas had consequences. One such idea was that world Communism had commenced a new offensive against the West. After the Leninist expectation of rapid world revolution had faded, the Soviets settled for Communism in One Country. Then came the advances of 1944–1948, followed by Western containment and an encircling network of Western alliances. Now there was seen to come a third phase of Soviet expansion: attack from the rear, which is to say from the Third World. American defeat in Vietnam would be followed by probes everywhere. By the end of the decade there were indeed Communist regimes in place in "Afghanistan, Angola, Cambodia, and, yes, Central America."

In fairness, in 1980 Boris Ponomarev had proclaimed a doctrine that went well beyond Leonid Brezhnev's celebrated "doctrine" set forth in 1968. Ponomarev, still a candidate member of the Politburo, had for a generation and more been responsible for Soviet relations with Communist parties abroad that were not in power. He now proclaimed that the boundaries of "socialism's" concerns had expanded to the Third World and that "fighters for true freedom" in these regions would qualify for the support of "Marxist-Leninists and internationalists" regardless of doctrinal niceties.[7] Too many Trotskyites, or other disqualifying flaws. This was openly an invitation to scattered groups of insurgents not previously under any Soviet discipline to receive Soviet aid. It was a call for more jungle war.

But the misunderstanding was to read the insurgencies as something *new,* as indeed a third phase in the expansion of Soviet empire. They were in fact something old; not the beginning but the end of a historical period. Thus in the regions cited by Mr. Reagan in his address at Fort McNair, a colonial era had come to an end, and preexisting Marxist insurgencies had come to power. These insurgencies had their origins in the period of Marxist triumphalism; when it seemed to so many that indeed this was to be the next stage in history. The doctrine had migrated from the metropolitan centers to the colonial periphery. In some instances the various schisms migrated also. Ho Chi Minh, who was in Paris writing his dissertation at the time of the Peace Conference in 1919, was later to kill his share of Trotskyites in Hanoi. The trouble in Cambodia to which the president referred involved the effort by Ho Chi Minh's red army to overcome the red army of Pol Pot, who had also studied in Paris. When ideas die at the center, it takes time for the news to reach the periphery. The pagans encountered by Christian Rome were often no more than acolytes of the gods of imperial Rome. By the 1970s the French Communist party had commenced terminal gerontological decline; but how was this to be known in Phnom Penh? It was all over for the party in Lisbon, all over in Madrid; but how was this information to reach Maputo or Managua at the level of changed expectation? How would Sendero Luminoso Maoists fighting in the jungles of Peru know that in Tiananmen Square there is now but one portrait left of Mao Tse-tung, and that verging on the inconspicuous?

In retrospect, the truly important event of 1980 took place in Gdansk, where a Polish electrician, Lech Walesa, having been fired from the Lenin shipyard for union activity climbed over the wall back *into* the yard and commenced the strike that before the decade was out would put an end to Communist rule in Poland. It was a drama of the highest moral order. In November 1989 Walesa would tell a joint meeting of the Congress:

> this struggle was conducted without resorting to violence of any kind—a point that cannot be stressed too much. We were being locked up in prison, deprived of our jobs, beaten and sometimes killed. And we did not so much as strike a single person. We did not destroy anything. We did not smash a single windowpane.[8]

All this while the United States government was translating "assassination manuals" for use by forces originally recruited in Central America by the Argentine junta that gave us the mothers of Plaza de Mayo holding photographs of their disappeared children.

Somehow the significance of Solidarity was never grasped by Washington during the Reagan years. For one thing it was not supposed to be possible: ideology held that authoritarian governments sometimes evolve toward democracy, but totalitarian governments *never*.

In part because the Reagan Doctrine was never formally proclaimed, there was little critique. Such efforts as were made tended to portray it as little more than a variant of the hawkish politics of the 1960s. At about this time I gave a commencement address at New York University suggesting that, in fact, we were dealing with something new; a response to a nonexistent challenge. Invoking the French theologian Georges Bernanos—"the worst, the most corrupting lies are problems poorly stated"—the address went on: "The truth is that the Soviet idea is spent. It commands some influence in the world; and fear. But it summons no loyalty. History is moving away from it with astounding speed ... Are there Marxist-Leninists here and about in the world? Yes: especially when the West allows communism to identify with nationalism. But in truth, when they do succeed, how well do they do? And for how long?"[9] But little heed was paid. In part *this* was due to Reagan's seeming revival of much older themes. In his celebrated 1983 address to the Annual Convention of the National Association of Evangelicals, Mr. Reagan invoked the British scholar C. S. Lewis on the nature of evil, brought up "the Hiss-Chambers case," declared that the United States faced the "aggressive impulses of an evil empire," and vowed not to waver in "the struggle between right and wrong and good and evil."[10] This may have been old material; but it was recycled on behalf of an essentially new thought, namely that Communism was winning!

In another pattern from the past, attention now turned to Central America. For some time a Marxist insurgency had been under way in El Salvador; now a neighboring insurgency, the Sandinistas, had come to power in Nicaragua. (The overthrow of the Somoza regime had been a broadbased effort, but when victory had come the Marxists forced out the democratic elements in the popular front.) The Nicaraguans had ties to the Salvadorans, who had apparently sent them money in the 1970s. This aid was now reciprocated. In 1980 Fidel Castro brought together the divided Salvadoran guerrilla factions and helped form a unified Farabundo Martí National Liberation Front. A headquarters was established in Managua. In 1981 the Reagan administration responded with presidential "findings" calling for counterinsurgency operations in the region. A group of former Somoza national guardsmen had crossed into Honduras at the end of the fighting in Nicaragua. The Argentine junta had sent officers to train them for some unspecified mission. The United States now took over this operation and the ranks of the "Contras," as they would come to be known, grew. So did difficulties with the Intelligence Committees of the House and Senate. The nominal mission of the Contras was to interdict arms shipments from Nicaragua into El Salvador. But no arms were interdicted at that point. Inevitably, the question arose: Did the administration really intend to use the Contras to overthrow the government of Nicaragua?

For those with a bent toward intrigue, a case could be made that a master tactician in the Kremlin had hit upon a device that would preoccupy the United States of America with matters of almost total inconsequence, leaving the Soviet Union to attend to issues that would influence the course of world events.

Let us turn for a moment to events in Grenada, the smallest independent nation in the Western Hemisphere. In 1979 a coup brought something called the New Jewel Movement to power with Maurice Bishop at the head of a People's Revolutionary Government. In the laconic summation of the *Political Handbook of the World, 1982–1983,* this "resulted in little more than the substitution of a leftist for a rightist dictatorship."[11] With this difference. Leftist dictatorships could alarm the United States by seeking aid from the Soviet Union. A new kind of cargo cult was delivering the goods! Transport planes would appear, filled with Kalishnikovs. Bishop cottoned onto this; the Russians responded; he in turn showed his gratitude, charging that 1981 NATO naval exercises off Puerto Rico were a rehearsal for an invasion of his own island home. (Puerto Rico is 500 miles from Grenada.) The next year, on a visit to Barbados (closer at hand), President Reagan responded that Grenada had joined Cuba, Nicaragua, and the Soviet Union in an effort to "spread the virus" of Marxism in the region.[12] Bishop in turn traveled to Moscow. Cuba, obviously merely a channel, offered aid for an airstrip that would bring in tourists. U.S. officials responded that it would bring in every aircraft in the Soviet-Cuban inventory.

In 1962 the Russian military had tried to slip ashore in Cuba, as they needed to be close in for their missiles to reach the mainland of the United States. By contrast, in 1982 Russian missiles were aboard nuclear submarines lying under the polar ice cap. There was no strategic advantage the Soviet Union could gain with "bases" in the Caribbean or Central America; any gain would consist solely in providing evidence that "the virus" of Marxism was indeed spreading. Curiously, the United States had not developed any coherent strategy for containing such an outbreak. A simple enough approach comes to mind; indeed, was argued at the time. Say we're sorry. Sorry, that is, for what would now happen to the hapless Grenadians. (Similarly, the unfortunate Nicaraguans.) Declare that they would continue to be eligible for disaster relief. Come the hurricane, come the earthquake, American C-5s would arrive with medical supplies and emergency rations. But, the *revolution* having come, there would be no assistance whatever with the first failure of the collectivized farms to grow food; the first debt default; the first purge of the revolutionary leadership. For all that, the luckless Grenadians, Nicaraguans, whatever, would have to look to Moscow and learn the joys of the bear's embrace. In point of fact, I tried this strategy out informally with Bishop, a pleasant enough type on first meeting, but with a short life span. He called on me in Washington on June 8, 1983, complaining that the CIA was plotting his overthrow. I told him to watch out for the KGB. He was dead by October 19, 1983; the United States invaded Grenada on the morning of October 25.

This was an action consistent with the Reagan Doctrine that there must be no more defections to Communism among the nations of the world. It was just as clearly a violation of the UN Charter. This is not a matter of opinion. Most things are, no doubt; but not *all* things. Henkin writes:

> As a matter of law, one cannot justify the U.S. action in Grenada or support for the contras and condemn the Soviet Union's role in Czechoslovakia. None of these is within the spirit of the Charter as conceived or as the United States interpreted it during its first thirty-

five years. Distinguishing between them as a matter of law is hopeless in a world where many of the 160 states claim to be socialist and few of them have authentic democracy. It is not permissible under the Charter to use force to impose or secure democracy; nor does the Charter contain a Monroe Doctrine exception that would permit the United States to use force to keep the Western Hemisphere free of communism.[13]

To anticipate, should a renewed Arab invasion of Israel take place, the United States under the Reagan Doctrine would have no grounds for objecting *at law,* nor would there be any basis *at law* for responding. We could respond. But no one in the United States government would be in a position to argue that under law we must, and that all involved had reason to understand in advance that we *would.* By this time the idea of law in the relations of states had at most a vestigial claim on United States policy where issues of this order were involved. Obviously the United States remained a meticulously law-abiding nation in its normal relations with friendly states. But where the spread of "the virus" of Marxism was concerned, we no longer felt bound by the Charter.

I was by now vice-chairman of the Senate Select Committee on Intelligence, Barry Goldwater of Arizona being chairman. The committee was intended to be, and was, bipartisan. (It is the only full, standing committee of the Senate with a vice-chairman, a member of the minority, who presides in the absence of the chairman.)[14] A practice developed of the Agency's reporting the most sensitive matters to only the chairman and vice-chairman, leaving it to them to decide whether to report to the full committee. Compartmentalization. The system had been working well for eight years, and worked well on this occasion. The evening before the invasion the deputy director of the CIA, John N. McMahon, came to my residence on Capitol Hill to inform me of the operation. I was appropriately flattered by the attention; but equally puzzled. This was an armed invasion, not an intelligence activity. It was practically under way, and would scarcely be covert. (There was a press "blackout," however. Journalists in small craft were taken aboard naval vessels and effectively detained. Eric Sevareid protested "piracy on the high seas.")[15]

In any event, the invasion was an elemental violation of the

Charter. Half a million persons protested in Holland; the Canadian government was hugely upset; even Mrs. Thatcher was not enthusiastic. Grenada was a member of the Commonwealth.

The following Sunday, October 30, Joan Barone, the producer of the CBS news program "Face the Nation," invited me to appear with Kenneth Dam, deputy secretary of state, to discuss the event. I had already given my view that the invasion was contrary to law. Moderator Leslie Stahl pressed the issue. The president had stated that the Soviets and the Cubans were setting up a base on Grenada from which to export terrorism, as the phrase was. Doctrine now decreed that the United States respond.

MS. STAHL: Now, the president hasn't really explained the legal justification for our going in there, and this seems to be one of the bases for our allies' being so up in arms. How are we going to turn world opinion around if we—if the president is out saying it's a military outpost, and we can't even prove it at this point?

SECRETARY DAM: Oh, I don't think that there is any doubt about the facts that there are all these weapons there, and so I don't think that's a question.

Ms. Stahl tried once more.

MS. STAHL: Mr. Dam, if there hadn't been any Americans on the island of Grenada, would we have gone in?

SECRETARY DAM: You would have had then, as I said in one of my appearances in the Congress, the situation where as a law professor I would have loved to have asked that question of my class. That's a totally hypothetical situation.

I joined in: "There is no ground in law for what we did . . ." Dam simply did not respond.[16] In an earlier period the second-ranking foreign policy official of the United States government might at least have troubled to deny such an allegation. On the record, at all events, Secretary Dam could have cared less. The invasion was by now a famous victory; 8,612 medals were awarded in testament thereof.[17]

Here we come upon an antecedent development. It is altogether possible that Dam, sometime Harold J. and Marion F. Green Professor at the University of Chicago Law School, director of the Chicago Council on Foreign Relations, author of *The GATT: Law and International Economic Organization,* an able, responsible public man, simply didn't care whether the invasion of Grenada did or did not comply with UN Charter or the Rio Treaty or whatever. A "realist" school had developed which looked upon international law as a delusion of the well-intentioned but inexperienced. A benefactors' creed. (Andrew Carnegie's biographer records that when the Carnegie Endowment for International Peace was established in 1910, the bequest, at Carnegie's direction, stipulated that "when the establishment of universal peace is attained, the donor provides that the revenue shall be devoted to the banishment of the next most degrading evil or evils, the suppression of which would most advance the progress, elevation and happiness of man.")[18] This view intensified as the decade progressed. In 1989, in the seventy-fifth anniversary issue of the *New Republic,* Charles Krauthammer would write of "The Curse of Legalism," contending that "the law—international law—is an ass. It has nothing to offer. Foreign policy is best made without it."[19] But a full ten years before Grenada, John Norton Moore had written in *Foreign Affairs:*

> international law is thought of as saying what cannot be done, solely as a system for restraining and controlling national actions. No one proposes to exclude military or political considerations from planning simply because they do not always determine policy. Yet because of a misleading image of law as a system of negative restraint, we make such a judgment when it comes to law. In fact, the legal tradition can play a variety of important roles in planning and implementing national security decisions.[20]

Not for nothing has mankind so often relegated the care of ultimate questions to priestly castes. To pierce the veil of authority in any social system is not something for the fainthearted. It is possible, after all, to ask, "*Why* does the Constitution bind us?" And it is not enough to answer, "Because." Yet, curiously, political scientists, whose work continuously involves issues of legitimacy, often have the greatest difficulty with the thought that international law is, well, real. Part of the difficulty is that this law has no recognizable enforcement system. Yet neither did most domestic law for most of history. Which is not to say that international law will necessarily "evolve," but only that many a system of law depends on self-enforcement. Alfred P. Rubin writes that such persons "don't even consider the possibility that international law is a very effective tort, contract, property, etc., system."[21] Law is confused with force. In this age, however, the greater difficulty is to be seen among those who study international politics and have thought much about the cold war. There is always, in statecraft as in law, the notion of emergencies in which laws are suspended. We have Jefferson's dictum that there are situations in which the niceties of congressional prerogatives may be put aside, lest scrupulous adherence put the nation at jeopardy, "absurdly sacrificing the end to the means."[22] From the *Caroline* affair of 1837 (Canadian militia having crossed onto the American side of the Niagara River and destroyed a steamboat used by rebels) we have Daniel Webster's celebrated dictum that the right of self-defense may extend to such incursions when "the necessity of that self-defence is instant, overwhelming, and leaving no choice of means, and no moment for deliberation."[23] Intervention is ever, of course, the issue. For the longest while Americans had reason to fear it, from the British. Out of this and on its own there came about a wide detestation of imperialism. The literature of anti-imperialism is extensive, ranging from Mr. Dooley's caricature of Theodore Roosevelt's exploits in "Cubia" during the Spanish-American War, to William Graham Sumner's not less sardonic essay, "The Conquest of the United States by Spain."[24]

The twentieth century changed all this. The law-abiding emerged as victims. None felt this more acutely than those on the anti-Communist left who migrated rightward under the duress of the cold war. They left behind persons whose sensibilities on this matter came across as "soft" and self-defeating, if not in fact self-destructive. Jeane J. Kirkpatrick represented this point of view in the Reagan administration. On April 12, 1984, six days after it became known that the United States had mined harbors in Nicaragua, now ambassador Kirkpatrick, the chief United States delegate to the United Nations and a member of the cabinet, addressed a joint meeting in Washington of the American Society of International Law and the Section on International Law and Practice of the American Bar Association. Speaking in general terms, she proposed that the United States could not practice "unilateral compliance" with the rules of international law which its adversaries violated with impunity. The UN Charter, she said, was not a "suicide pact." "Unilateral compliance with the Charter's principles of non-intervention and non-use of force may make sense in some specific, isolated instances, but are hardly a sound basis for either U.S. policy or for international peace and stability." In essence, "the legalistic approach to international affairs" was inadequate to cope with the realities of Communist aggression.[25] Stuart Taylor, Jr., of the *New York Times* observed that the ambassador "stopped short of saying that the United States should disregard international law."[26] But the address came as near as makes no matter:

> If there is to be a rule of law—and we are as committed to that proposition today as ever in our history and as any other nation in the world—that rule of law must be universally accepted, a day which we would welcome.
>
> But we cannot permit, in defense not only of our country but of the domain of law . . . in which democratic nations must rest . . . ourselves to feel bound to unilateral compliance with obligations which do in fact exist under the Charter, but are renounced by others. This is not what the rule of law is all about. As we confront the clear and present dangers in the contemporary world, we must recognize that the belief that the U.N. Charter's principles of individual and collective self-defense require less than reciprocity is simply not tenable.

The nub of her argument was that "the legalistic approach to international affairs" was inadequate to cope with the realities of Communist aggression and subversion. Nicaragua was "engaged in a continuing determined armed attack against its neighbors" and had "initiated the violation of international law through the use of violence against its neighbors."[27] Putting aside any argument as to the facts on the ground, it is surely the case that in two centuries of national existence, no American official had ever before espoused the view that international law was *optional,* that the United States was free to abide by it or not to abide by it according to its assessment as to whether others were doing so. The Russians, the Chinese, the Bhutanese, whoever. This case can be made, but only by moving to a nihilist extreme. If international law exists, it exists independently of whether any one state agrees with or abides by it. If one state violates international law—as surely the Soviet Union has repeatedly done—this in no way releases other states from their obligations under law. International law has its own set of permissible responses to violations, including violent responses. If the Soviets "renounce" international law by, let us say, invading Afghanistan, the United States is not free to respond by invading Grenada. Yet, in the setting of Washington at that time, the ambassador's address went unremarked. The setting, of course, was the aftermath of the mining of harbors in Nicaragua. In October Stahl had asked Secretary Dam, "Is the United States government planning an invasion of Nicaragua?" Dam: "No." Stahl: "Flatly no?" Dam: "No, flatly no." In point of fact the United States was at that moment planning the mining of Nicaraguan harbors; not exactly an invasion, but just as clearly an act of aggression.

The invasion of Grenada was a military operation, the mining of Nicaraguan harbors an intelligence operation. Here we come upon an anomaly. As the United States became more committed to the advancement of democratic values in the world at large, it came more and more to do so by means of covert strategies, concealed from the world and not least from the American public. This is not difficult to explain; it is difficult to defend. It costs too much, it achieves too little; and it gives power to presidents to do things that come to seem merely extralegal, rather than illegal. Not lawless, simply above the law. The intelligence community cannot help but make presidents feel this is what they are there for.

It must be insisted that the American intelligence community is not lawless; anything but. The ethos of the individual officers and of the different agencies and their respective divisions is, simply, intensely *president*-directed and threat-oriented. It is a military ethos without the intermediating loyalties to the regiment, the ship, the fighter wing, thereafter the services, only finally the president.

For a period there were perhaps too many agents whose notion of adventure was to be dropped behind enemy lines into a three-star restaurant, but the greatest number of intelligence officers are quiet, resilient, persistent adjuncts of the Executive Office of the President. The military have a Uniform Code of Military Justice and a manual for courts-martial. This law extends very much to the rules of cross-national conduct as codified and agreed to in treaties. There is nothing such in the intelligence service. Nor is there an Arlington Cemetery. CIA agents killed in action must settle for an unidentified gold star set in the marble wall of the lobby of agency headquarters in Langley, Virginia.

Ponder the testimony of Donald Phinney Gregg at a hearing on May 12, 1989, of the Committee on Foreign Relations concerning his nomination by President George Bush to be ambassador to the Republic of Korea. Ambassador Gregg had served for thirty years in the Central Intelligence Agency, before becoming national security adviser to then vice-president Bush. He was present at a meeting of the National Security Planning Group in December 1983. The subject was the mining of harbors in Nicaragua. At his nomination hearing, he discussed the meeting in the following terms:

DPM: Could I ask [when] . . . in the course of the 1983–84 events which were involved here, when did you learn of the CIA decision to mine harbors in Nicaragua—there were three—and to do it directly from an American mother ship, as they say, under American command?

MR. GREGG: Those decisions were discussed at the—I have forgotten the names, but the normally constituted groups in the NSC [National Security Council] system.

DPM: The planning group?

MR. GREGG: . . . I was at some of the meetings when those options were discussed. I remember that the CIA officers whose job it was going to be to come down to tell the Congress about such things were always very concerned about congressional reactions . . .

DPM: Could I ask you about ... one of the meetings where this option was discussed ... This was in advance of the actual operation?

MR. GREGG: Yes.

DPM: Did anybody ever say at this meeting, at the meeting you were at, or the number of meetings, whichever ... that for the United States to lay mines in Nicaraguan harbors was a violation of treaty obligations and under the Constitution of the United States a violation of the supreme law of the land?

MR. GREGG: I do not remember that particular point being raised. I think there had been discussions of what our relations were with Nicaragua, but I do not remember that particular concern being voiced.

DPM: ... The Constitution of the United States says that treaties are the supreme law of the land ... our Executive Branch ... deliberately violated that law ... Did no one ever say that was against the law? ...

MR. GREGG: Which treaty and which law are you referring to ... ?

DPM: I will start with The Hague—is it the 9th Hague Convention of 1908? ... Treaty law and conventional law would declare mining of harbors a belligerent act.

MR. GREGG: ... I remember there was a discussion of the fact that the mines to be used were low power; that the effort was to try to sink, I believe, a Soviet ship or a ship bringing supplies— military supplies—in to the Sandinistas or to block a channel through which a lot of the military supplies to the Sandinistas came and there was discussion of trying to do this in a way so that casualties would be nonexistent, or at least minimized.

Senator Paul Simon of Illinois continued the line of questioning:

MR. SIMON: Then in response to Senator Moynihan, you said first, there was no discussion when you were talking about mining the harbor in Nicaragua, no discussion of a violation of international law, which I find a little incredible.

But then you said in response . . . "Our aim was to sink a Soviet ship or a ship bringing supplies." Was there any discussion of what would happen if a Soviet ship were sunk?

MR. GREGG: Yes, there was. And there was concern about it. And there was—you are getting me into an area where I am feeling uncomfortable, because I do not remember the dénouement of what was discussed there. And I did not realize that Senator Moynihan was talking about international law, I thought he was talking about American law.[28]

(Remember the *Maine*? In the immediate aftermath of the incident in Havana harbor a U.S. naval inquiry determined that the battleship was sunk by "the explosion of a mine situated under the bottom of the ship." Years later the navy disavowed this finding. A report written by Admiral Hyman G. Rickover in 1976 determined that "in all probability, the *Maine* was destroyed by an accident which occurred inside the ship."[29] The most likely culprit: spontaneous combustion in a coal bunker. No matter. The mining of Caribbean harbors, real or imagined, can have large consequences. Is our institutional memory that poor? And has it never occurred to us that the Spanish-American War—McKinley sent his war message to Capitol Hill within a few weeks of the mining report—was possibly not the best idea we ever had as a nation?)

It is not clear that there ever was a presidential "finding" authorizing the mining of the harbors. Either way, we have Gregg's testimony, in response to a further question by Senator Simon, that as the White House group discussed the plan, "there was anticipation of a tremendously negative reaction from Congress."[30] They got one thing right.

A curious role reversal had taken place. For the first 150 years or so of American history, issues such as international law were pretty much the province of presidents. They were to be heard advocating, sometimes preaching, international norms. Congress, sometimes agreeing, sometimes disagreeing, was at most reactive. In the second half of the twentieth century, however, the idea of

normative, "legalistic" behavior took hold within the Congress—
sections of the Congress—even as it waned within the precincts of
the presidency. You could put it that Congress was still lagging,
still behind the times. Or you could put it that Congress was com-
mencing an active assertion of what had been, for the most part,
latent convictions. Some pronouncements, attaining the level of
legislation, were explicit in this regard. Thus, on November 18,
1983, it fell to me to present the report of the Conference Committee on the Intelligence Authorization Act for the next fiscal year.
I stated:

> As I noted on the floor the day the Senate passed the Intelligence
> Authorization Act (November 3), the distance between the House
> and the Senate was not as large as many might have thought. Both
> committees understood the Government of Nicaragua to be in vio-
> lation of international law. This was recognized by an express
> finding in the Intelligence Authorization bill passed by the House.
> The finding states:
>
>> By providing military support (including arms, training and
>> logistical command and control, and communications facilities)
>> to groups seeking to overthrow the government of El Salvador
>> and other Central American governments, the Government of
>> National Reconstruction of Nicaragua has violated article 18
>> of the Charter of the Organization of American States which
>> declares that no state has the right to intervene directly or indi-
>> rectly, for any reason whatsoever, in the internal or external
>> affairs of any other state.
>
> The United States, in upholding these covenants, has a duty to
> respond to these violations of law. Our response, however, must be
> both proportional and prudent.
>
> Along with my colleagues, I pressed the administration to redefine
> its covert program to assure that it was in accord with our obliga-
> tions under international law. I believe the new Presidential finding
> reflects this counsel. Thus, the goal with this program is as it should
> be—to bring the Government of Nicaragua into conformity with
> accepted norms of international behavior.[31]

This floor statement is scarcely to be compared to Senator
Lodge's Round Robin letter of March 4, 1919, but just as surely
by ignoring it the Reagan administration consigned its Central
American policy to failure. Ironically, it was *fear* of failure that

was driving policy in the White House. Vietnam, the previous jungle war, was seen to have failed. This one must succeed. But nothing seemed to be happening on the ground. (Nothing would. In a situation of revolutionary triumph we had aligned ourselves with persons easily depicted as counterrevolutionaries. We had chosen as our staging area the Central American equivalent of Dien Bien Phu, a landlocked inaccessible terrain north of the Coco River, with the Sandinistas on the southern perimeter and the Honduran Department of Extortion on the northern. But that is another story.) The president seems to have been growing edgy. In the summer of 1983 he told a small meeting of career ambassadors, "I want to win one."[32] And so, on the advice of his counselors, he set about ensuring that he would lose. And in what way? By ignoring, for a period suborning, the clearly indicated will of the Congress that his actions be lawful. It may be asked: If the editorial board of the *Wall Street Journal* had known in the fall of 1983 that the imminent mining of Nicaraguan harbors would set in motion events that came close to destroying the presidency of Ronald Reagan, would they have been so dismissive of the counsel of international lawyers? It may, of course, be that the *Journal* covertly desired the president's ruin. In the event, he narrowly escaped.

What follows is not agreeable and is best got over quickly. It is not agreeable, because so many honorable men dishonored themselves; did things they would never normally undertake to do but found themselves doing. Some years later David Hoffman, White House correspondent for the *Washington Post*, began an article, "Official Lies: The Real Issue behind the [Colonel] North Trial," with this summation:

> They lied to us—to the media, the Congress, and the American people. The record of misrepresentation runs all the way from CIA-Director William Casey's failure to inform Congress about the mining of Nicaraguan harbors in 1984, through national security adviser Robert McFarlane's false promises to Congress that the White House was following the "letter and spirit" of the law, to Reagan's own statement that news reports of arms sales to Iran had "no foundation."[33]

Please note the first specific: "the mining of Nicaraguan harbors." But then, it seemed like a good idea at the time. Grenada was a triumph with the public. In the parking lot at Langley, the jeep of the CIA agent who planned the harbor mining carried a bumper sticker, "Nicaragua Next."[34] "Next" was early January. The first mine was laid on the seventh of that month. More than thirty mines were laid through March 30. (The CIA regards these dates as being now in the public record.) The fact that mines had been, were being, laid was always known. What was not known was that the United States was laying them. This fact was reported by the *Wall Street Journal* on April 6.

Senator Goldwater was stunned. The Reagan administration represented in many ways the triumph of his own political career; he was paternal, trusting, and assumed this trust was reciprocated, especially with regard to the Intelligence Committee, where trust is everything. Even so, events in Central America had been unsettling. In May of 1983, the Committee had asked for a new presidential finding. *What* had they in mind? On September 20, 1983, the new finding was presented to the committee by William J. Casey, director of the CIA, and Secretary of State George P. Shultz. By now the harbor mining decision had been made, as well as the more serious decision not to inform the Congress. (Recall Gregg's testimony.) I *believe* the concern was that the committee would say "no." Technically, the administration could have gone ahead anyway, but at risk to the next year's budget authorization. They *might* have had in mind that the Senate committee would raise questions of international law; this happened recurrently in closed committee meetings. In any event, they chose deception.

A thought: Leaving aside the question of whether "law" in this instance made any claims on conduct, it would have been clear to some of those involved in the cabinet that the harbor mining was illegal, for all that this might be dismissed as irrelevant under the Kirkpatrick rule. Did this even so entail a degree of secrecy and evasion within the circle of presidential advice, such that no one ever found out who might have asked, "Are you out of your minds? It won't work!" The mining could have had no conceivable effect on Soviet policy, save to stir world indignation at the United States. (Imagine a Bulgarian ship captain who, arriving at Puerto Sandino with a hold full of helicopters, or whatever, and facing the prospect of sustaining some hull damage, deciding to return to Varna on the

Black Sea!) Open government typically defeats secret government owing to a greater facility at concealing strength.

By springtime there was murmuring in Capitol Hill corridors about the mining. On March 27 I wrote Dam asking for a legal opinion from the Department of State as to our involvement. (At minimum, we would have been putting up the money.) But Goldwater and I, at all events, were not prepared for the April 6 report in the *Journal*. We agreed he would write Casey, which was done three days later. Among other things, he wrote:

> All this past weekend, I've been trying to figure out how I can most easily tell you my feelings about the discovery of the President having approved mining some of the harbors of Central America.
>
> It gets down to one, little, simple phrase: I am pissed off! . . .
>
> The President has asked us to back his foreign policy. Bill, how can we back his foreign policy when we don't know what the hell he is doing? Lebanon, yes, we all knew that he sent troops over there. But mine the harbors in Nicaragua? This is an act violating international law. It is an act of war. For the life of me, I don't see how we are going to explain it.[35]

The statement that this was "an act of war" was Senator Goldwater's. I had offered the further thought that it was "an act violating international law." It was in substance a joint letter.

On April 12, Robert C. McFarlane, national security adviser to the president, gave an address at the Naval Academy in which he said, in effect, that Senator Goldwater was a liar. The *Washington Times* recounted the event:

> Every important detail of United States secret warfare in El Salvador and Nicaragua—including the mining of Nicaraguan harbors—was "shared in full by the proper congressional oversight committees," insists President Reagan's assistant for national security affairs, Robert C. McFarlane.
>
> Mr. McFarlane said he "cannot account for" Sen. Barry Goldwater's contention that he was kept ignorant about the CIA-sponsored harbor minings.[36]

With this statement, the chairman being out of the country, I announced I would resign as vice-chairman. An episode now followed which we could well have done without. Four years later, Robert R. Simmons, Goldwater's staff director of the Senate committee, recalled: "in 1984 the Agency engaged in what can only be called a domestic disinformation campaign against the U.S. Congress in which they alleged that the [intelligence committees] had been fully briefed on the harbor mining program."[37] Nothing like this had ever happened. The intelligence community, on behalf of the president, set out to discredit portions of the Congress. There were men whose conduct came very near to treason.

The agency's involvement with the mining had been alluded to in briefings *after* the mining had taken place. The Senate committee might indeed have picked this up; there is no excuse for our not having done so. But Goldwater's complaint went to the statute. By any reckoning the committee should have been informed *in advance*. Informed in a workmanlike, explicit manner that left no doubt on the part of the briefers that the briefing had been absorbed. This was not done.

The disinformation campaign, for it was that, took the form of directing press attention to the question of when the respective committees and the various members learned of the mining *after* it had commenced. This was an easily muddled issue. The administration assault on Goldwater was vicious. On April 13, four days after his letter was sent and three days after it was reported in the *Washington Post,* William Safire wrote about it on the editorial page of the *New York Times.*

> But why didn't the C.I.A. inform Senator Goldwater, chairman of the Senate Intelligence Committee, of this covert action?
> It did, on March 8 and again on March 13, in single, identical sentences amid secret testimony that ran 54 pages and 84 pages. Some believe that the Senator, 75, who will retire in 1986, was not listening; but his top aide, Rob Simmons, characterizes that repeated sentence as implying that the contras would undertake the action on their own. After reading about our participation in the mining in the papers, the grand old toothless tiger's fulmination helped the doves whip up their firestorm.

Now Safire, too, had been lied to. The issue was not why the chairman—"grand old toothless tiger"—had not been alert during briefings in March; the issue was why he had not been informed the previous September. Or December. All this was lost on the press. A *New York Times* editorial summed up the general reaction: "The Case of the Incurious Congress."[38]

We knew better, and promptly cut off all further aid for the Contras. Whereupon the search for third-country funding began. Nothing Woodrow Wilson envisioned at St. Louis remotely resembled the constitutional subordination that followed, presided over by an amiable chief magistrate whose only concern seemed to be that they not get caught, lest we all "be hanging by our thumbs outside the White House."[39] After the mining episode, Goldwater told an aide, "I feel betrayed." But nothing approached the extent to which those who betrayed him now betrayed the Constitution they were sworn to uphold against "all enemies foreign *and* domestic." In one document introduced in the trial of Lt. Colonel Oliver North, Secretary Shultz told a National Security Planning Group meeting on June 25, 1984, that "Jim Baker . . . said that if we go out and try to get money from third countries, that is an impeachable offense."[40] Casey and Caspar Weinberger, lawyers, thought otherwise. Serious men discussing whether pursuing marginal policies in marginal regions of the world would result in the impeachment of the president in whose cabinet they were serving, and deciding to take the chance. The president is bound by the Constitution to see that the laws are faithfully executed. He takes an oath to do so. So do cabinet members. The whole setting was normless to the point of nihilism. The plain fact is that the president did invite and almost certainly did deserve impeachment.[41]

Soon administration officials were secretly soliciting the aid of the governments of Israel, Saudi Arabia, the People's Republic of China, Taiwan, South Korea, Guatemala, Honduras, El Salvador, Brunei, Panama, and other unnamed nations, seeking support for the Contras. "Incentives" were offered.

Even as accusations flew about in Washington, Nicaragua prepared to take the United States to the International Court of Justice. It had a formidable case, but a broad defense could have been mounted. Nicaragua most assuredly had intervened in the affairs of El Salvador, supporting forces seeking to overthrow the government there. The possibility of turning the tables on the Sandinistas does not even seem to have occurred to the Department of State. The United States chose instead to run away from the issues of law. Three days before Nicaragua filed its complaint against the United States, the administration gave notice that, effective immediately, the United States would not consider the Court's jurisdiction compulsory. This hiatus would last for two years and would apply solely to "disputes with any Central American State or arising out of or related to events in Central America."[42] This was asserted notwithstanding the express terms of the commitment made by the United States in its 1946 declaration accepting the compulsory jurisdiction of the statute of the Court that it would give at least six months' notice before terminating its declaration. The Committee on Foreign Relations had been quite explicit about this provision in its 1946 report on the United States declaration: the provision had and was intended to have "the effect of a renunciation of any intention to withdraw our obligation in the face of a threatened legal proceeding."[43]

In two centuries of national existence no more pusillanimous act was ever contemplated, much less carried forward, by American officials responsible for our relations with international tribunals. In 1794 John Jay got into trouble at home for negotiating a treaty with Great Britain which established arbitration panels to settle issues left over from the Revolutionary War and the Treaty of Paris. George Washington stood by him. Generally speaking, this was the record thereafter. Upon the filing of the Foreign Relations Committee report, the Senate, on August 2, 1946—having already adhered to the UN Charter by a vote of eighty-nine to two—also accepted the "Optional Clause" in the Statute of the International Court of Justice, giving the Court compulsory jurisdiction over the United States in disputes with other nations that had also agreed to this arrangement.

The Senate did attach conditions to the United States' acceptance in addition to the routine requirement of reciprocity. Those conditions came to be known as the Connally and the Vandenberg Reservations. The former states that the United States will not accept compulsory jurisdiction in cases involving matters "which are essentially within the domestic jurisdiction of the United States of America as determined by the United States of America." This deprived the Court of the power to determine for itself whether it had jurisdiction in a given case.[44] The Vandenberg Reservation states that the United States will not accept compulsory jurisdiction in "disputes arising under a multilateral treaty" unless "all parties to the treaty affected by the decision are also parties to the case before the Court."[45] Nicaragua's claims were based in part on multilateral treaties (the Charter of the United Nations and the Charter of the Organization of American States), and the United States argued before the Court that El Salvador, Costa Rica, and Honduras would be affected by and yet were not participating in the case. El Salvador did petition the Court to be allowed to argue the U.S. position in the case, but its request was rejected. Thus, the United States maintained that the Vandenberg Reservation vitiated the Court's compulsory jurisdiction.

In 1946 the American Bar Association had adopted a resolution deploring the restrictions adopted by the Senate. By 1985 the United States was no longer willing to accept compulsory jurisdiction even with these restrictions. Bar associations were left to pass resolutions deploring the decision to withdraw from compulsory jurisdiction altogether.

Thomas Franck and Jerome Lehrman record that

> in 1959, President Dwight D. Eisenhower asserted that "the time has come for mankind to make the role of law in international affairs as normal as it is now in domestic affairs . . ." He called for global acceptance of the World Court's compulsory jurisdiction, and held that it would be far "better to lose a point now and then in an international tribunal and gain a world in which everyone lives at peace under the rule of law."

They also note that his vice-president, Richard Nixon,

> had previously stated that "the rule of law must somehow be established to provide a way of settling disputes among nations as it does among individuals . . ." Nixon did not think it a waste of time to set a good example, even one not likely soon to be requited. The United States, [Nixon] said, "should be prepared to show the world by our example that the rule of law, even in the most trying circumstances, is the one system which all free men of good will must support."[46]

But by the 1980s, the United States would not even honor the explicit statement of the Senate that we would not withdraw from the Court's jurisdiction because we felt we had a weak case coming up.

On November 26, 1984, the Court ruled that it did have jurisdiction to hear the merits of the case, both parties having agreed in advance to accept the Court's jurisdiction. The Court also ruled that it had jurisdiction to hear Nicaragua's claims on the narrower grounds that a provision of a 1956 Treaty of Friendship, Commerce and Navigation between the two countries gave the Court jurisdiction over disputes relating to the interpretation or application of the treaty.

In January 1985, two months later, the United States announced that it would no longer participate in the Court's proceedings.[47] Moreover, toward the end of 1985 the administration made its two-year withdrawal from compulsory jurisdiction permanent.[48] And whereas the two-year hiatus had been limited to cases concerning Central America the new announcement had no geographic limits. Specifically, the United States announced on October 7, 1985, that the United States had deposited with the UN secretary general notice of termination of the 1946 declaration accepting the compulsory jurisdiction of the International Court of Justice. This termination would become effective in six months.

The following month the Executive Committee of the Association of the Bar of the City of New York endorsed a report by its Committee on International Law concluding that the decision of the United States to withdraw from the compulsory jurisdiction of the World Court "is unwise and should be reconsidered":

> Termination of the United States' acceptance of the compulsory jurisdiction of the World Court represents a fundamental departure from the long-standing policy of the United States to support the compulsory jurisdiction of the Court. This policy has been based on the premise that over the long run, the United States has far more to gain than lose by championing the observance of international law by all nations and that an important element in extending the reach and role of international law in the peaceful settlement of disputes is supporting the compulsory jurisdiction of the World Court.
>
> We believe . . . that the interests of the United States and the values that we espouse would be better served by continuing our staunch and consistent support for the compulsory jurisdiction of the Court than by following the example of those states that have not accepted the Court's compulsory jurisdiction.[49]

But again, there was otherwise little stir. In 1986 the Court ruled against the United States in the case concerning "Military and Paramilitary Activities in and against Nicaragua" (*Nicaragua v.*

United States of America). The United States was held to have violated international law in a variety of ways, including mining Nicaraguan harbors, arming the Contras, attacking oil installations, ports, and shipping, and allowing distribution of a manual on guerrilla warfare techniques, which the Court found to be contrary to "general principles of humanitarian law."[50] This was the first time in the history of the Court that the United States was found in violation of international law in a matter involving the use of force against another nation.

There was a pattern of such events in the middle years of the Reagan administration. Henkin summarizes:

> the United States appears to have adopted the view that under international law a state may use force in and against another country for the following reasons:
>
> > to overthrow the government of that country in order to protect lives there;
> >
> > to counter intervention there by another state and carry the attack to the territory of the intervening state;
> >
> > to overthrow the government of that country on the ground that it is helping to undermine another friendly government;
> >
> > in reprisal for that country's suspected responsibility for terrorist activities in the hope of deterring such acts in the future;
> >
> > to overthrow a communist (or "procommunist") government or to prevent a communist (or "procommunist") government from assuming power, even if it was popularly elected or emerged as a result of internal forces.[51]

One intrigue led to another intrigue which required in turn a third intrigue. It seemed to be working; it was not. Robert Byron, an English writer, a friend of Waugh's lost at sea in the Second World War, had remarked on a similar sense of invulnerability that had insinuated itself in his nation at the end of the last century. "Misfortune comes to the complacent, brought not by some moral law, but because complacence is the parent of incompetence."[52] The Reagan conspirators got caught. There was a nice touch; their secret was revealed by a weekly magazine published in Beirut. They had decided they could not trust the proceedings of the International Court of Justice, but they could trust the Ayatollah Khomeini.

Journalists in Washington began to connect specific events with more general attitudes. Edwin M. Yoder, Jr., wrote: "if you elect presidents with a contempt for government, you're all too likely to get contemptible government."[53] Meg Greenfield observed that the men in the White House National Security Council apparatus and their associates "who were involved in this pathetic, foolish and costly conspiracy had one thing in common: a grand contempt for the government."[54] Not for the first time, we are learning the cost of such contempt. Liberals had to do so; now it is the conservatives' turn. George Will described the conspirators as the "White House's fallen cowboys," whose "self-congratulatory exchanges reek of contempt for people who practice the patience demanded by democracy and who accept the procedural accommodations required by anything as orderly as government."[55] Complacency involves more than taking institutions of government for granted. It also suggests we no longer realize why the system of government was created in the first place. Reston wrote that the Constitution

> didn't, of course, tell us how to handle the Russians, or compete with the Japanese, or preserve our cities, or elect the most qualified men and women to public office, or educate our children. In fact, it assumed human stupidity, ambition, greed and religious fanaticism, and merely suggested a few rules to hold things together.
>
> One of these rules was that no one person, not even the President, let alone Colonel North, had the right to impose his will or ideology in secret on the elected representatives of the people.[56]

Another might have been that for a nation of laws, the obligation of compliance extends to the law of nations. There is a continuum of law and a corresponding continuum of lawlessness. If treaties don't matter, men easily enough come to think that statutes don't matter either.

· · · · ·

Thesis. A political culture from which the idea of international law has largely disappeared places its initiatives in jeopardy. This is not to assert that international law provides a ready guide to policy, a convenient compendium of readily accessible solutions, or any such thing. On the other hand the United States did begin this century with a persistent, openly proclaimed effort to expand the role of law in international affairs, our own included. One consequence is that there are a good many treaties around, including the United Nations Charter, which frequently provide us with considerable leverage in situations of conflict.[57] International law is not a scheme for surrender; it is not a unilateral, self-imposed restriction on the law-abiding; it is not a suicide pact. To the contrary, where relevant, it is a framework for deciding how and when to use force. It is correspondingly a mode of marshaling support. To the degree that law, the law of the Charter included, is seen to be, and is, the basis for our international conduct, a bipartisan foreign policy does not require a party out of office to agree with policies of the party in power, but rather simply to agree with the principles of law on which those policies are based. Principles prior, as you might say, to whatever the present emergency; the incumbent president; prospects for the next election. The same principle applies to allied and nonaligned nations, who can far more readily support (or at least accept) American policies if our conduct is seen to be based on law that binds them as well as us. Thus, L. F. E. Goldie: "Long respected and adhered to in America, the moral commitment to international legality is an essential cement for the international community and one which exchanges anarchy for common action, and Realpolitik for peace . . . Obedience to law . . . is not only a categorical value but also a prudential one."[58]

Matthew Nimitz has argued that the United States has a unique interest in international law because it cannot "match the Russians in deviousness or the Libyans in irresponsibility or the Iranians in brutality." Americans seem uninterested in international law today because they do not recognize that it is the United States "which stands to lose the most in a state of world anarchy."[59]

Hard cases make bad law. It may be that in the international arena hard cases make no law. However, a state that finds itself tempted by self-interest to erode traditional norms may in time regret its conduct. Indeed, it may not take very long. When it invaded Goa, India argued that borders established by a colonial conquest do not command full international legal rights. A year later the Chinese Communists invaded India, making precisely the same point. The Indian prime minister, Jawaharlal Nehru, promptly appealed to the United States and to Britain for military assistance. The Chinese took what territory they wanted, declared a unilateral cease-fire, and the matter rests there. The American and British aid missions having departed, the Indians resumed their ritual denunciations of American and British imperialism, but these charges rang hollow for years thereafter. The more painful, then, was the United States' drift away from the position it had sustained well into the 1960s.

When the Reagan administration left office, the Sandinistas were still in power. By contrast, the Soviet Union had announced it was withdrawing its troops from Afghanistan. This was truly an extraordinary event. (One I predicted would never happen.) Russian expansion into Central Asia had for two centuries been characterized by indifference to tribal resistance no matter how prolonged. In the end the fighting would stop and the Russians would still be there. Now, after a mere decade, they were leaving. What had changed? The United States sent a fortune in sophisticated weaponry to the Afghan resistance, and in the end, Soviet helicopters were no match for American hand-held surface-to-air missiles. This in no way detracts from the valor of the Afghans. But in colonial wars of the previous four centuries valor was rarely a match for technology.[60] How did this weaponry reach Afghanistan? By virtue of sustained, uninterrupted bipartisan support in the Intelligence Committees of the Congress from the Carter administration onward. Everyone knew it. No one said a word about it. The Soviet Union said little, if, indeed, anything, at all about it. What was there to say? The Soviets were in clear violation of the Charter, the United States was just as clearly upholding the Afghan right to self-defense as proclaimed in the Charter.

·   ·   ·   ·   ·

With the opening of the 101st Congress in 1989, it appeared that the world of the previous seven decades was changing enough to suggest that the Committee on Foreign Relations hold a series of hearings on the state of world affairs. George F. Kennan was the first witness. He announced to the Committee that the era of containment was finally over, that the Soviet Union should now be regarded essentially as another great power like other great powers—one, that is, whose aspirations and policies are conditioned outstandingly by its own geographic situation, history and tradition, and are, therefore, not identical with our own, but are also not so seriously in conflict with ours as to justify any assumption that the outstanding differences could not be adjusted by the normal means of compromise and accommodation.

I asked Kennan that if this was true, what did that mean for the Wilsonian project? Kennan replied, "I was long skeptical about Wilson's vision with relation to the time at which it was brought forward. But I begin today in the light of just what has happened in the last few years to think that Wilson was way ahead of his time in his views about the international organization."[61]

At the level of pronouncement, at all events, the Soviet Union was certainly cooperating. In an article in *Pravda* in September 1987 Mr. Gorbachev addressed the subject of international law.

> One should not forget the capacities of the international court either. The General Assembly and the Security Council could approach it more often for consultative conclusions on international law disputes. Its mandatory jurisdiction should be recognized by all on mutually agreed upon conditions. The permanent members of the Security Council, taking into account their special responsibility, are to make the first step in that direction.[62]

Until that time, the Soviets had accepted the jurisdiction of the International Court of Justice only in the most arcane of instances. But since Gorbachev's pronouncement, they have proposed compulsory ICJ jurisdiction over six multilateral conventions to which they are a party, and have entered into discussions with the other permanent members of the Security Council to enumerate rules under which all five will accept the jurisdiction of the Court.[63]

Now came a yet more extraordinary statement from Eduard Shevardnadze, Soviet minister for foreign affairs. Referring to the withdrawal of the United States, the United Kingdom, and Singapore, he told a UNESCO meeting in Paris that October:

> UNESCO could not escape the influence of political and ideological storms of this century . . . It found itself on the threshold of a crisis. It could not fully use its rich potentials. Three highly respected members suspended their participation. As we delve into the roots of the

trouble, we don't try to shift the blame on others. We submitted to the influence of confrontation, and adopted its spirit as we sought to repulse ideas alien to us. The exaggerated ideological approach undermined tolerance intrinsic to UNESCO.

We refuse to act as judges, and we start our criticisms with ourselves. We call on everybody to learn the lessons of the past as [the] UNESCO revival is starting . . . UNESCO shall embark on the course determined in its Charter and become a genuine center of cooperation. Thus we see the goal of its revival . . .

Surely this change in attitudes has had an impact on our foreign policy, which today is underpinned and guided by the concept of new political thinking.

The basic principles of this concept are these:

free choice, which implies that one must not claim the right to final judgment, nor impose ideas, doctrines or models of development;

political and cultural pluralism, which implies that no commitment to one's beliefs can . . . justify their messianic promotion.[64]

The Soviet foreign minister went on to speak of the "exclusion of the self-acting component of ideological differences," which is a fair summary of the Brezhnev Doctrine; and indeed, addressing the Council of Europe in Strasbourg the following July, Mr. Gorbachev said: "Social and political orders in one or another country changed in the past and may change in the future. However, that is exclusively the affair of the peoples themselves. It is their choice. Any interference in internal affairs of whatever kind, any attempts to limit the sovereignty of states, both of friends and allies, no matter whose it is, is impermissible."[65] Soviet pronouncements regarding international law and international cooperation now came regularly, a pattern of Soviet decision making. Attention was called to the possibilities of international cooperation in environmental matters and also, and with great specificity, to existing agreements on human rights. During his Western European trip in the spring of 1989, Gorbachev called for all manner of cooperation in the common "European home." There were, for example, "climatic disasters" to be dealt with.

It would probably be beneficial too to involve the military services of different countries, first and foremost the medical and engineering services, for international rescue and restoration activities. The humanitarian content of the common European process is a decisive one. A world in which it is possible to reduce military arsenals, but in which human rights will be violated, cannot feel sure of itself. We have ourselves finally come to this conclusion and there is no turning back. The decision adopted at the Vienna meeting signifies a genuine breakthrough in this sense. A whole program of joint activities for the European countries has been outlined, packed with an extremely wide variety of measures. Mutual understanding has been achieved on many issues, which until quite recently were a stumbling block in relations between East and West. We are convinced that a reliable, law-based foundation must underlie the common European process. We think of the common European home as a law-based community, and for our part, we have started moving in that direction.

The decision of the USSR Congress of People's Deputies incidentally states that proceeding from international norms and principles, including those contained in the general declaration on human rights, the Helsinki agreements and accords, and bringing its internal legislation into line with them, the USSR will promote the establishment of a world community of law-based states. Here Europe could set an example. Naturally its international law-based integrity includes the national and social peculiarities of the states. Every European country, the United States, and Canada, has its own laws and traditions in the humanitarian sphere, although generally recognized norms and principles do exist.[66]

Later in July advice came from an unusual source. An editorial in the *Wall Street Journal* noted that a wave of strikes in Soviet coalfields had prompted Gorbachev's regime to undertake a revision of the laws on trade unions. The *Journal* suggested that Gorbachev call on respected labor experts to help: the International Labor Organization.[67] As noted earlier, the ILO had been critical to events in Poland. The fact that Poland had ratified the ILO conventions on freedom of association was at one point the only hold the free trade union Solidarity had on its right to exist. The Polish Communist government dared not denounce the treaty; and while the treaty was there, Solidarity was legal in the eyes of the world. Poland was the first ever society to free itself from totalitarianism, something it was being argued could never be done. But it was done. Is it too much by way of hyperbole to argue that it came about much as Woodrow Wilson and Franklin D. Roosevelt conceived that it might?

. . . . .

George Bush was by now president of the United States. Less an ideologue than his predecessor, he was on that account more open to ideas. His first national office had been as permanent representative to the United Nations, an experience of world politics no previous president had, nor indeed had much sense of. (He was the first president since James Buchanan to have previously been an American ambassador.) Ronald Reagan had survived the Iran-Contra calamity less damaged than the government he headed, if only because of a mood in Washington that above all we could not wish another ruined presidency. Instead, the president was sentenced to the internationalist equivalent of community service. In his first term Mr. Reagan's emissaries had been dismissive of the United Nations. In 1983 one Charles Lichenstein, in a squabble with the Soviets over where Foreign Minister Andrei A. Gromyko could land on his way to the General Assembly, invited the organization to leave New York.

> If in the judicious determination of the members of the United Nations, they feel that they are not welcome and that they are not being treated with the hostly consideration that is their due . . . then the United States strongly encourages such member states seriously to consider removing themselves and this organization from the soil of the United States . . .
>   We will put no impediment in your way . . . The members of the U.S. mission to the United Nations will be down at dockside waving you a fond farewell as you sail into the sunset.[68]

(This would have been difficult to do, as the sun in that vicinity sets over Hoboken, New Jersey, and not the Atlantic Ocean.) The White House spokesman promptly assured the diplomatic community that Lichenstein's statement did not reflect administration policy. Just as promptly, the president stated that it did.[69] Gromyko had gone to great lengths to ensure that the headquarters of the new international organization would be in the *United States*, not in Geneva or some other place where we would not feel our absence. Nineteen forty-five was a complex time. But the Soviets did not respond to our envoy, which is one we owe them. The Reagan years could have ended with the United States a debtor nation, burdened with a defunct and disgraced foreign policy, the headquarters of the world organization in Vienna, and of world finance in Tokyo. But unlike most ideologues, this one was lucky. Mr. Reagan's farewell address to the Forty-third Session of the UN General Assembly—a speech given at a "moment of hope"—was lyrical.

> I stand at this podium then in a moment of hope—hope, not just for the peoples of the United States or the Soviet Union but for all the peoples of the world; and hope, too, for the dream of peace among nations, the dream that began the United Nations. Precisely because of these changes, today, the United Nations has the opportunity to live and breathe and work as never before.[70]

The Bush administration marked a return to normalcy in American government. The terrible reign of doctrine was over once again; information regained some of its authority, in foreign affairs at all events. As information is more difficult to come by than ideas, foreign policy became cautious once again.[71] In this first summer it began a reconciliation with the World Court. Sofaer, who had to deal with the squalor bequeathed him in the aftermath of the Iran-Contra Affair, stayed on as legal adviser. In his Coudert Lecture he had proposed that the United States might make more use of "special chambers" of the Court. The Court statute provides that parties to a dispute may, instead of having it heard by the full Court, bring it before a picked panel. (Typically, the judge or judges from each side pick an additional judge who can have the deciding vote.) In August 1989 the United States and the Soviet Union proposed such an arrangement, in disputes over six treaties dealing with terrorism and drug trafficking.[72] Verdicts would be final. This was actually a Soviet initiative. In 1987 Gorbachev had proposed strengthening the Court by having the five permanent members of the Security Council enter such agreements for binding arbitration and inviting other nations to follow. It remains to be seen whether anything will come of these initiatives of the Gorbachev period. Still, the United States was responding. Also, in August the United States agreed to let the World Court try the case brought by Iran involving an Iran Air flight shot down by the USS *Vincennes* over the Persian Gulf in 1988.

That part of the law of nations which matters most will never be enforced by courts, or even referred to courts. The United States recognizes a "distinction between judicially enforceable rights and rights enforceable only by the political branches."[73] Some disputes are justiciable; indeed in some areas this has become almost routine. In other areas, however, especially where the use of force is involved, rights are resolved in the political realm. If the time should come when the use of force by sovereign nations is in fact adjudicated, that will only mean that the nations involved are no longer sovereign. The General Agreement on Tariffs and Trade adjudicates international disputes by the hour. If such disputes seem marginal today, it may be remembered that for centuries European powers routinely went to war over trade issues. (It may also be noted that GATT began as a wholly informal arrangement—mainly Eric Wyndham White, formerly a British civil servant, and three French-speaking secretaries in a villa above Geneva—after the Senate Committee on Finance rejected the UN proposal for an International Trade Organization with headquarters in Havana.)[74] The formally constituted "world courts" have not done much judging. In the 1920s and 1930s the chief clerk of the Permanent Court of International Justice made his way about the capitals of Europe as a kind of *agent provocateur* talking up border disputes the court could adjudicate. From 1946 to 1988, the International Court of Justice (renamed in 1945) dealt with only sixty cases, though handling 174 orders and some twenty advisory opinions. The decisions that were handed down generally dealt with matters of little consequence. In one such, eleven hectares of land claimed by Holland were solemnly declared to be the territory of Belgium. Issues of war and peace did not come before international courts in this stage of history, and may never do so.

It is in this sense only that Wilson may be said to have had reservations about law; he did not expect that serious disputes between nations would ever be litigated, and could be impatient with those who evidently did. This is not to deprecate law, but rather, to take it seriously and consider how it *is* to be enforced, or rather brought about. This is the spirit in which in the summer of 1989 Robert S. McNamara, former secretary of defense, set forth an East-West Code of Conduct:

circumstances have changed, and a mutually beneficial Code of Conduct can perhaps be negotiated . . .

Perhaps more important, the Soviets are retracting a good many of their costly Third World commitments . . . and Gorbachev himself has suggested that "new rules of coexistence" might be drafted.

Such "new rules" could provide that:

1. Each bloc's political interests will be pursued through diplomacy, not military threats or the use of force.
2. Consistent with number one, each bloc's military forces will be restructured to defensive postures and reduced to a balance at substantially lower levels.
3. The super powers will not become involved in regional conflicts.
4. The nations of East and West, and in particular the super powers, will utilize international organizations to solve regional and global problems, including conflicts within and between Third World nations.

The Code of Conduct would have precluded such unilateral postwar actions as Soviet intervention in Afghanistan, Angola (via the Cubans), Indochina (via the North Vietnamese) and Korea (via the North Koreans); U.S. intervention in Vietnam, the Dominican Republic, Nicaragua, Grenada and the Persian Gulf; and British and French intervention in Egypt.[75]

One may wonder at the seeming "equivalence"—as the term was used with such ferocity by the advocates of the Reagan Doctrine —accorded the Soviet intervention in Afghanistan and the "U.S. intervention in Vietnam." And this from the man who intervened, if that is the term to use. (If the Reagan administration lied, and shielded its lies by classifying the truth as something that the American people could never be trusted to know, let it be clear that this practice was rampant during the Johnson administration also.) McNamara also discusses how the code of conduct would be applied to a number of conflicts. The most important of these is the Arab-Israeli problem, both for the subject itself and for the context.

·   ·   ·   ·   ·

This still unresolved conflict dates back to the mandatory system established by the Treaty of Versailles. The context is the issue of self-determination, which in that period developed into a "right" that is easy enough to assert, but often dauntingly difficult to realize. There are 171 nations in the world; evidently some 6,170 languages. Will there someday be 6,170 nations? Obviously not that many, but there *will* be more. Walker Connor estimates that nearly half of the independent countries in the world have in recent years experienced some degree of "ethnically inspired dissonance."[76] A general pattern perceived by Donald Horowitz is that less advanced groups attack more advanced groups; the issues are fairly described as those of inequality, but the sources of inequality and its forms are seemingly infinite.[77]

The post-totalitarian world faces a storm of regional ethnic conflicts. In our entry on "Ethnicity" for *The Harper Dictionary of Modern Thought* in 1988, Nathan Glazer and I forecast that "ethnic conflict within the Soviet empire is likely to prove a major element in 21st-century world politics."[78] Already the timing is off. The world news of 1989 has been filled with ethnic conflict within the Soviet empire. "Ukraine Stirs; Kremlin Shudders"; "Azerbaijan Blockades Rail Transport of Critical Supplies to Armenia"; "Lithuania Declares Annexation by Moscow Void"; "Soviet Official Warns of 'Homemade' Lebanon.'"[79] In the United States the spell of Marxism really did suppress understanding of the ethnic antagonisms in the Soviet Union. In contrast, that is, to class solidarity. We would have been far less impressed with Soviet power during the long confrontation of the cold war had we realized just how fragile the Russian empire was. Similarly, we might be better prepared today to accommodate the centripetal forces that threaten to tear the Soviet state apart.

Nor was this conflict limited to the Soviet Union's internal empire: "Hungary Accuses Romania of Human Rights Violations"; "Hungarian Accuses Rumania of Military Threats."[80] The Soviets will have to deal with this, as will the Chinese, the Yugoslavs, the Indochinese, the Bulgarians, the Hungarians, the Rumanians. Much of the world is now caught up in such conflict, and it will certainly not diminish.

Is it possible that the mitigation of ethnic conflict can become an area of deliberate international collaboration? In a sense this has already happened. Granted, nothing came to the great schemes of 1944–45 for the creation of a United Nations military force. It has been observed that diplomats as well as generals are disposed to fighting the last war. The founders of the League wished to be able to prevent wars from breaking out through impulsiveness, as seemed to have happened in 1914. The founders of the UN had in mind the model of German and Japanese aggression: methodical, deliberate. (The Germans could be said to have reached a written agreement to begin the Second World War.) But virtually from the moment that the United Nations came into existence, it found itself dealing with warring ethnic groups that inhabit the same territory, as epitomized by the Arab-Jewish warfare that began in anticipation of the British departure in 1948. The oldest UN "peacekeeping force" still in place, the UN Commission for India and Pakistan, established in January 1948, will be found amidst the Mogul glory and natural splendor of the Vale of Kashmir, a dispute left over from the Muslim-Hindu cleavage that preceded and followed the British departure from the subcontinent. There is a homeopathic sense in which the UN itself gives rise to the conflicts it seeks to restrain. The Charter proclaims "the principle of equal rights and self-determination of peoples." The problem is that only rarely do we come across groups living together at equal levels of achievement.

Is it possible to imagine the evolution of something like international arbitration and mediation in the manner of the Hague conferences? The essential fact is that the nations of the world are committing themselves to the proposition that there is a category of individual entitlement called "human rights." These rights go beyond the elemental rights of citizenship. They extend to *group* identity. Each of the Geneva Conventions of 1949 dealing with the treatment of prisoners of war and the protection of civilians in time of war has the same Article 3 (known as "common Article 3"), which provides that during "armed conflict not of an international character" those caught up in the event must be treated humanely "without any adverse distinction founded on race, colour, religion or faith." The International Convention on the Prevention and Punishment of the Crime of Genocide recognized a right of "national, ethnical, racial or religious groups" to be free from genocide and imposes obligations on the states that are parties to the convention to prevent genocide.[81]

Other major human rights instruments speak primarily in terms of individual rights, but not exclusively so. The Universal Declaration of Human Rights, adopted by the General Assembly in 1948, recognizes the family as "the natural and fundamental group unit of society" and states that it "is entitled to protection by society and the State."[82] The International Covenant on Economic, Social, and Cultural Rights recognizes the right of trade unions to exist and to "function freely subject to no limitations other than those prescribed by law and which are necessary in a democratic society in the interests of national security or public order or for the protection of the rights and freedoms of others."[83] The International Covenant on Civil and Political Rights recognizes the right of "ethnic, religious or linguistic minorities . . . to enjoy their own culture, to profess and practice their own religion, or to use their own language."[84] The Final Act of the Conference on Security and Cooperation in Europe, Helsinki, recognizes the right of "national minorities" to "equality before the law" and to "the full opportunity for the actual enjoyment of human rights and fundamental freedoms."[85]

All of which guarantees fission, and arguably makes a claim on the attention of those who advanced these propositions in the first instance, notably the United States. Arguably. Meg Greenfield makes the point that whether or not the cold war is over, "What *is* clearly over is the intellectually easy cold-war period in which there seemed to be only two sides in the world and only two ways of thinking about their relationship here at home" (my emphasis). The new complexity of world affairs is not especially inviting. She asks:

> Do we give a hoot what kind of domestic political lives other countries lead? If Third World disputes were not overlaid with East-West meaning, would we care how they came out? Would we be concerned only as our economic interests were affected? Outside the cold-war context, does any of the currently burgeoning ethnic mayhem around the world matter to us, warfare between peoples with exotic names who have been trying to annihilate each other for centuries and whom most of us probably never even heard of until the 6 o'clock news tonight?[86]

Most of these peoples with exotic names will be found among the 100 nations of the "Non-Aligned," as they designate their organization. So also is the Palestine Liberation Organization. In the main these are not attractive societies from the point of view of political liberties or civil rights. A majority of them rank at the very bottom of the Freedom House comparative survey for 1988–89.[87] Yet without significant exception these nations will be parties to all the assorted conventions that in the emerging field of human rights law oblige them to act otherwise. When "conflict not of an international character" breaks out in such regions, the international community is even so somewhat on notice; somewhat obligated. We shall see.

For the moment the Non-Aligned are in an unenviable position. They bet wrong on the cold war. This is not altogether their own doing. The movement, which dates back to the Bandung Conference of 1955, was intended to be an Afro-Asian affair. In all, some twenty-nine countries attended that first gathering. With one or two exceptions each had just obtained independence after a period of colonial domination by a Western democracy. The most significant exception, the People's Republic of China, represented by Chou En-lai, had been sufficiently subjected to Western dominion and was, in any event, a Communist regime. Had the delegates come from newly independent former Soviet Republics the disposition might have been different. The Movement was formally organized in 1961 in a conference in Belgrade. Jawaharlal Nehru, who seems to have been genuinely committed to the idea of non-alignment, found the other delegations still caught up with anti-colonialism. By the end of that decade the Non-Aligned were part of the Soviet bloc. In part there was a fellow-traveling impulse acquired in European universities and suchlike settings. In part there was understandable resentment. Part *schadenfreude* at the seeming decline of the West, or at least its travail. Then there was the prospect of booty if the United States Congress determined to save you from Communism. Alternatively, there was the more limited but typically more lethal largess of the U.S.S.R.

It proved a woefully bad bargain, not least in the degree to which the Soviet connection reinforced the already powerful attraction of state-directed economies. In any event, it was clear by 1989 that it was all over. In September the heads of state or government of the Non-Aligned returned to Belgrade for their ninth summit conference. A muted declaration emerged. The world learned that "The

Non-Aligned favour concordance rather than confrontation." There were problems with the environment and with debt. "We appeal to the developed world to face, with maximum will and determination and without prejudice, the conflict which is older and deeper than the cold war and bloc confrontation—the conflict between affluence and poverty." A bit late. Then this: "Peace and harmony among peoples and nations require strict observance and further enhancement of international law. In this context the outcome of the recent meeting of Non-Aligned countries at The Hague and its initiative for the Decade of International Law represents an important contribution."[88]

From the perspective of the United States the test of this proposition has to be the position of the Non-Aligned, or rather the member states, toward the state of Israel. This hostility was not present at the creation. For a considerable period Israel was a developing nation in good standing. Relations with most African countries were exemplary. The Soviet Union was friendly at first. Israel declared itself to be an independent state on the day the British relinquished their mandate, May 14, 1948. The United States recognized the state instantly, as did the Soviets. On the same day. Israel was pretty much a neutral nation until the 1967 war. By then Syria, previously a portion of the French mandatory territory in the Middle East, had become a Soviet client state while Egypt was at very least much dependent on Soviet arms. Syria and Egypt were defeated by Israel. The Soviets became openly anti-Israeli. Again, almost nothing is known of the internal deliberations of the Kremlin, but the outward facts will do. A vicious, raging propaganda assault commenced. The central charge appeared in a two-part article, "Anti-Sovietism—Profession of Zionists," published in *Pravda* February 18 and 19, 1971. The Jews, we learned, had been collaborators of the Nazis. Zionism was racism. The Non-Aligned took up this cause, with considerable additional pressure coming from the oil-producing Arab principalities. The campaign culminated on November 10, 1975, when the General Assembly of the United Nations formally adopted Resolution 3379 declaring that "zionism is a form of racism and racial discrimination."[89]

The impact, the import, of this event within Israel is somehow not appreciated in the United States, and still less in Europe. Israel had set out to be a model, lawful, law-abiding member of the society of nations, and of course of the United Nations. It cannot be said that it owed its existence to the United Nations, and yet the partition of Palestine was formally agreed to by the General Assembly on November 29, 1947, the United Nations having succeeded to the League's trusteeship of the region. *This* history is well known, including American involvement at the Paris Peace Conference. Toward the end of 1948 the Israelis made public the text of a proposed constitution, beginning, "WE, THE PEOPLE OF ISRAEL," Articles 11 and 12 of which stated:

> The State of Israel shall seek to settle all international disputes of whatever nature or origin in which it may be involved by pacific means only. *The generally recognized rules of international law shall form part of the municipal law of Israel* [my emphasis].
>
> The State shall ensure the sanctity of human life and uphold the dignity of man. There shall be no penalty of death, nor shall anyone be subjected to torture, flogging or humiliating punishment. The application of moral pressure or physical violence in the course of police interrogations is prohibited; evidence obtained by such methods shall not be admissible in Court.[90]

This was a state founded in the aftermath of the Holocaust, a racist crime that still defies description or understanding. Now at the United Nations Israel was declared to be all that it was founded *not* to be. Inevitably Israeli opinion turned away from the United Nations as an institution, and imperceptibly at first the Israeli government began to act less committed to the norms of the Charter, which had after all for them been desecrated in an unfathomable, unforgivable manner. But the world was not especially sympathetic or understanding.

As for the Non-Aligned, now two-thirds of the UN membership, they remained committed to their declaration at their seventh summit, which met at New Delhi in 1983. By that time it was routine for such pronouncements to declare "Jerusalem" to be "occupied Palestinian territory." If pressed on the matter, Non-Aligned ambassadors and such would explain that meant only East Jerusalem, or the Old City or something such. Now the declaration was changed to read: "West Jerusalem is part of the occupied Palestinian territory and Israel should withdraw completely and unconditionally from it and restore it to Arab sovereignty."[91] This is no more than to call for extinction of the state. It is wholly in violation of international law, and in truth it has not been repeated. But neither has the Zionism resolution been overturned or disavowed. While that resolution stands the United Nations is essentially on record favoring the annihilation of a member state. For racism is the one public policy that can deprive a state of legitimacy—even legality—in the modern world. This is singularly the case with Israel, for it was founded to be a *Jewish* nation. A. M. Rosenthal does not overstate.

> Every Israel-hating government, every anti-Semite in office around the world, has used that resolution to spread fear of Jews among their own people and, more important, among people who never saw a Jew and hardly ever heard of them before.
>
> To hundreds of millions of people, "racism" is a curse word meaning exploitation of and contempt for people exactly like themselves—black, brown, Latin, Oriental or just newly independent.
>
> Through constant, obsessive, vicious Zionism-is-racism propaganda wrapped in a United Nations cloak, racists and Jews were connected in the minds of people all over the world and still are.[92]

In 1986 the Australian Parliament adopted a resolution condemning Resolution 3379 of the thirtieth General Assembly. In 1987 by joint resolution, the United States Congress adopted this word for word. It was hoped the "Australian Resolution" could then make its way to democratic parliaments around the world. It did not. Thirty days after President Reagan signed the joint resolution, the *intifada* began. Israel's isolation became ever more evident. But it cannot be left there. Resolution 3379 *must* go. For this to happen two things are necessary. The Non-Aligned nations have got to be brought to understand that disavowing that infamous act is a condition of regaining the respect, and the support, they lost during their years in the "Soviet camp." But this will happen only if the United States convinces the democracies that it is *serious* about the matter; and to do this it must demonstrate that it is once again serious about the United Nations and the law of nations from which the UN emerged. More is at stake than the survival of Israel; but that would be more than sufficient. If the United States should give up on the idea of a law of nations, or fritter away its commitment in a fit of absentmindedness, do we give up also on the viability of Israel? Along with what else?

In late September 1989 it was President Bush's turn to address the General Assembly, which he did in the best of spirits and at times with great specificity on issues such as trade and the environment. He affirmed the end of ideology: "Today we are witnessing an ideological collapse, the demise of the totalitarian idea of the omniscient, all-powerful state." And he stated the elemental truth: "The founders of this historic institution believed that it was here that the nations of the world might come to agree that law, not force, shall govern."[93] In mid-October, however, the president was of a different view. Asked at a White House news conference about an aborted attempt to overthrow Panamanian general Manuel Antonio Noriega, the president defended himself against charges of fecklessness. "I wouldn't mind using force," he said, "if it could be done in a prudent manner."[94]

On that same day, October 14, the *New York Times* reported that the Department of Justice, reversing an earlier position of the Carter years, had given the Federal Bureau of Investigation legal authority to apprehend fugitives from United States law in foreign countries and bring them to the United States without either the knowledge or consent of the country involved.[95] This ruling was prepared by the Office of Legal Counsel and was not made public —a defensible position, as the legal counsel is the attorney general's lawyer. Press coverage simply reported that an attempt to kidnap Noriega was probably afoot. The following month, however, the assistant attorney general involved, William P. Barr, testified on the matter before the Subcommittee on Civil and Constitutional Rights of the House Committee on the Judiciary, one of the few, all-but-hidden crannies in the Congress where questions of international law continue to be of any interest. Barr's testimony—"On the Legality as a Matter of Domestic Law of Extraterritorial Law Enforcement Activities That Depart from International Law"— attained to the condition of a state paper, and was the ablest work to appear in Washington in decades.[96] To be sure, the subject was a narrow one, but the perspective was as broad as could possibly be wished, and the candor without precedent. A 1980 opinion of the Office of Legal Counsel had "suggested that the President and the Congress are legally powerless under United States law to authorize action in a foreign country that departs from customary international law." Accordingly, the FBI had no authority "to arrest a fugitive in a foreign country without that country's consent."[97] However, this was now to change. And why? Because the United States had decided to act differently. The paper next ranges knowledgeably among the various decisions of the Supreme Court which might bear on the subject, principally Justice Marshall in *The Schooner Exchange* (1812) to Justice Gray in *The Paquete Habana* (1900), returning to *Brown* (1814), wherein Marshall observed that the rule of customary international law "is a guide which the sovereign follows or abandons at his will. The rule, like other precepts of morality, of humanity, and even of wisdom, is addressed to the judgement of the sovereign; and although it cannot be disregarded by him without obloquy, yet it may be disregarded."[98]

Next a passage of compelling candor:

> Moreover, the conclusion that the President has the authority to depart from customary international law is consistent with the very nature of customary international law. Customary international law is not a rigid canon of rules, but an evolving set of principles founded on the common practices and understandings of many nations. It is understood internationally that this evolution can occur by a state's departing from prevailing customary international law principles, and seeking to promote a new rule of international custom or practice (although a state remains liable under international law for breaches until a new rule develops). In the absence of authority under the Constitution to take actions departing from customary international law, the United States would be absolutely bound under its own fundamental law to international customs and practices, and largely powerless to play a role in shaping and changing those customs and practices itself. Under our constitutional system, where the President is primarily responsible for the conduct of our foreign affairs, it therefore makes sense that the President has the discretion to depart from customary international law norms in the exercise of his constitutional authority.[99]

This is the doctrine of presidential prerogative, ever more frequently invoked by American administrations of the late twentieth century. One may wholly disagree—as I do—while just as wholly admiring the openness of the proposition. The president may break the law if he will take the consequences, and who knows but we might all get used to it!

Three days after the Justice Department came out for kidnapping—we are now just three weeks from the president's speech at the UN—the Central Intelligence Agency came out for assassination. In an interview with the *New York Times,* published under the title "C.I.A. Seeks Looser Rules on Killings during Coups,"

> William H. Webster, the Director of Central Intelligence, called . . . on the President and Congress to consider giving the Central Intelligence Agency greater latitude in supporting potentially violent efforts to overthrow foreign dictators.
>
> Mr. Webster, in an interview, said a longstanding Presidential executive order barring American involvement in assassinations had been interpreted to prohibit American assistance to any coup that could lead to the death of a country's leader, even in the heat of battle.
>
> Asked if he would like to see this interpretation relaxed, Mr. Webster said, "I don't think you're misreading me."[100]

This from William H. Webster, a former federal district judge. At that time the Department of the Army field manual *The Law of Land Warfare* explicitly forbade any such conduct. Under the heading "Assassination and Outlawry," the manual stipulates that the Annex to Hague Convention No. IV of 1907 provides:

> *It is especially forbidden *** to kill or wound treacherously individuals belonging to the hostile nation or army . . .*
>
> This is construed as prohibiting assassination, proscription, or outlawry of an enemy, or putting a price upon an enemy's head, as well as offering a reward for an enemy "dead or alive."[101]

The manual is dispositive; no assassinations. The law applies in any circumstance in which the United States has resorted to the use of military force. The manual, just like the 1907 treaty it cites, is still in force. But seemingly makes no claim further up the south bank of the Potomac.

We know what happened. Even as the army was codifying the assorted texts on the laws of warfare, having reference especially to the Geneva Conventions of 1949, which grew out of the Nuremberg trials, a postwar school of opinion was emerging which, in reaction to the very same events that led to Nuremberg and the affirmation of law, led to the emergence of a postwar school of *Realpolitik* that held there was no such thing. This was not the view of the Right; it was far more, in Judith Shklar's term, that of "disillusioned liberals" shaken by the lawlessness of that war. And yet if there were those disillusioned with law, it was possible for others to be troubled by its increasing absence from our counsels.

It happens I was one of a small company assembled in the big southwest corner office of the West Wing of the White House in the early afternoon of November 22, 1963, waiting word from Dallas. In the event, no message came; leastwise, none that I recall. Rather, at one point we all seemed to come to the same realization. John F. Kennedy was dead. Assassinated.

Within minutes Hubert Humphrey burst into the room, tears streaming, grabbing Ralph Dungan by both arms: "What have they done to us?" We all knew who *they* were. The right wing in Dallas. And yet, later in the day we learned on radio that an arrest had been made of a man who had been connected with Fair Play for Cuba. Oh, God, I said to myself. They will kill him, too. I began to plead that the federal government must get physical custody of Lee Harvey Oswald. Else we would never know. There would be no end to conspiracy theories. Late that evening I went out to Andrews Air Force Base to meet the plane bringing the cabinet back from its aborted trip to Japan. *We must get custody of Oswald!* I really worked at this. Dean Joan Konner of the Columbia School of Journalism recalls my coming into her studio at Channel 13 on 56th Street and Ninth Avenue to plead the case. Assassinations, you see, linger. Societies sicken.

I had more than Castro in mind. Obviously we had tried without success to assassinate him. Had he succeeded in an attempt at revenge? But there was something more. It happened that at the time I also knew that we had been in on the assassination of Ngo Dinh Diem in Vietnam. We did not order it. We certainly did not do it. But we were involved.

William Colby, a career intelligence officer, later director of the Central Intelligence Agency, served in Vietnam. He writes:

it is clear that the overthrow of President Ngo Dinh Diem left a legacy of anarchy in South Vietnam to Johnson. Many contributing causes can be blamed for the overthrow . . . but the American Government's role clearly was crucial. And the basis for that role still seems almost incomprehensible: the beliefs that greater democratization and effectiveness could be brought to the Vietnamese by an unidentified general or generals than by Diem's continued rule, and that American interests would be better served by assuming the responsibilities of fine-tuning Vietnamese political leadership and policies than by supporting what existed.

The coup against Diem, then, must be assigned the stigma of America's primary (and perhaps worst) error in Vietnam.

Colby continues:

There is much evidence that the lessons of Vietnam have been ignored or not learned. The Reagan Administration, in its determination to oust the Sandinista regime from Nicaragua, clearly put its faith in a military—even if paramilitary—approach through support of the contra forces and put this cart in front of the essential horse of a political cause and structure. Mining harbors, sending raiding forces supported by a covert airlift, and building border base camps preceded the development of the political ideas to attract support away from the Sandinistas.[102]

Which *is* the point. The United States has every right to try to bring about regimes it approves, especially in places we consider important. But there are rules.

On December 20, 1989, in its largest military operation since Vietnam, the United States invaded Panama. The legality of the action *was* considered within the administration; there were simply too many treaties involved for the issue to be ignored as it had been in Grenada. As, for example, the Charter of the Organization of American States, a regional organization as contemplated by the UN Charter, and chockablock with the same propositions. "IN THE NAME OF THEIR PEOPLES, THE STATES REPRESENTED" pledged themselves to "good neighborliness" and "the essential rights of man." Article 20 holds:

The territory of a State is inviolable; it may not be the object, even temporarily, of military occupation or of other measures of force taken by another State, directly or indirectly, on any grounds whatever. No territorial acquisitions or special advantages obtained either by force or by other means of coercion shall be recognized.

Article 21, however, affirms the right of self-defense, and not long after the invasion began a Justice Department "spokesman" told the *New York Times* that this was what the American forces were about. At the OAS the American representative invoked the "inherent right of nations to act in self-defense" under international law.[103] Back at the Justice Department the spokesman further invoked Article 4 of the 1977 Treaty concerning the Permanent Neutrality and Operation of the Panama Canal, known as the Neutrality Treaty.[104] This gave either party the right to use force to maintain the neutrality of the canal. The Justice Department in 1978 could not have been more explicit as to the restrictions on this right. An opinion by the department presented to the Committee on Foreign Relations stated:

> A legitimate exercise of rights under the Neutrality Treaty by the United States would not, either in intent or in fact, be directed against the territorial integrity or political independence of Panama. No question of detaching territory from the sovereignty or jurisdiction of Panama would arise. Nor would the political independence of Panama be violated by measures calculated to uphold a commitment to the maintenance of the Canal's neutrality which Panama has freely assumed. A use of force in these circumstances would not be directed against the form or character or composition of the Government of Panama or any other aspect of its political independence; it would be solely directed and proportionately crafted to maintain the neutrality of the Canal.[105]

This was restated in a reservation set forth in the instrument of ratification. The Neutrality Treaty "shall be only for the purpose of assuring that the Canal shall remain open, neutral, secure, and accessible and shall not have as its purpose or be interpreted as a right of intervention in the internal affairs of the Republic of Panama or interference with its political independence or sovereign integrity."[106]

It was also said that the new Panamanian government had requested our intervention, although at the United Nations the newly arrived representative of that government said that the decision to invade "was a unilateral decision by the U.S. We were not part of it."[107] All that was missing from this miscellany was the notion of "hot pursuit" of General Noriega. A spokesman for the attorney general let it be known that a detailed description of the legal justifications would be presented to Congress. None was expected, and by week's end none had arrived. Indeed, by week's end the department was no longer aware anything had been promised.[108] None of this elicited any serious objection from the Congress, the press, or the public at large. The United States was seen to have done the right thing, even though we acted in seeming violation of all manner of previous undertakings. An eminent professor of international law put it that this was no time for "mechanical fidelity to black letters." The issue was the restoration of democracy. In a press briefing Secretary of State James A. Baker III declared: "The actions we have taken, in our view are fully in accordance with international law." He continued: "Both the United States and the Soviet Union today are supporting democracy . . . The difference is that the Soviet Union supports democracy by staying out of countries and thus permitting democracy to proceed. In this one and very unique instance, the United States did it by going in."[109] (Still, later, Secretary Baker suggested that the Soviet Union might also support democracy by "going in" to Rumania to help with the overthrow of Nicolae Ceausescu.)[110]

The day after the Panama invasion, in a letter to the speaker of the House of Representatives and the president pro tempore of the Senate, President Bush asserted:

> The deployment of U.S. Forces is an exercise of the right of self-defense recognized in Article 51 of the United Nations Charter and was necessary to protect American lives in imminent danger and to fulfill our responsibilities under the Panama Canal Treaties. It was welcomed by the democratically elected government of Panama. The military operations were ordered pursuant to my constitutional authority with respect to the conduct of foreign relations and as Commander in Chief.[111]

And so at the end of our tour we come round to the point at which we began. It is clear that the United States has commenced to hold views or to take positions with respect to international law which are considerably at variance with earlier positions. It is impossible, for example, to suppose that the drafters of the UN

Charter would have judged the right of self-defense to extend to the invasion of Panama. In the view of some, William Pfaff for one, the United States has commenced a general challenge to international convention and law. Perhaps. What is certain is that many of our views are not what they once were. We have a right to change our mind, and to attempt to persuade others to join us. What is to be pleaded is that this be an open, acknowledged process, and that above all the Congress be involved, for it is *law* that is being rewritten.

There is a risk that we will jettison the whole idea of international law where the unilateral use of force is concerned. Just as the Panama invasion was getting underway the *National Interest* published an article by Robert H. Bork, titled "The Limits of 'International Law.'"[112] The quotation marks suggest the point of view, which is that the whole notion is an illusion at best, and at worst an obstacle to the pursuit of legitimate American interests. Chief Justice John Marshall had no more difficulty with the idea than did the framers. "By the law of nations," he held in *The Schooner Exchange,* "all independent powers stand upon an equality, as regards their rights and duties, whether relatively weak or powerful."[113] Bork, who was nominated for the Supreme Court by President Reagan, clearly, on the bench or off, would be uneasy with this view. Among conservatives it was increasingly to be heard that nations were not equal at law because they were not equal in moral worth. This view began, albeit slowly, with the advent of the totalitarian state and now was carrying over to merely Marxist regimes, or merely criminal ones. Here is Bork on the eve of Panama.

> ... by eliminating morality from its calculus, international law actually makes moral action appear immoral. It can hardly be doubted that, in the American view, it would be a moral act to help a people overthrow a dictatorship that had replaced a democratic government by force, and to restore democracy and freedom to such people. Yet when our leaders act for such moral reasons, they are forced into contrived explanations. The implausibility of such explanations then reverses the moral stance of the parties.
>
> International law thus serves, both internationally and domestically, as a basis for a rhetoric of recrimination directed at the United

States. Those who disapprove of a President's actions on the merits, but who fear they may prove popular, can transform the dispute from one about substance to one about legality. The President can be painted as a lawbreaker and perhaps drawn into a legalistic defense of his actions. The effect is to raise doubts and lower American morale. The Soviets and other nations have no such problem.

As currently defined, then, international law about the use of force is not even a piety; it is a net loss for Western democracies. Senator Moynihan, speaking of international relations in Woodrow Wilson's time, said, approvingly, that "the idea of law persisted, even when it did not prevail." That is precisely the problem. Since it does not prevail, the persistence of the idea that it exists can be pernicious. There can be no authentic rule of law among nations until nations have a common political morality or are under a common sovereignty. A glance at the real world suggests we have a while to wait.[114]

At the level of formal analysis, Judge Bork's position is difficult to sustain. International law is made up of customary law and treaty law. The latter is of much the greater relevance now, whether we are concerned with the status of Antarctica, or the condition of the ozone layers of the atmosphere. Or, once again, Panama. In the course of the Panama invasion American forces occupied the residence of the Nicaraguan ambassador. When, thereafter, the Security Council took up the matter, the U.S. representative defended our action as an "honest mistake," adding that the "United States not only fully accepts but supports" the "pertinent articles" of the 1961 Vienna Convention on Diplomatic Relations.[115] That is to say, we acknowledge the existence of international law providing for the immunity of diplomatic missions. A matter of some consequence to us in Iran earlier on.

It is to be noted, further, that for the United States *treaty* law is not just the "supreme Law of the Land," but that it comes into being through a singularly exacting sequence. Treaties are entered into by the United States with other nations, either directly or through adherence to a common document. They are signed by a member of the executive branch. Thereafter the Senate of the United States must by resolution, two-thirds of the senators present concurring therein, give its advice and consent to ratification. This advice and consent having been given—by an extraordinary majority—the president then ratifies and confirms the treaty in an instrument of ratification. At that point, under Article VI of the Constitution the said treaty "shall be the supreme Law of the Land." It may be that Judge Bork did not take this course when at law school. But that, at all events, answers the question as to the existence of international law so far as the president of the United States is concerned; which president, under Article II of the Constitution, is bound to "take Care that the Laws be faithfully executed."

At a practical level, however, Judge Bork's argument commands attention. It begins as a reprise of the Kirkpatrick position. The Soviets don't, so why should we? If one is prepared to have the Soviet Union set standards of conduct for the United States, well and good. One suspects that Judge Bork is not. To the contrary, what worries him is that in situations such as Operation Just Cause in Panama (which commenced after Bork's article appeared) "The President can be painted as a lawbreaker and perhaps drawn into a legalistic defense of his actions." This is more than a fair comment; it is urgent counsel. In Washington, in the first year of the last decade of the century, international law is no longer internalized as a body of specific or fairly specific obligations, entitlements, sanctions. It is widely seen as a formal reproach thought up by others. At most an extension of Anglo-American tort law. In these circumstances, absent advisers who understand this law and care about it, a president is not much to be faulted if he simply decides to do what he wants to do in the reasonable expectation that in time someone in the Executive Office Building or somewhere will put out a brief demonstrating that, whatever the decision, it was legal.

In the case of the invasion of Panama this role was carried out by Lloyd N. Cutler, who had been counsel to President Carter at the time of the Iranian hostage crisis and the signing of the Panama Canal treaties. Writing in the *Washington Post* a week after the invasion had been decided upon, Cutler, a certifiable liberal, argued in the "he-had-it-comin'-to-him" tradition of American jurisprudence. It was "harder to tell what is lawful under international law than under national law," but there was no doubt about the fact that the Panamanian had asked for it through his belligerent behavior. Further, we had the right to defend the canal under the Neutrality Treaty. Regrettably, the American action against Gen. Manuel Noriega is likely to produce as many legal battles as military ones. It has revived the favorite cottage industry of the international law community—opining whether or not one nation may lawfully use its military forces to help either side in another nation's internal struggle for political power.

Oh for the good old days.

In the simpler times of the American Revolution, intervention was unquestionably lawful. We are an independent nation today because the French fleet and army helped us win the Battle of Yorktown. Vattel, one of the fathers of international law, stated the rule in his Law of Nations, published in 1758:

> To give help to a brave people who are defending their liberties against an oppressor by force of arms is only the part of justice and generosity. Hence, whenever such dissension reaches the state of civil war, foreign nations may assist that one of the two parties which seems to have justice on its side. But to assist a detestable tyrant . . . would certainly be a violation of duty.

> But Vattel's rule is out of fashion today. The UN Charter obliges all member nations to "refrain . . . from the threat or use of force against the territorial integrity or political independence of any other state." The OAS Charter states that "no State . . . has the right to intervene, directly or indirectly, for any reason whatever, in the internal or external affairs of any other State." Both charters, however, recognize the right to use force in self defense.[116]

Two cases do not establish a pattern, but in this instance they do illustrate one. Here are two Washington lawyers of large intellectual powers and wide experience bumbling the most elemental parts of this particular subject. The French did not intervene in the American revolution because Vattel had decreed this could be done on behalf of "a brave people . . . defending their liberties." The French intervened because the colonists had won the battle of Saratoga, the first major defeat by an overseas British army in history. (An achievement that had eluded the French for four centuries.) The Americans had rushed the news to Versailles. The French were perfectly within their rights to recognize the new state, and they did so. That they might well have done so when no possible case could be made is beside the point. There were ascertainable rules then; there is a great range of explicit rules now. Do we or do we not wish to make such rules more salient in our conduct as a nation?

When Iranian students seized embassy buildings protected by the Vienna Convention of 1961, the United States argued that such conduct should be vigorously denounced by all nations. But when U.S. troops in Panama raided the Nicaraguan ambassador's residence during their search for General Noriega, President Bush's response was so mild that a *Washington Post* editorial said that he was virtually "condoning" the raid.[117] Even as the administration testified that the United States is free to seize fugitives abroad, the Iranian parliament approved a bill allowing Iranian officials to arrest Americans anywhere in the world if they violate Iranian law.[118] As Lars-Erik Nelson summed up the situation: "Since the Bork view appears to be prevailing, America's message to the world is that we are strong, we are good, we are moral and we will do whatever we think is right. Most Americans will probably agree with this. Just don't be surprised if nobody else does."[119] From Paris the indomitable Pfaff commented yet again on the "anarchic" implications of the ever more obvious, at times insistent American disavowal of international legal norms. "It is time indeed for a 'political branch' of government, the Congress, to restore to the practice of American government that 'decent respect' for the interests and opinions of the rest of mankind which the nation's founders enjoined upon their fellow citizens."[120]

The subject needs attention. There is clear evidence that the United States is moving away from its long-established concern for and advocacy of international legal norms of state behavior. It would be quite wrong to site this along some liberal–conservative spectrum. It would seem more a reflection of relative power. Weak nations will hope that strong nations will be law-abiding. Law does impose restraints. We were once weak; later powerful. We have noted the impassioned advocacy of international law and organization on the part of Wilson and Roosevelt at moments of unsurpassed power. We have also noted how casually these very same presidents broke all manner of rules, not least those that they themselves most proclaimed. The praise of Wilson and of Roosevelt is that at times when American power was so clearly preeminent, they advocated restraints on the use of power, even if they did not always abide by such restraints. There is, of course, a constitutional dimension; presidents pull, Congress tugs. The American Constitution provides for a great diffusion and separation of power. Yet it almost goads presidents to ignore the limits of presidential authority. In any event, it is the Congress as much as or more than the president that needs to raise its consciousness of international law as *our* law; American law. Enacted by Congress; executed by the president; demanding the attention of both. International law changes, just as domestic law changes. We are fully within our rights to propose changes; to limit or withdraw commitments. What we must not do is act as if the subject was optional, essentially rhetorical. For it is a fearfully dangerous thing, *the* thing most to be feared, to hold that some laws bind the president but others do not. That leads us, and, by example, others, in the very opposite direction from the one that we have hoped and trusted and rightly believed that history has been taking us and the rest of the world. In the second half of 1989, one by one the totalitarian regimes of the Warsaw Pact collapsed. First Poland. Then Hungary. Next East Germany. Then Bulgaria. On to Czechoslovakia. Finally Rumania. In the closing tumult of the year it was scarcely noted that the Soviet Union declared the invasion of Afghanistan and the Molotov-Ribbentrop pact to have been illegal. Hannah Arendt was prophetic. It came suddenly. Just as suddenly the threat to world order emerged not so much from the danger of Soviet expansion as from internal Soviet collapse. New world-order questions emerge. Control of weapons among many, not just a few, nations. Human rights as international obligations. Environmental concerns that obliterate boundaries. Old-order concerns persist: armies will still cross boundaries. These most extraordinary events of the year—of the century—argue that the United States, which inspired so many of them, might well pause to consider that this inspiration was authentic, a legacy not to be frittered away by forgetfulness of our own past, or by frustration with the behavior of others.

Notes

Index

Notes

INTRODUCTION

1. Arthur Conan Doyle, "Silver Blaze," in *The Memoirs of Sherlock Holmes* (London: John Murray, 1974), p. 34.
2. Quoted in Louis Henkin, "Use of Force: Law and U.S. Policy," in *Right v. Might: International Law and the Use of Force* (New York: Council on Foreign Relations Press, 1989), pp. 42–43.
3. Daniel Patrick Moynihan, "The Idea of Law in the Conduct of Nations," in *Loyalties* (San Diego: Harcourt Brace Jovanovich, 1984), pp. 59–96.
4. *Wall Street Journal*, November 1, 1983.
5. William Wordsworth, "Rob Roy's Grave."
6. Moynihan, "The Idea of Law," p. 77.
7. Extracts from the letter also appeared in the press, e.g., *New York Times*, November 29, 1989, p. A20.
8. *Report of the Congressional Committees Investigating the Iran-Contra Affair*, S. Rept. no. 100–26, H. Rept. no. 100–433, 100th Cong., 1st sess. (Washington, D.C.: Government Printing Office, 1987), p. 411.
9. George Will, *Washington Post*, June 8, 1989; Leon Wieseltier, "Spoilers at the Party," *National Interest*, no. 17 (Fall 1989), p. 12.
10. Sir Robert Chambers, *A Course of Lectures on the English Law, 1767–1773*, vol. 1, ed. Thomas M. Curley (Madison: University of Wisconsin Press, 1986), pp. 91, 90.
11. Ibid., p. 94.
12. Ibid., p. 92.
13. Alfred P. Rubin to Daniel Patrick Moynihan, October 25, 1989.
14. Hans J. Morgenthau, *Politics among Nations*, 4th ed. (New York: Alfred A. Knopf, 1967), p. 265.
15. Lawrence S. Eagleburger, "Uncharted Waters: U.S. Foreign Policy in a Time of Transition" (Samuel D. Berger Lecture, Georgetown University, Washington, D.C., September 13, 1989), p. 3.
16. Daniel Patrick Moynihan with Susan Weaver, *A Dangerous Place* (Boston: Little, Brown, 1978), pp. 270–271.

17. Quoted in Daniel Bell, "Thinking Aloud: Sidney Hook at Sixty," *New Leader,* March 4, 1963.

CHAPTER ONE: PEACE

1. James Kent, *Commentaries on American Law,* vol. 1 (New York: O. Halstead, 1826), p. 1.
2. Johnny H. Killian and Leland E. Beck, eds., *The Constitution of the United States of America: Analysis and Interpretation* (Washington, D.C.: Government Printing Office, 1987), p. 332. On Saturday, May 22, 1779, the Continental Congress approved a letter to the minister plenipotentiary of France assuring him that in judging the legality of the seizure of certain vessels the Congress "will cause the law of nations to be most strictly observed"; Worthington Chauncey Ford, ed., *Journals of the Continental Congress: 1774–1789,* vol. 14: *1779, April 23–September 1* (Washington, D.C.: Government Printing Office, 1909), p. 635. On Friday, November 23, 1781, the Congress recommended that the states "enact laws for punishing infractions of the laws of nations"; Gaillard Hunt, ed., ibid., vol. 21: *1781, April 23–September 1* (Washington, D.C.: Government Printing Office, 1912), p. 1136.
3. *The Federalist* is, of course, filled with citations of Greek and Roman practice, frequently intermixed: "Minos, we learn, was the primitive founder of the government of Crete, as Zaleucus was of that of the Locrians. Theseus first, and after him Draco and Solon, instituted the government of Athens. Lycurgus was the lawgiver of Sparta. The foundation of the original government of Rome was laid by Romulus, and the work completed by two of his elective successors, Numa and Tullius Hostilius. On the abolition of royalty the consular administration was substituted by Brutus, who stepped forward with a project for such a reform, which, he alleged, had been prepared by Servius Tullius, and to which his address obtained the assent and ratification of the senate and people. This remark is applicable to confederate governments also. Amphictyon, we are told, was the author of that which bore his name. The Achaean league received its first birth from Acheaus, and its second from Aratus"; Alexander Hamilton, James Madison, and John Jay, *The Federalist Papers,* ed. Clinton Rossiter, No. 38 (New York: New American Library 1961), p. 232.

On the condemnation of enemy property, we learn from Chancellor Kent: "This species of reprisal for some previous injury, is laid down in the books as a lawful measure, according to the usage of nations; but it is often reprobated, and it cannot well be distinguished from the practice of seizing property found within the territory upon the declaration of war. It does not differ in substance from the conduct of the Syracusans, in the time of Dionysius the Elder, (and which Mitford considered to be a gross violation of the law of nations,) for they voted a declaration of war against Carthage, and immediately seized the effects of Carthaginian traders in their warehouses, and Carthaginian richly laden vessels in their harbour, and then sent a herald to Carthage to negotiate. But this act of the Syracusans, near four hundred years before the Christian era, was no more than what is the ordinary practice in England, according to the observation of Lord Mansfield, in *Lindo* v. *Rodney*. 'Upon the declaration of war or hostilities, all the ships of the enemy,' he says, 'are detained in our ports, to be confiscated, as the property of the enemy, if no reciprocal agreement is made,'"; Kent, *Commentaries on American Law*, 1: 58–59.

Nor is the practice lost. When on January 18, 1985, the agent of the United States declined the jurisdiction of the International Court of Justice in the case of the mining of Nicaraguan harbors, the Department of State offered a gratuitous comment about the nationality of two of the judges who would be involved. In an acerbic response, Judge Manfred Lachs, a Pole, stated: "By way of an opening motto I cite Diodorus of the high court of ancient Egypt, where judges were chosen 'ten each from Heliopolos, Thebes and Memphis.' 'This Court,' he said, was 'in no way inferior to the Athenian Areopagus or the Spartan senate.' Despite their differing origins, these magistrates were thus held in no lower esteem than the highest national courts of the Hellenic polity"; Judge Manfred Lachs, "A Few Thoughts on the Independence of Judges of the International Court of Justice," *Columbia Journal of Transnational Law*, 25 (1987), 594–600.

4. J. L. Brierly, *The Law of Nations: An Introduction to the International Law of Peace* (Oxford: Clarendon Press, 1928), p. 8. By the fifth edition, published in 1955, Brierly had revised his observation to this extent: "Fortunately, however, at the very time when political development seemed to be leading to the complete separateness and irresponsibility of every state, other causes were at work which were to make it impossible for the world to accept the absence of bonds between state and state, and to bring them into more intimate and constant relations with one another than in the days when their theoretical unity was accepted everywhere" (p. 6). Unless otherwise indicated, citations are to the 1955 edition.

5. Ibid., pp. 6–7.

6. William Blackstone, *Commentaries on the Laws of England*, vol. 1, bk. 1 (Philadelphia: Childs & Peterson, 1860), p. 41.

7. Brierly, *Law of Nations*, p. 23.

8. Ibid., pp. 39–41.

9. Samuel Johnson, "Taxation No Tyranny" (1775), quoted in Donald Greene, "'Sweet Land of Liberty': Libertarian Rhetoric and Practice in Eighteenth-Century Britain," *American Revolution & 18th Century Culture* (New York: AMS Press, 1986), p. 130.

10. Donald Greene to Daniel Patrick Moynihan, August 20, 1989.

11. Quoted in ibid.

12. Ibid.

13. Quoted in R. Coupland, *The Quebec Act: A Study in Statesmanship* (Oxford: Clarendon Press, 1925), p. 211.

14. Henry Steele Commager, ed., *Documents of American History,* 6th ed. (New York: Appleton-Century-Crofts, 1958), p. 74.

15. John C. Miller, *Dictionary of American History,* ed. James Truslow Adams, vol. 3 (New York: Charles Scribner's Sons, 1946), p. 389.

16. Brierly, *Law of Nations,* p. 20.

17. Kent, *Commentaries,* pp. 3–4.

18. The Paquete Habana, 175 U.S. 677, 700 (1900).

19. Charles Krauthammer, "The Curse of Legalism," *New Republic,* November 6, 1989, pp. 44–50.

20. There is a particularly interesting account of these developments in a recently published history of those early days of the Congress. See Charlene Bangs Bickford and Kenneth R. Bowling, *Birth of the Nation: The First Federal Congress, 1789–1791* (Washington, D.C.: First Federal Congress Project, 1989), pp. 67–75.

21. Michael Barone and Grant Ujifusa, *The Almanac of American Politics, 1990* (Washington, D.C.: National Journal, 1989), p. 841.

22. *New York Times,* September 16, 1872, p. 1.

23. Ibid., p. 4.

24. Abraham D. Sofaer, "Adjudication of the International Court of Justice: Progress through Realism," *Record of the Association of the Bar of the City of New York,* 44 (June 1989), 468.

25. Ibid., p. 469.

26. "The Lotos Club," *Roster of the Lotos Club, 1985–86,* p. 7.

27. Sofaer, *Adjudication,* p. 462.

CHAPTER TWO: WAR

1. Evelyn Waugh, *When the Going Was Good* (London: Penguin Books, 1951), p. 8.

2. Evelyn Waugh, *The Diaries of Evelyn Waugh,* ed. Michael Davie (London: Weidenfeld and Nicolson, 1976), p. 653.

3. Evelyn Waugh, *Scott-King's Modern Europe* (Boston: Little, Brown, 1949), p. 5.

4. Ibid., p. 6.

5. Ibid., p. 87.

6. George Orwell, Review of *Scott-King's Modern Europe, New York Times Book Review,* February 20, 1949, p. 1.

7. J. L. Brierly, *The Law of Nations: An Introduction to the International Law of Peace,* 5th ed. (Oxford: Clarendon Press, 1955), pp. 25–26.

8. Hannah Arendt, *The Origins of Totalitarianism* (New York: Harcourt, Brace, 1951), p. vii.

9. "A friend came to see me on one of the evenings of the last week—he thinks it was on Monday, August 3. We were standing at a window of my room in

the Foreign Office. It was getting dusk, and the lamps were being lit in the space below on which we were looking. My friend recalls that I remarked on this with the words: 'The lamps are going out all over Europe; we shall not see them lit again in our life-time'"; Edward Grey, *Twenty-Five Years: 1892–1916*, vol. 2 (New York: Frederick A. Stokes, 1937), p. 20.

10. James Kent, *Commentaries on American Law*, vol. 1 (New York: O. Halsted, 1826), pp. 1–2.

11. William Pfaff, *Barbarian Sentiments: How the American Century Ends* (New York: Hill and Wang, 1989), p. 106.

12. Ibid., p. 107.

13. Ivan S. Turgenev, *Fathers and Sons*, trans. Bernard Guilbert Gurney (New York: Modern Library, 1961), pp. xii–xiii, 70–71.

14. Leopold Labedz, "Nihilism," in *The Harper Dictionary of Modern Thought*, ed. Alan Bullock and Stephen Trombley (New York: Harper & Row, 1988), p. 584.

15. Daniel Patrick Moynihan, "The 'New Science of Politics' Vindicated or The Founders Rediscovered" (Britannica Lecture, Woodrow Wilson Center, Smithsonian Institution, Washington, D.C., September 12, 1986).

16. "Bolshevism is not merely a political doctrine; it is also a religion, with elaborate dogmas and inspired scriptures. When Lenin wishes to prove some proposition, he does so, if possible, by quoting texts from Marx and Engels"; Bertrand Russell, *Bolshevism: Practice and Theory* (New York: Harcourt, Brace and Howe, 1920), p. 6.

17. John Dollard, "Guilt as a Political Motive" (Mimeograph, n.d.), pp. 25–26. In correspondence Mrs. Joan Dollard surmises that the date was 1975, which is my recollection. He sent it to me, as best I can recall, while I was at the United Nations. Although Dollard never published this essay, and might well have rejected it on further consideration, it is an important manuscript.

18. "The party grew rapidly. It doubled in the first three years of the Depression; it doubled again in the first two years of the New Deal; it almost doubled again in the following two years. And then for twelve years, from 1938 to 1950, the party was able to muster a membership of at least 50,000. Its power to recruit rose even more rapidly: 11,000 were brought into the party in 1931, 19,000 in 1932, 17,000 in 1933. And by the late thirties it could recruit 30,000 in a single year. (It lost almost as many—but that is another story.)"; Nathan Glazer, *The Social Basis of American Communism* (New York: Harcourt, Brace & World, 1961), pp. 90–91.

CHAPTER THREE: WILSON

1. "An Address to a Joint Session of Congress, April 2, 1917," in *The Papers of Woodrow Wilson*, ed. Arthur Link, 57 vols. to date (Princeton: Princeton University Press, 1966–), 41: 521 (cited hereafter as *Wilson Papers*).

2. Ibid., p. 520.

3. "I communicate to Congress certain documents, being a continuation of those heretofore laid before them on the subject of our affairs with Great Britain . . . British cruisers have been in the continued practice of violating the American flag on the great highway of nations, and of seizing and carrying off persons sailing under it, not in the exercise of a belligerent right founded on the law of nations against an enemy, but of a municipal prerogative over British subjects. British jurisdiction is thus extended to neutral vessels in a situation where no laws can operate but the law of nations and the laws of the country to which the vessels belong, and a self-redress is assumed which, if British subjects were wrongfully detained and alone concerned, is that substitution of force for a resort to the responsible sovereign which falls within the definition of war"; "Special Message to Congress," *The Writings of James Madison: 1808–1819*, ed. Gaillard Hunt, vol. 8 (New York: G. P. Putnam's Sons, 1908), pp. 192–193.

4. Wilson, "Address to Joint Session," p. 523.

5. "Wilson sought to add to the treaty provisions making Nicaragua an American protectorate, but the Senate rebuffed him while accepting the treaty's other features. Critics noted that the new administration was making Taft's dollar diplomacy more nearly resemble ten-cent diplomacy"; Louis W. Koenig, *Bryan: A Political Biography of William Jennings Bryan* (New York: G. P. Putnam's Sons, 1971), p. 515.

6. Wilson, "Address to Joint Session," pp. 526–527.

7. "Wilson and his secretary of state, William Jennings Bryan, began their foreign policy early in 1913 on a high note of idealism, which most Democrats and progressives in Congress applauded. Bryan quickly negotiated conciliation treaties with twenty-nine countries, providing for six-month or year-long cooling-off periods during which it was hoped that antagonisms would evaporate. Signatories agreed to refer disputes to investigatory commissions and to refrain from going to war or increasing armaments until after receiving the commissions' reports. 'No one except Bryan,' complained one of the dissidents, Senator Henry Ashurst, 'believes that his treaties will preserve the peace.' But, nevertheless, the Senate consented to ratify twenty of them"; Robert C. Byrd, *The Senate: 1789–1989, Addresses on the History of the United States Senate*, ed. Mary Sharon Hall, vol. 1 (Washington, D.C.: Government Printing Office, 1988), p. 414.

8. Koenig, *Bryan*, p. 503.

9. Ibid., p. 501.

10. Kenneth Waltz, *Man, the State, and War: A Theoretical Analysis* (New York: Columbia University Press, 1954).

11. Ruhl Bartlett, *The League to Enforce Peace* (Chapel Hill: University of North Carolina Press, 1944), p. 51.

12. Robert Lansing, *The Peace Negotiations: A Personal Narrative* (Boston: Houghton Mifflin, 1921), pp. 34, 37.

13. Ibid., pp. 44–45.

14. Waltz, *Man, the State, and War*, p. 113.

15. Lansing, *Peace Negotiations*, p. 135.
16. Theodore Roosevelt, "International Peace," Address before the Nobel Prize Committee, Christiania, Norway, May 5, 1910, Manuscript Division, Library of Congress, Washington, D.C. The prize was awarded to Roosevelt in 1907.
17. "An Address to a Joint Session of Congress, 8 Jan'y, 1918," *Wilson Papers*, 45:536–537.
18. Ibid., pp. 526–527.
19. Koenig, *Bryan*, p. 536.
20. Ibid., p. 538.
21. Robert Lansing, *War Memoirs of Robert Lansing* (New York: Bobbs-Merrill, 1935), p. 112.
22. Alvin M. Josephy, Jr., *The American Heritage History of the Congress of the United States* (New York: McGraw-Hill, 1975), p. 302.
23. Abrams et al. v. United States, 250 U.S. 616 (1919).
24. Byrd, *Senate*, p. 418.
25. Quoted in ibid., p. 414.
26. *The Federalist Papers*, ed. Clinton Rossiter (New York: New American Library, 1961), p. 452.
27. Edward S. Corwin, *The President: Office and Powers, 1787–1957* (New York: New York University Press, 1957), p. 171.
28. "Committee or Cabinet Government?" *Wilson Papers*, 2:617–619.
29. Ibid., p. 640.
30. "An Address in Philadelphia to Newly Naturalized Citizens, May 10, 1915," ibid., 33:149.
31. Woodrow Wilson to E. G. Conklin, in Ray Stannard Baker, *Woodrow Wilson: Life and Letters*, vol. 4 (New York: Greenwood Press, 1968), p. 55.
32. Abraham D. Sofaer, "Adjudication of the International Court of Justice: Progress through Realism," *Record of the Association of the Bar of the City of New York*, 44 (June 1989), 471.
33. Address at auditorium in St. Paul, Minnesota, September 9, 1919, *Addresses of President Wilson*, Senate Document no. 120, 66th Cong., 1st sess. (Washington, D.C.: Government Printing Office, 1919), p. 109.
34. Warren F. Kuehl, *Seeking World Order: The United States and International Organization to 1920* (Nashville: Vanderbilt University Press, 1969), p. 309.
35. William E. Leuchtenberg, Foreword to Byrd, *Senate*, pp. ix–xi.
36. Byrd, *Senate*, p. 423.
37. Ibid., p. 424.
38. *Congressional Record*, 66th Cong., 1st sess., p. 5112.
39. Ibid., p. 5113.
40. Wilson, *Addresses*, pp. 369–370.
41. Byrd, *Senate*, p. 427.
42. Herbert Hoover, *The Ordeal of Woodrow Wilson* (New York: McGraw-Hill, 1958), p. 300.

43. Colin Rowe and Fred Koetter, *College City* (Cambridge, Mass.: MIT Press, 1978), p. 4.
44. Address to crowd outside house in S Street, November 11, 1923, Papers of President Wilson, reel 478, series 7A, box 15, Manuscript Division, Library of Congress.

CHAPTER FOUR: ROOSEVELT

1. "Instructions of Prince Bismarck to the German Ambassadors and Ministers, 8 February 1890, Inviting the Powers to a Conference at Berlin, March 1890," quoted in *The Origins of the International Labor Organization*, ed. James T. Shotwell, vol. 1 (New York: Columbia University Press, 1934), pp. 470–471.
2. "Resolutions of the International Conference on Labor Legislation, Berlin, 29, March 1890," in ibid., pp. 472–475.
3. Sir Malcolm Delevingne, "The Pre-War History of International Labor Legislation," in ibid., p. 36.
4. *Congressional Record*, 66th Cong., 1st sess., vol. 58, pt. 9, pp. 8703, 8718–19.
5. Woodrow Wilson to Royal Meeker, July 19, 1919, Wilson Papers, Library of Congress.
6. Congressional colloquy: *Congressional Record*, 66th Cong., 1st sess., vol. 58, pt. 4, p. 3584; Joint resolution and Wilson note quoted in Daniel Patrick Moynihan, "The United States and the International Labor Organization, 1889–1934" (Ph.D. diss., Fletcher School of Law and Diplomacy, Tufts University), pp. 296, 298.
7. This incident is recounted in an unpublished manuscript on which Sir Harold Butler was working at the time of his death in 1951 (cited hereafter as Butler MS). Titled "American Initiation," it was intended to be the first chapter of the second volume of his memoirs.
8. Woodrow Wilson, "Speech at Des Moines, September 6, 1919," in *Senate Documents*, 66th Cong., 1st sess., vol. 11 (Washington, D.C.: Government Printing Office, 1920), p. 61.
9. *New York Times*, September 19, 1919.
10. Quoted in Moynihan, "Organization," p. 308.
11. Butler MS, in ibid., p. 309.
12. Ibid., p. 310.
13. Ibid., pp. 311–312. (This dinner probably took place between October 8 and 18, 1919.)
14. Quoted in ibid., pp. 575–576.
15. Ibid., p. 577.
16. Ibid.
17. Ibid.
18. Ibid.
19. *Manchester Guardian*, June 23, 1934.

20. *New York Times,* June 18, 1934.
21. W. Cole, *Roosevelt and the Isolationists* (Lincoln: University of Nebraska, 1981), p. 123.
22. Robert D. Schulzinger, *The Wise Men of Foreign Affairs: The History of the Council on Foreign Relations* (New York: Columbia University Press, 1984), p. 93.
23. Richard H. Rovere, *The American Establishment and Other Reports, Opinions, and Speculations* (New York: Harcourt, Brace & World, 1962), p. 8.
24. Outrage at the perceived contumely of the Morgan banks was one of few unifying forces in American life in the 1930s. It was a doctrine shared across the spectrum of sophistication, or of self-delusion, as you like. Richard Rovere tells of the consequence of reviewing Walter Lippmann's 1956 book, *The Public Philosophy*: "One day, soon after the review was published, I met . . . Edmund Wilson in the corridor outside my office. He stopped me and said he had been terribly disappointed by my review. Assuming he had read the book and liked it better than I had, I asked him what he himself had liked in it. He said he hadn't read it, but had been put off by my general praise of Lippmann. I said that I admired the man very much, particularly in his latest phase, when he was bedeviling Eisenhower and Dulles for their foreign policy. 'Have you been reading him lately, Mr. Wilson?' I asked . . . 'I haven't read him since 1926, when I discovered that he was an agent of the House of Morgan'"; Richard H. Rovere, "Walter Lippmann," *American Scholar,* 44 (Autumn 1975), 596.
25. "Opinion of the Attorney General," August 27, 1940, in *Documents on American Foreign Relations,* ed. S. Shepard Jones and Denys P. Myers, vol. 3 (Boston: World Peace Foundation, 1941), p. 207. The "comma that saved a kingdom" did not go unnoticed at the time. Several critical analyses of the attorney general's opinion appeared in the *American Journal of International Law,* 34 (1940), 680–697.
26. Franklin D. Roosevelt, "Peace, like War, Can Succeed Only Where There Is a Will to Enforce It, and Where There Is Available Power to Enforce It," Radio address at the Foreign Policy Association, New York City, October 21, 1944, in *Public Papers of Franklin D. Roosevelt,* ed. Samuel Rosenman, 1944–45 (New York: Harper & Bros., 1950), pp. 345, 351, 353.
27. Ibid., p. 350.
28. Text of fourth draft, Roosevelt Library, Hyde Park, N.Y.
29. Memorandum from Edward R. Stettinius, Jr., to President Roosevelt, "Public Opinion on International Organization," October 19, 1944, National Archives, Washington, D.C.
30. "Organization for Peace and Security," in *Foreign Relations of the United States, Diplomatic Papers,* 79th Cong., 1st sess., House Document no. 303, pt. 1, vol. 1: *1944* (Washington, D.C.: Government Printing Office, 1966), p. 661.
31. Cordell Hull, *The Memoirs of Cordell Hull,* vol. 2 (New York: Macmillan, 1948), p. 1665.
32. Ruth B. Russell, *A History of the United Nations Charter: The Role of the*

United States, 1940–1945 (Washington, D.C.: Brookings Institution, 1958), p. 264.

33. *Congressional Record,* 78th Cong., 2d sess., vol. 90, pt. 6, pp. 7920–21.
34. October 11, 1944, p. 8.
35. Memorandum from Edward R. Stettinius, Jr., to President Roosevelt, October 13, 1944, file PSF, Dumbarton Oaks folder, pp. 3–44, National Archives.
36. Duff Cooper, *Old Men Forget: An Autobiography of Duff Cooper (Viscount Norwich)* (London: Century, 1986), pp. 269–270.

CHAPTER FIVE: "BIG WHITE SPACE"

1. Mikhail Gorbachev, "U.S.S.R. Arms Reduction, Rivalry into Sensible Competition," Speech delivered before the United Nations on December 7, 1988; reprinted in translation in *Vital Speeches of the Day,* 55 (February 1, 1989), 229–236.
2. "Soviet Foreign Minister Speaks at UNESCO," *Newsletter of Americans for the Universality of UNESCO,* 5 (January 1989), 14.
3. William Pfaff, *Barbarian Sentiments: How the American Century Ends* (New York: Hill and Wang, 1989), p. 124.
4. Francis Fukuyama, "The End of History?" *National Interest,* no. 16 (Summer 1989), 3 and 13.
5. Seymour Martin Lipset, "The End of Ideology and the Ideology of the Intellectuals," in *Culture and Its Creators: Four Essays in Honor of Edward Shils,* ed. Joseph Ben-David and Terry Nichols Clark (Chicago: Chicago University Press, 1977), pp. 15–42.
6. Quoted in ibid., p. 19.
7. See Daniel Patrick Moynihan, "Peace," in *Coping: On the Practice of Government* (New York: Random House, 1975), p. 420.
8. Robert Warshow, "The Legacy of the 30's: Middle-Class Mass Culture and the Intellectuals' Problem," *Commentary,* 4 (December 1947), 538.
9. Norman Podhoretz, *Making It* (New York: Random House, 1967), p. 319.
10. Daniel Bell, *The End of Ideology: On the Exhaustion of Political Ideas in the Fifties* (1960; reprint, Cambridge, Mass.: Harvard University Press, 1988), p. 404.
11. Mostafa Rejai, W. L. Mason, and D. C. Beller, "Empirical Relevance of the Hypothesis of Decline," in *Decline of Ideology?* ed. Mostafa Rejai (Chicago: Aldine/Atherton, 1971), p. 275.
12. Seweryn Bialer, *The Soviet Paradox: External Expansion, Internal Decline* (New York: Vintage Books, 1986), p. 263.
13. Nikita S. Khrushchev, "Speech in Tbilisi, February 7, 1961," *Notes: Soviet Affairs,* no. 252 (May 5, 1961), 46.
14. "Khrushchev Out, Brezhnev and Kosygin Appointed," *Current Digest of the Soviet Press,* 16 (October 28, 1964), 5.

15. Vadim Zagladin, International Department, Soviet Central Committee, conversation with the author, Moscow.

16. Correspondence from Assistant Secretary of State Janet G. Mullins to Senator Lloyd Bentsen, December 18, 1989, enclosing Secretary of State James Baker's responses to questions submitted by Senator Daniel Patrick Moynihan, Senate Committee on Finance, Washington, D.C.

17. Murray Feshbach, testimony before a joint hearing of the Subcommittee on Economic Goals and Intergovernmental Policy of the Joint Economic Committee and the House Subcommittee on Europe and the Middle East of the Committee on Foreign Affairs, *The Political Economy of the Soviet Union,* 98th Cong., 1st sess., September 29, 1983, S. Hrg. 98–691 (Washington, D.C.: Government Printing Office, 1984), pp. 88–162.

18. William Pfaff to Daniel Patrick Moynihan, September 27, 1989.

19. Leon Wieseltier, "Spoilers at the Party," *National Interest,* no. 17 (Fall 1989), 12.

20. See Daniel Patrick Moynihan, "The 'New Science of Politics' and the Old Art of Governing," in *Came the Revolution: Argument in the Reagan Era* (New York: Harcourt Brace Jovanovich, 1988), p. 301.

21. Bert Horwitz to Daniel Patrick Moynihan, August 16, 1989.

22. Hannah Arendt, *The Origins of Totalitarianism* (New York: Meridian Books, 1958), p. 510.

23. Gorbachev, "U.S.S.R. Arms Reduction," p. 234.

24. Quoted in Rudolf L. Tokes, "A Talk with Hungary's Imre Pozgay," *New Leader,* June 12–26, 1989, p. 9.

25. Robert Conquest, *Tyrants and Typewriters: Communiqués from the Struggle for Truth* (Lexington, Mass.: Lexington Books, 1989), p. xii.

26. Melor G. Sturua, *New York Times,* August 5, 1989, p. A24.

27. Foreign Broadcast Information Service, Soviet Union, June 2, 1989, pp. 21–22.

28. The text of the various agreements is reproduced in the *Congressional Record,* May 18, 1989, vol. 135, no. 64, daily ed., unbound, pp. S5587–94.

29. *New York Times,* August 25, 1989, p. A1.

30. *New York Times,* August 20, 1989, sec. 4, p. 1.

31. Franklin D. Roosevelt, "Peace, like War, Can Succeed Only When There Is a Will to Enforce It, and When There Is Available Power to Enforce It," Radio address at the Foreign Policy Association, New York City, October 21, 1944, in *Public Papers of Franklin D. Roosevelt,* ed. Samuel Rosenman, *1944–1945* (New York: Harper and Brothers, 1950), p. 344.

32. George F. Kennan, "The Sources of Soviet Conduct," *Foreign Affairs,* 25 (July 1947), 566–582.

33. *New York Times,* January 1, 1980, p. A1.

34. *Washington Post,* February 26, 1988.

35. Fukuyama, "The End of History?" p. 13.

36. Gorbachev, "U.S.S.R. Arms Reduction," p. 231. In February 1990 Gorbachev went further, stating: "We should abandon the ideological dogmatism that became ingrained during past decades, outdated stereotypes in

domestic policy and outmoded views on the world revolutionary process . . .
We should abandon everything that led to the isolation of socialist countries
from the mainstream of world civilization"; quoted in *New York Times,*
February 6, 1990, p. A16.

CHAPTER SIX: *"PACTA SUNT SERVANDA!"*

1. Abraham D. Sofaer, "Adjudication in the International Court of Justice:
   Progress through Realism," *Record of the Association of the Bar of the City
   of New York,* 44 (June 1989), 475.
2. Mikhail Gorbachev, "U.S.S.R. Arms Reduction: Rivalry into Sensible Competition," Speech delivered before the United Nations on December 7, 1988;
   reprinted in translation in *Vital Speeches of the Day,* 55 (February 1, 1989),
   234.
3. Ibid., p. 233.
4. Ibid.
5. Richard Gardner, "Superpower Cooperation in the UN: Dream or Reality?"
   Freedom at Issue, November/December 1989, p. 19.
6. Woodrow Wilson, "Address at Luncheon, Palace Hotel, San Francisco,
   Calif., September 18, 1919," in *Addresses of President Wilson,* Senate Document no. 120, 66th Cong., 1st sess. (Washington, D.C.: Government
   Printing Office, 1919), p. 250.
7. Frederick E. Schortemeier, ed., *Rededicating America: Life and Recent
   Speeches of Warren G. Harding* (Indianapolis: Bobbs-Merrill, 1920), p. 226.
8. Melvin Small and J. David Singer, *Resort to Arms* (Beverly Hills: Sage Pub-
   lications, 1982), pp. 50–69.
9. See Zeev Maoz and Nasrin Abdolali, "Regime Types and International Conflict, 1816–1976," *Journal of Conflict Resolution,* 33 (March 1989), 3–35.
10. Michael Doyle, "Kant, Liberal Legacies, and Foreign Affairs," pts. 1 and 2,
    Philosophy and Public Affairs, 12 (Summer and Fall 1983), 204–235, 322–
    353.
11. Warner R. Schilling to Daniel Patrick Moynihan, August 24, 1989.
12. John Mueller, *Retreat from Doomsday: The Obsolescence of Major War*
    (New York: Basic Books, 1988), p. 245.
13. Thucydides, *The Peloponnesian War,* trans. Richard Crawley (New York,
    Modern Library, 1982), pp. 351–353.
14. Daniel Patrick Moynihan, *Counting Our Blessings: Reflections on the Future
    of America* (Boston: Little, Brown, 1980), p. 19.
15. Samuel Huntington notes that, although critics claim that the presence of a
    United States military base "demonstrates the subservience of the local gov-
    ernment to U.S. wishes," in fact the opposite is true: "the base and the price
    paid for it are evidence of the autonomy of those governments"; Samuel P.
    Huntington, "Transnational Organizations in World Politics," *World Poli-
    tics,* 25 (April 1973), 356.

16. Raymond Gastil, *Freedom in the World—Political Rights and Civil Liberties, 1988–1989* (New York: Freedom House, 1989).

17. Central Intelligence Agency, *Handbook of Economic Statistics* (Washington, D.C.: Government Printing Office, 1989).

18. Wilson, "Address at Coliseum, St. Louis, Mo., September 5, 1919," in *The Papers of Woodrow Wilson,* ed. Arthur Link, vol. 63 (Princeton: Princeton University Press, 1990), p. 46.

19. Ibid., pp. 46–47.

20. Conversation with the author.

21. Charter of the United Nations, Chapter VII, Article 39.

22. Robert C. Byrd, *The Senate, 1789–1989: Addresses on the History of the United States Senate,* ed. Mary Sharon Hall, vol. 1 (Washington, D.C.: Government Printing Office, 1988), p. 560.

23. Ibid., p. 561.

24. Dean Acheson, "We Can Only Help Where We Are Wanted," *Vital Speeches of the Day,* 16 (February 1, 1950), 238.

25. Byrd, *Senate,* p. 555.

26. "Creation of a United Nations Emergency Force: Resolution 1000 (ES-1)," adopted by the United Nations General Assembly on November 5, 1956, in United Nations General Assembly, *Official Records, First Emergency Special Session,* Supplement No. 1, Doc. A-3354, pp. 2–3; reprinted in U.S. Senate Committee on Foreign Relations, *A Select Chronology and Background Documents Relating to the Middle East* (Washington, D.C.: Government Printing Office, 1975), p. 206.

27. UN Participation Act of 1945; 22 U.S.C.A., sec. 287d.

28. "Arming the United Nations," *U.S. Department of State Bulletin,* 17, no. 422A (August 3, 1947), 239.

29. Constitution of U.S.S.R., 1936, Chapter II, Article 18a. Each republic had the right to enter into "direct relations with foreign states and to conclude agreements and exchange diplomatic and consular representatives."

30. The ability to completely eradicate another nation is not, however, unique in history. In 146 B.C. the Romans celebrated their victory in the Third Punic War by obliterating Carthage. Sadly, history records many attempts to achieve what has since been known as "a Carthaginian peace."

31. It is indicative of the expectations of 1947 that Article 51 of the Indian constitution, adopted that year, instructed Indian officials to strive to "foster respect for international law and treaty obligations" and to "encourage settlement of international disputes by arbitration." Fourteen years later India would, nonetheless, flagrantly violate international law and its treaty obligations under the Charter and eschew arbitration in favor of force.

32. Robert H. Jackson, *The Supreme Court in the American System of Government* (London: Oxford University Press, 1955), pp. 6–7.

33. "Condemnation of Soviet Interference in Hungary: Resolution 1131 (XI)," adopted by the United Nations General Assembly, December 12, 1956;

reprinted in *American Foreign Policy: Current Documents,* Document 148 (Washington, D.C.: Department of State, 1959), p. 487.

34. *Congressional Record,* November 20, 1979, 96th Cong., 1st sess., vol. 125, pt. 25, p. S33401.

35. Edward Luttwak writes that command and control over the mission were so divided that a disaster was virtually inevitable. He reports that "British, French and Israeli commando experts were astonished" by the division of responsibility; *The Pentagon and the Art of War* (New York: Simon & Schuster, 1985), pp. 44–45.

36. "Case concerning United States Diplomatic and Consular Staff in Tehran" (United States v. Iran), International Court of Justice, May 24, 1980, reproduced in *International Legal Materials,* 19 (May 1980), 44, 52.

CHAPTER SEVEN: A NORMLESS NORMALCY?

1. Theodore Draper, "Getting Irangate Straight," *New York Review of Books,* October 8, 1987, p. 47.

2. Daniel Patrick Moynihan, "Democratic Response," Radio broadcast following President Reagan's broadcast of November 29, 1986.

3. Louis Henkin, "Use of Force: Law and U.S. Policy," in Council on Foreign Relations, *Right v. Might: International Law and the Use of Force* (New York, 1989), p. 53.

4. Ibid., p. 54.

5. Remarks to the students, faculty, and guests of the National Defense University, and the signing of the Department of Veterans Affairs Act, October 25, 1988, *Weekly Compilation of Presidential Documents,* 24, no. 43 (October 31, 1988), p. 1368.

   Somewhat earlier William R. Bode, the special assistant to the under secretary of state for security assistance, science, and technology in the Reagan administration, offered a synopsis of the doctrine in "The Reagan Doctrine," *Strategic Review,* Winter 1986, pp. 21–29: "A 'Reagan Doctrine' has evolved in pace with a remarkable phenomenon of global dimensions: the spontaneous combustion of resistance to direct and surrogate prongs of the Soviet Union's expansion in such disparate regions as Asia, Africa and Central America. The Doctrine, as an expression of American values, calls for support, in various forms, to those forces of resistance. On a global scale, it seeks not only to fend against the time-honored and recently accelerating Soviet strategy in the developing world, aimed at outflanking the centers of capitalist power, but to exploit the vulnerabilities opening in the Soviet strategy in order to turn the offensive back" (p. 21).

6. Jeane J. Kirkpatrick, "Why We Don't Become Republicans," *Common Sense,* 2, no. 3 (1979), 27–35.

7. Quoted in Daniel Patrick Moynihan, *Loyalties* (New York: Harcourt Brace Jovanovich, 1984), p. 85.

8. Lech Walesa, "Address to a Joint Session of Congress," *Congressional*

Record, November 15, 1989, 101st Cong., 1st sess., p. H8633 (unbound daily edition).

9. Daniel Patrick Moynihan, Commencement address at New York University, May 24, 1984; reprinted in idem, *Came the Revolution: Argument in the Reagan Era* (New York: Harcourt Brace Jovanovich, 1988), p. 190.

10. Ronald Reagan, "Remarks at the Annual Convention of the National Convention of the National Association of Evangelicals," in *Public Papers of the Presidents, Ronald Reagan, 1983, Book I* (Washington, D.C.: Government Printing Office, 1984), p. 364.

11. Arthur S. Banks et al., eds., *Political Handbook of the World: 1982–1983* (New York: McGraw-Hill, 1983), p. 189.

12. Ronald Reagan, "Remarks at Bridgetown, Barbados, following a Luncheon Meeting with Leaders of Eastern Caribbean Countries," in *Public Papers of the Presidents, Ronald Reagan, 1982, Book I* (Washington, D.C.: Government Printing Office, 1983), p. 448.

13. Henkin, "Use of Force," p. 56.

14. Two special committees—the Impeachment Trial Committee and the Special Committee on Investigations—have a similar arrangement.

15. Eric Sevareid, transcript of speech accepting the Fourth Estate Award, National Press Club, Washington, D.C., March 6, 1984, p. 3.

16. Transcript from CBS News, "Face the Nation," October 30, 1983, pp. 11–14.

17. *Washington Post,* March 30, 1984, p. A17.

18. Quoted in Joseph Frazier Wall, *Andrew Carnegie* (New York: Oxford University Press, 1970), p. 898.

19. Charles Krauthammer, "The Curse of Legalism," *New Republic,* November 6, 1989, p. 50.

20. John Norton Moore, "Law and National Security," *Foreign Affairs,* 51 (January 1973), 415.

21. Alfred P. Rubin to Daniel Patrick Moynihan, November 13, 1989.

22. Quoted in Arthur M. Schlesinger, Jr., *The Imperial Presidency* (Boston: Houghton Mifflin, 1973), p. 25.

23. Quoted in Henkin, "Use of Force," p. 45.

24. Peter Finley Dunne, "Cuba vs. Beet Sugar," in *Observations by Mr. Dooley* (New York: Harper and Bros., 1906), p. 94; William Graham Sumner, "The Conquest of the United States by Spain," in *The Conquest of the United States by Spain and Other Essays,* ed. Murray Polner (Chicago: Henry Regnery, n.d.), pp. 139–173.

25. Jeane J. Kirkpatrick, "Law and Reciprocity," *Proceedings of the 78th Annual Meeting, American Society of International Law* (Washington, D.C., 1984), p. 67. The reference was to Justice Robert H. Jackson's decision in Torminiello v. Chicago, in which he held: "There is danger that, if the Court does not temper its doctrinaire logic with a little practical wisdom, it will convert the constitutional Bill of Rights into a suicide pact"; 337 U.S. 1, 37 (1949). The subject, however, was rigidity in applying the law rather than

the existence thereof. Jackson, of course, was the American member of the international military tribunal convened at Nuremberg, Germany, in 1945. In his opening address he declared: "The first trial in history for crimes against the peace of the world imposes a grave responsibility. The wrongs which we seek to condemn and punish have been so calculated, so malignant and so devastating that civilization cannot tolerate their being ignored because it cannot survive their being repeated"; Robert H. Jackson, "Opening Address," in *Trial of German War Criminals*, Senate Doc. no. 129, 79th Cong., 1st sess. (Washington, D.C.: Government Printing Office, 1946), p. 1. The distance from Jackson's address to Kirkpatrick's suggests the turbulence that the cold war brought to the liberal Democratic tradition in American politics.

26. Stuart Taylor, "Mrs. Kirkpatrick Chides Latin Critics," *New York Times*, April 13, 1984, p. A3.

27. Kirkpatrick, "Law and Reciprocity," pp. 65, 67.

28. Transcript, nomination hearing for Donald Phinney Gregg as ambassador to the Republic of Korea, Committee on Foreign Relations, U.S. Senate, May 12, 1989, pp. 90–93, 152.

29. Hyman G. Rickover, *How the Battleship Maine Was Destroyed* (Washington, D.C.: Government Printing Office, 1976), p. 104. The conclusion of the 1898 court of inquiry is quoted in ibid., p. 70.

30. Transcript, nomination hearing for Gregg, p. 153.

31. *Congressional Record*, vol. 129, no. 161, pt. 2, November 18, 1983, 98th Cong., 1st sess., p. S-16859.

32. Bob Woodward, *Veil: The Secret Wars of the CIA, 1981–1987* (New York: Simon and Schuster, 1987), p. 136.

33. *Washington Post*, April 16, 1989, p. B1.

34. David Rogers and David Ignatius, "The Contra Fight," *Wall Street Journal*, March 6, 1985, p. A20.

35. Quoted in Moynihan, *Came the Revolution*, pp. 178–179.

36. *Washington Times*, April 13, 1984, p. 1.

37. Robert R. Simmons to Daniel Patrick Moynihan, October 13, 1988.

38. "The Real Intelligence Failure," *New York Times*, April 18, 1984. My notes from this period record a friend in the White House calling to warn that the word previously being passed from there was that Goldwater was "senile" and I was "lying." Journalists might usefully inquire into the event. Were there persons in the Reagan administration shrewd enough to calculate that a "liberal" press would collaborate in discrediting Barry Goldwater? That Safire would give the attack conservative cover? It had come to this in Washington.

For the record, the following exchange took place in the Iran-Contra hearings between Senator Paul S. Sarbanes of Maryland and McFarlane on May 12, 1987 (Transcript of Joint Hearings before the Iran-Contra Committees, Testimony of Robert McFarlane, p. 157):

MR. SARBANES: Did you know about the mining of the Nicaraguan harbor?

MR. MCFARLANE: Yes, sir.

MR. SARBANES: Did you think that should have been consulted with the Intelligence Committees?

MR. MCFARLANE: Yes, sir.

MR. SARBANES: It wasn't done.

MR. MCFARLANE: No, sir.

McFarlane, a victim in his own right, later pleaded guilty to criminal charges arising from these and subsequent events.

As is known, Director Casey later apologized to the Senate Intelligence Committee for earlier statements that he had kept us properly informed. Was this simply more deception? I don't believe so. On April 26 Mr. Casey came to my office in the Russell Senate Office Building to offer, in his words, "my apologies," "mea culpas." He agreed with me that he had broken the law. The Intelligence Oversight Act, that is; he had no interest in treaty law. I grant the awkwardness of citing the words of a dead man; but they do not do Mr. Casey discredit. To the contrary, as I see it they bespeak the confusion that attends the dismissal—an institutional dismissal—of international law as a point of reference.

39. Minutes of the National Security Planning Group, June 25, 1984, reprinted in *Congressional Record,* July 17, 1989, 101st Cong., 1st sess., p. S-8028 (unbound daily edition).

40. Ibid.

41. Louis Fisher has written in "How Tightly Can Congress Draw the Purse Strings?" *American Journal of International Law,* 83 (October 1989), 764–765: "If President Reagan had defied the Boland amendment by seeking financial or other assistance from foreign countries or private individuals, at a minimum this would have subjected the United States to ridicule and humiliation. Having been rebuffed by Congress, the President would go, hat in hand, to foreign governments and private citizens for assistance in implementing the administration's foreign policy. Such conduct would risk a major collision with Congress, with the President acting in the face of a congressional policy enacted into law. In such circumstances, I believe a President would invite, and deserve, impeachment proceedings. He would fail in his constitutional duty to see that the laws are faithfully executed, and he would precipitate a constitutional crisis by merging the power of the sword with the power of the purse."

42. Reprinted in Lori Fisler Damrosch, ed., *The International Court of Justice at a Crossroads* (Dobbs Ferry, N.Y.: Transnational Publishers, 1987), p. 471.

43. "International Court of Justice," Senate Report No. 1835, Committee on Foreign Relations, July 25, 1946, 79th Cong., 2d sess., p. 5.

44. The Connally Reservation so restricted the United States' acceptance that Sir Hersch Lauterpacht maintained that the United States had *not* accepted

compulsory jurisdiction; Switzerland v. United States, 1959 I.C.J. 6, pp. 116–117 (dissenting opinion of Judge Lauterpacht).

45. Declaration of the United States of America under Article 36(2) of the I.C.J. Statute, August 26, 1946, reprinted in Damrosch, *The International Court,* p. 469.

46. Thomas M. Franck and Jerome M. Lehrman, "Messianism and Chauvinism in America's Commitment to Peace through Law," in Damrosch, *The International Court,* pp. 5–6.

47. Declaration reprinted in ibid., p. 473.

48. Notice reprinted in ibid., p. 477.

49. Committee on International Law, Association of the Bar of the City of New York, "Report on the U.S. Withdrawal from the Compulsory Jurisdiction of the World Court," November 21, 1985.

50. This was the celebrated "assassination manual," *Operaciones sicologicas en querra de guerrillas,* prepared by the CIA for use by the Contras. It has a painful history. Early in the Vietnam War, during the Kennedy administration, Americans began to be impressed by the effectiveness of the Viet Cong in winning over villagers. How was this done? In time a good deal was learned about their political techniques, which were quite disciplined and routinized. One routine was to choose a landowner or someone such, accuse him of being an enemy of the people, hold a trial, take a vote . . . Fire! Thereafter the villagers were implicated with the guerrillas. The thought had been that American forces might emulate their adversaries; on further thought this did not seem wise. At minimum some G.I. was going to write home: "Dear Mom, we shot another Mayor today . . ."

However, the army commenced to teach the subject at the Special Warfare School at Fort Bragg, North Carolina. The CIA now decided to practice it. Materials from there were now translated into a manual for use by the Contras. It is a strange affair; almost *naif.* Peasant soldiers in the Honduran jungle, for the most part illiterate, are asked to ponder the following: "Oratory is a quality so tied to political leadership that it can be said that the history of political orators is the political history of humanity, an affirmation upheld by names such as Cicero, Demosthenes, Danton, Mirabeau, Robespierre, Clemenceau, Lenin, Trotsky, Mussolini, Hitler, Roosevelt, etc." They are instructed in rhetoric: "Appraisal or Argumentation: Arguments are presented, EXACTLY IN THIS ORDER: First, the negative arguments, or against the thesis that is going to be upheld . . ." Given hints on diction, tips on approaches: "As far as possible, it is recommended that all speeches be based on syllogism." Even so, it proposed a lot of "Selective Use of Violence for Propagandistic Effects." Aryeh Neier, sometime professor of law at New York University, has detailed the ways in which the manual violated, for example, Common Article 3 of the Geneva Conventions; "The Legal Implications of the CIA's Nicaragua Manual," in *Psychological Operations in Guerrilla Warfare* (New York: Vintage Press), pp. 99–124.

51. Henkin, "Use of Force," p. 55.

52. Quoted in Moynihan, *Came the Revolution*, p. 176.
53. Edwin M. Yoder, Jr., "... And a President Who Fell Short," *Washington Post*, March 3, 1987, p. A23.
54. Meg Greenfield, "Assessing the Damage," *Newsweek*, March 9, 1987, p. 76.
55. Quoted in Moynihan, *Came the Revolution*, p. 328.
56. James Reston, "The State of the Union," *New York Times*, January 18, 1987, sec. 4, p. 29.
57. As of June 1989 the Department of State had logged some 893 treaties and 5,117 other international agreements in force.
58. L. F. E. Goldie, Review of Moynihan, *Loyalties*, *Syracuse Journal of International Law and Commerce*, 2 (Summer 1984), 184–185.
59. Matthew Nimitz, "Respect World Law," *New York Times*, April 19, 1984, p. A19.
60. As Hilaire Belloc's jingle proclaimed: "Whatever happens / we have got / the Maxim gun / and they have not."
61. Testimony of George F. Kennan, "The Future of U.S.-Soviet Relations," Hearings before the Committee on Foreign Relations, U.S. Senate, 101st Cong., 1st sess., April 4, 12, 19; May 3, 15, 18; and June 1, 20, 1989 (Washington, D.C.: Government Printing Office, 1990), pp. 13, 28.
62. Mikhail Gorbachev, "The Reality and Guarantees of a Secure World," Foreign Broadcast Information Service, *Daily Report: Soviet Union*, September 17, 1987, p. 27.
63. *New York Times*, October 8, 1989, p. A4.
64. "Soviet Foreign Minister Speaks at UNESCO," *Americans for Universality of UNESCO*, 5 (January 1989), 3, 15.
65. Ibid.; Mikhail Gorbachev, "Speech to Council of Europe," Foreign Broadcast Information Service, *Daily Report: Soviet Union*, July 7, 1989, p. 29.
66. Gorbachev, "Speech to Council of Europe," p. 34.
67. "Soviet Workers Arise," *Wall Street Journal*, July 21, 1989, p. A14.
68. *New York Times*, September 20, 1983, p. A1.
69. "I think the gentleman who spoke the other day had the hearty approval of most people in America in his suggestion that we weren't asking anyone to leave, but if they chose to leave, goodby"; "Appointment of Richard Herbert Pierce as a Member of the Commission on Presidential Scholars, September 21, 1983," in *Public Papers of the Presidents, Ronald Reagan, 1983, Book II* (Washington, D.C.: Government Printing Office, 1985), p. 1325.
70. Ronald Reagan, "Address before the 43rd Session of the United Nations General Assembly on September 26, 1988," *Weekly Compilation of Presidential Documents: October 8, 1988*, vol. 24, no. 39 (Washington, D.C.: Government Printing Office, 1988), p. 1206.
71. The Bush administration promptly disengaged from Nicaragua but could not keep its hands off Panama. What with all those underemployed, Spanish-speaking agents. But when yet another coup failed in the autumn of 1989, the political public wanted to know why the president had not done more.

The *Washington Post* offered a refreshing comment on October 10, 1989: "We have a question: When did it become not just acceptable, but downright fashionable for political observers of every stripe in this country to call for the United States to help in the military overthrow of the ruler of another country and to lament to high heaven our government's failure to (we use the critics' own preferred phrase) 'get rid' of him? We don't know the answer, but it wasn't just this past week that the phenomenon occurred, without so much as an embarrassed footnote or explanation on the part of those— liberals mostly—who have spent so much of the past two decades arguing against this kind of American military intervention in the affairs of other countries. Since the later days of the Reagan administration—and never mind the criticism of moves against the rulers of Libya, Grenada, Nicaragua, et al.—it has somehow been allowed to pass without noticeable comment, let alone complaint, that suddenly the U.S. government was easily and publicly announcing not just its wish that Gen. Manuel Noriega would be deposed by his countrymen but its own disposition to help out."

72. *New York Times,* October 8, 1989, p. A4.

73. U.S. Government, *amicus curiae* brief, June 6, 1980, filed in Filartiga v. Pena-Irala, 630 F. 2d 876 (2d Cir. 1980), reproduced in Marian Nash Leich, *Digest of United States Practice in International Law, 1980* (Washington, D.C.: Government Printing Office, 1986), p. 254.

74. Frank Stone, *Canada, the GATT and the International Trade System* (Montreal: Institute for Research on Public Policy, 1987), p. 18.

75. Robert S. McNamara, *Out of the Cold* (New York: Simon and Schuster, 1989), p. 157.

76. Walker Connor, *Mexican Americans in Comparative Perspective* (Washington, D.C.: Urban Institute, 1985), p. 2.

77. Donald L. Horowitz, *Ethnic Groups in Conflict* (Berkeley: University of California Press, 1985).

78. Nathan Glazer and Daniel Patrick Moynihan, "Ethnicity," in *The Harper Dictionary of Modern Thought,* ed. Alan Bullock (New York: Harper and Row, 1988), p. 286.

79. *Washington Post,* September 11, 1989, p. A1; *New York Times,* September 26, 1989, p. A3; ibid., September 24, 1989, p. A5; *Washington Post,* October 2, 1989, p. A23.

80. *Washington Post,* February 28, 1989, p. A18; *New York Times,* July 11, 1989, p. A3.

81. 7 U.N.T.S. 277 (1951).

82. G.A. Res. 217 (1948); U.N. Doc. A/811, art. 16(3).

83. 993 U.N.T.S. 3, art. 8(1)(c) (1976).

84. 999 U.N.T.S. 171, art. 27 (1976).

85. *International Legal Materials,* 14 (1975), 1292.

86. Meg Greenfield, "Needed: A New Compass," *Washington Post,* September 26, 1989, p. A28.

87. Freedom House ranks nations for "political freedoms" on a seven-

point scale, with 7 being the worst and 1 being, essentially, the Netherlands. Fifty-one of the members of the Non-Aligned Movement rank in the worst two categories (7 and 6). An overwhelming 70 of the 100 members are in the worst three. Raymond D. Gastil, *Freedom in the World: Political Rights and Civil Liberties, 1988–1989* (New York: Freedom House, 1989).

88. Declaration of the Ninth Conference of Heads of State or Government of Non-Aligned Countries, Belgrade, September 7, 1989, paras. 6, 10, 16 (pp. 2, 3, 5).

89. G.A. Res. 3379 (1975), in UNGA *Official Records: 30th Session,* suppl. 34 (Doc. A-10034), pp. 83–84.

90. *New York Times,* December 10, 1948, p. 6.

91. Declaration of the Seventh Conference of Heads of State or Government of Non-Aligned Countries, New Delhi, March 1983, para. 101(d), p. 23.

92. *New York Times,* December 19, 1989, p. A27.

93. George Bush, "Outlines of a New World Freedom," address before the 44th Session of the UN General Assembly, September 25, 1989, in *Current Policy,* no. 1207 (Washington, D.C.: U.S. Department of State, 1989), p. 2.

94. *New York Times,* October 14, 1989, p. A1.

95. Ibid., p. A6.

96. Testimony by William P. Barr, Assistant Attorney General, U.S. Department of Justice, "On the Legality as a Matter of Domestic Law of Extraterritorial Law Enforcement Activities That Depart from International Law," Subcommittee on Civil and Constitutional Rights of the Committee on the Judiciary, U.S. House of Representatives, 101st Cong., 1st sess., November 8, 1989, pp. 1–14.

97. Ibid., p. 2.

98. Ibid., pp. 4–5, citing The Schooner Exchange v. M'Faddon, 11 U.S. (7 Cranch) 116 (1812); The Paquete Habana, 175 U.S. 677 (1900); Brown v. United States, 12 U.S. (8 Cranch) 110, 128 (1814).

99. Barr, "Legality," pp. 11–12.

100. *New York Times,* October, 17, 1989, p. A1.

101. U.S. Department of the Army, *Field Manual FM 2710: The Law of Land Warfare* (Washington, D.C.: Government Printing Office, 1956), p. 17.

102. William Colby, *Lost Victory: A Firsthand Account of America's Sixteen-Year Involvement in Vietnam* (New York: Contemporary Books, 1989), pp. 366, 368.

103. *New York Times,* December 21, 1989, p. A22.

104. Treaty concerning the Permanent Neutrality and Operation of the Panama Canal, September 7, 1977, United States–Panama, 33 U.P.S.T. 1, T.I.A.S. No. 10029.

105. *Panama Canal Treaties,* Committee on Foreign Relations, U.S. Senate, 95th Cong., 2nd sess., Executive Rpt. no. 95-12 (Washington, D.C.: Government Printing Office, 1978), p. 7.

106. Reproduced in *Senate Debate on the Panama Canal Treaties: A Compen-*

dium of Major Statements, Documents, Record Votes and Relevant Events, Committee on Foreign Relations, U.S. Senate, 96th Cong., 1st sess. (Washington, D.C.: Library of Congress, 1979), p. 547.

107. *Washington Post,* December 22, 1989, p. A29.

108. *New York Times,* December 21, 1989, p. A22.

109. Transcript of press conference by James A. Baker III, U.S. Department of State, December 20, 1989, Washington, D.C., pp. 5, 8.

110. Transcript of NBC News, "Meet the Press," December 24, 1989, pp. 7–8.

111. George Bush, "Letter to the Speaker of the House and the President Pro Tempore of the Senate on United States Military Action in Panama, December 21, 1989," in *Weekly Compilation of Presidential Documents: December 25, 1989,* vol. 25, no. 51 (Washington, D.C.: Government Printing Office, 1989), p. 1985.

112. Robert H. Bork, "The Limits of 'International Law,'" *National Interest,* no. 18 (Winter 1989), pp. 3–10.

113. The Schooner Exchange, p. 137.

114. Bork, "Limits," p. 10.

115. Statement by Ambassador Thomas R. Pickering, United States Permanent Representative to the United Nations, in the Security Council, on "the Complaint of Nicaragua, January 17, 1990," Press Release USUN 02-(90), January 17, 1990, pp. 5, 8.

116. Lloyd N. Cutler, "Noriega's Actions Gave Us Justification," *Washington Post,* December 24, 1989, p. C7.

117. *Washington Post,* January 3, 1990, p. A14.

118. *New York Times,* November 1, 1989, p. A11.

119. *New York Daily News,* December 29, 1989, p. 17.

120. William Pfaff, *Chicago Tribune,* March 5, 1990, p. 17.

Index